ACUTE GRIEF AND THE FUNERAL

ACUTE GRIEF AND THE FUNERAL

Edited by

VANDERLYN R. PINE
AUSTIN H. KUTSCHER
DAVID PERETZ
ROBERT C. SLATER
ROBERT DeBELLIS
ROBERT J. VOLK
DANIEL J. CHERICO

With the Editorial Assistance of

Lillian G. Kutscher

CHARLES C THOMAS · PUBLISHER
Springfield, Illinois, U.S.A.

Published and Distributed Throughout the World by
CHARLES C THOMAS · PUBLISHER
BANNERSTONE HOUSE
301-327 East Lawrence Avenue, Springfield, Illinois, U.S.A.

With THOMAS BOOKS *careful attention is given to all details of manufacturing and design. It is the Publisher's desire to present books that are satisfactory as to their physical qualities and artistic possibilities and appropriate for their particular use.* THOMAS BOOKS *will be true to those laws of quality that assure a good name and good will.*

Printed in the United States of America
H-II

Library of Congress Cataloging in Publication Data

Main entry under title:

Acute grief and the funeral.

  Bibliography: p.
  Includes index.
  1. Grief. 2. Funeral rites and ceremonies—Psychological aspects.
Pine, Vanderlyn R.
BF575.G7A28 393'.01'9 75-8626
ISBN 0-398-03434-6

CONTRIBUTORS

Vanderlyn R. Pine, Ph.D.

Associate Professor
Department of Sociology
State University of New York
at New Paltz
New Paltz, New York

Austin H. Kutscher, D.D.S.

Associate Professor and Director
New York State Psychiatric Institute
Dental Service
School of Dental and Oral Surgery
Columbia University
New York, New York,
President, The Foundation of
Thanatology

David Peretz, M.D.

Assistant Clinical Professor
Department of Psychiatry
College of Physicians and Surgeons
Columbia University
New York, New York

Robert C. Slater

Professor and Director
Department of Mortuary Science
University of Minnesota
Minneapolis, Minnesota

Robert DeBellis, M.D.

Assistant Professor of Medicine
(Oncology)
College of Physicians and Surgeons
Columbia University
New York, New York

Daniel J. Cherico, Ph.D.

Assistant Professor of Health and
Physical Education
Queensborough Community College
Bayside, New York

Robert J. Volk

Funeral Service Director
Teaneck, New Jersey

Joyce Ayers, M.A.

Department of Psychology
Western State Hospital
Hopkinsville, Kentucky

Joanne Bernstein, Ph.D.

Assistant Professor
School of Education
Brooklyn College
City University of New York
Brooklyn, New York

James O. Carpenter, Ph.D.

Assistant Professor
Public Health Administration
Associate Director
Program in Health Gerontology
School of Public Health
University of Michigan
Ann Arbor, Michigan

Ned H. Cassem, M.D.

Department of Psychiatry
Harvard Medical School
Massachusetts General Hospital
Boston, Massachusetts

[v]

Marcelle Chenard, Ph.D.
Assistant Professor of Sociology
College of Saint Elizabeth
Convent Station, New Jersey

Shirley J. Conroy
Department of Psychiatry
University of Florida
Gainesville, Florida

John P. Danglade, CAE
Executive Vice-President
American Cemetery Association
Columbus, Ohio

Edith S. Deck, R.N., M.S.
Assistant Professor of Nursing
School of Nursing
University of Vermont
Burlington, Vermont

Kermit Edison
Funeral Service Director
Stoughton, Wisconsin

Patricia B. Farris
Department of Psychiatry
University of Florida
Gainesville, Florida

Rev. Vincent Fish
Vicar
Church of the Holy Family
Lake Villa, Illinois

Edward J. Fitzgerald
First Vice-President
Board of Governors
National Funeral Directors
Association
Albuquerque, New Mexico

Regina Flesch, Ph.D.
Medical Research Scientist
Eastern Pennsylvania Psychiatric
Institute
Philadelphia, Pennsylvania

Jeannette R. Folta, Ph.D.
Assistant Dean
College of Arts and Sciences
Associate Professor of Sociology
The University of Vermont
Burlington, Vermont

Robert Fulton, Ph.D.
Professor of Sociology
University of Minnesota
Minneapolis, Minnesota

Robert A. Furman, M.D.
Director
Cleveland Center for Research in
Child Development
Cleveland, Ohio

Frank Galante
President
Board of Governors
National Funeral Directors
Association
Newark, New Jersey

Francis J. Gomez
Funeral Service Director
Lakeville, Connecticut

Erwin H. Greenberg, LL.B.
President
National Association of Colleges
of Mortuary Science
President
Worsham College of Mortuary
Science, Inc.
Chicago, Illinois

Rev. Albert B. Hakim

Seton Hall University
South Orange, New Jersey

William G. Hardy, Jr.

Past President
National Funeral
Directors Association
Louisville, Kentucky

C. Stewart Hausmann

Executive Director
The New Jersey State Funeral
Directors Association
Union, New Jersey

Florence M. Hetzler, Ph.D.

Adjunct Associate Professor
Department of Philosophy
Fordham University
Bronx, New York

Gene S. Hutchens

Funeral Service Director
Florissant, Missouri

Rev. Paul E. Irion

The Lancaster Theological Seminary
of the United Church of Christ
Lancaster, Pennsylvania

Royal Keith

Treasurer
National Funeral Directors
Association
Yakima, Washington

Baheej Khleif, Ph.D.

Professor
Department of Sociology
Worcester State College
Worcester, Massachusetts

Ann S. Kliman, M.A.

Director
Situational Crisis Service
The Center for Preventive Psychiatry
White Plains, New York

Corliss Lamont, Ph.D.

Author
New York, New York

Robert E. Markush, M.D.

Center for Epidemiologic Studies
Rockville, Maryland

Rabbi Steven A. Moss

Chaplain
Memorial Hospital,
for Cancer and Allied Diseases
New York, New York

Howard C. Raether, LL.B.

Executive Director
National Funeral Directors
Association
Milwaukee, Wisconsin

Rev. Robert B. Reeves, Jr.

Chaplain
The Presbyterian Hospital in
the City of New York
Columbia-Presbyterian Medical
Center
New York, New York

Carol F. Ruff

Chief Psychologist
Western State Hospital
Hopkinsville, Kentucky

John J. Schwab, M.D.
Chairman and Professor
Department of Psychiatry
and Behavorial Sciences
University of Louisville
School of Medicine
Louisville, Kentucky

Robert G. Shadick, Ph.D.
Professor
School of Education
Brooklyn College
City University of New York
Brooklyn, New York

Donald Templer, Ph.D.
Formerly, Director of
Psychology Research
Pleasant Grove Hospital
Anchorage, Kentucky;
Department of Psychology
Waterford Hospital
St. John's, Newfoundland, Canada

Robert G. Twycross, M.D.
Research Fellow
Department of Clinical Research
St. Christopher's Hospice
London, England

Wendy Veevers-Carter
Author
Mombasa, Kenya

Avery D. Weisman, M.D.
Advisor-at-Large
The Foundation of Thanatology;
Department of Psychiatry and
Project Omega
Massachusetts General Hospital and
Harvard Medical School
Boston, Massachusetts

Morris A. Wessel, M.D.
New Haven, Connecticutt

INTRODUCTION

WHY IS A FUNERAL?

Avery D. Weisman

When primitive man stopped eating one another, he discovered the solidarity and continuity of his clan. We could even say that *Homo sapiens*, cast in our image, began with funerary customs. Formal disposition of the dead has been known since paleolithic times. Neanderthal man built monuments, and had special territories for his dead; there were special sites as well as postures in which dead clan members were placed. It is more than likely that primitive man also had special beliefs about death which accompanied the brute fact of being killed or dying.

Burial, burning, dessication, and exposure of dead bodies are not only rituals, but also signs of observing a directive, that the dead always signify something sacred and sinister. Funeral customs do not represent new traditions for us; they are only more modern procedures for ensuring our own survival and safety.

Probably no society exists that does not provide for its dead. It is conceivable, of course, that a roving band of marauders or a pack of anthropoids might desert the bodies of those who fall behind, who are killed or who die from other causes. But it does not require much social organization to mark the passage of the dead, even if the passage is simply the opening of a symbolic door from this world into oblivion.

Could there be a funeral so meaningless that the deceased is immediately forgotten, without token bereavement? The John Doe, buried in Potter's Field, at least lingers in our thoughts for a while as a dismal terror which reminds us that we, too, can not only pass from this world into oblivion, but also be wholly anonymous from beginning to end. Empty ceremonials are desecrations in themselves, regardless of the trappings and rhetoric. An authentic funeral, which is as simple as unadorned burial or as complex as bereavement itself, fills the heart and mind of the true survivor. The funeral is a symbol of the moment of death, not a depiction of it. This, not copulation between parents, is the real Primal Scene.

Almost all humans dread the moment of death. The most desolate creature hangs onto the thread of life. Suicides, killing off only an unwanted part of themselves, may still hope to exert a lasting, unforgettable influence upon survivors. For reasons unknown, most people scrape away at their existence, searching for something beyond food and elemental fulfillment, striving for sanity, hoping that somehow they can make sense out of what is so often chaotic.

Why is a funeral? Not even societies which glorify death rejoice when someone important dies. Mourning may not be a necessary part of bereavement, but grief is a human quality which is brought to a focus at death. Anticipatory grief is genuine enough, but we come to expect grief or its equivalent when death actually occurs. One scene of a drama closes, leaving the audience aghast. The sense of reality is undeniably undermined; they wait for the curtain to rise for the next act.

In reading the papers that make up this book, I urge people to imagine their own deaths, to consider what kind of funeral they would find acceptable, and then to discover for themselves that what is visualized is nothing more than a consummatory strategy for letting others know what we were all about.

Why is a funeral? In the beginning, there was death. After that, life as we know it began; death receded to the shadows. But like every shadow death demands light, and we interpret darkness in different ways. How and why mankind generally fears death would require a special treatise. Nevertheless, the moment of death, the Primal Scene, is a practical, contemporary, and very moot point, quite apart from its psychological significance.

That a sense of death is a prerequisite for a sense of being alive is no mere oxymoron. It has a long history. Death questions every value, appetite, fear, and enterprise sought and shunned during life.

The sense of death, if not the moment itself, is an excellent way to gain a perspective on life.

Perhaps it is perculiar to us moderns that we fret so much about "getting more out of life." Maybe we want more than there is to be found. Naturally, we want to survive and survive well, without suffering, surrounded by the materials that mean most. These supernumerary rewards assume that there is something better (which might be true) and that death concludes all striving. The concept of "virtue" originally meant a "potentiality for betterment." However, it is an open question as to how betterment occurs, and in which direction it should be sought. If our passion for betterment is destined to fail because of false expectations, then life is an empty enticement, death is a hypocritical betrayal, and funerals are the raw stuff of comedy.

Why is a funeral? I can offer several answers. The obvious and concrete reason is to dispose of the dead with dispatch, because someone has died. It is equally obvious that this is an insufficient reason. An enemy might die, but we would scarcely conduct a funeral on his behalf, unless to celebrate our own survival.

A funeral is a rehearsal of death in reminding us of our mortality. It is also a mirror of the clan in which we can observe the values and expectations that we have for each other. For example, if a person belongs to a group that values control, discipline, and self-reliance, the clan's funerals will discourage open emotional expression of grief. In contrast, if a clan has a tradition of suffering and strong family dependencies, the funeral catalyzes catharsis and paralyzes action. If the reigning beliefs are that a dead person will rejoin his ancestors in one way or another, everything possible will be done to achieve that end. The body may be equipped with food, clothing, and other suitable necessities for the trip. In short, the format follows custom; the custom fuses substance and symbol; the ceremonies muffle the shock to the bereaved, not by denial, but through implicit assurances that their ego ideals are genuine and worth the effort.

A funeral is more than the mere fact that someone has died. It is that someone has died whom we wish to honor. By doing so, we also honor ourselves and endow the situation with dignity. However, it is not just another testimonial, for memorials usually exceed the people they memorialize. I attended a funeral where the chief speaker acted like a toastmaster introducing the deceased to the audience. The bereavement was missing.

Therefore, a funeral is a custom whereby authentic survivors come together for mutual consolation that the salient values of the clan have been preserved, if not accentuated by the death. With or without elaborate rituals, the common ceremonial situation does something positive for the participants. The strategy of shared concern, even clustering together in common calamity, blunts the differences between people, suspends animosities, confronts everyone with his or her own vulnerability. Floods, tornados, and bombings may also bring people together for the same reasons, though without ceremony. We must assume that it is not ceremony alone that makes a funeral. Rather, it is the symbolism pertaining to a person that helps to contain our fear of death, while simultaneously honoring the clan's values.

Were it not for pervasive fear of death and awareness of its inexorability, funerals might be rather pleasant occasions in which we remembered all the nice things about the deceased, long after the acute grief had subsided. We honor the dead lest we feel guilty if we fail to do so. Guilt is difficult to define, but, in general, it is a highly individualized experience of dishonor, lapse in status, a shortcoming for which one can be punished or die.

Violation of a prohibition is often followed by death. Whether these prohibitions are called "laws" or "taboos" is irrelevant. Both are punished, not in order to rectify a wrong, but because it is the only way for a miscreant to be forgiven. When an untimely or unexpected death occurs, many mourners plaintively ask, "Why him— why her?" It is as if the death was a case of mistaken identity, and no one should die unless there was a very good reason for it—a clear compromise and confusion between need and necessity.

Why is a funeral? The most general reason is that it is a *socially sanctioned act of responsibility*, in which we look for the best in people, ignoring the worst (unless it is for the sake of drawing an exculpatory parallel), praising the clan and its continuity, tacitly blaming someone else, simultaneously accepting death and finding a reason for it in the person who died. For many people, ceremony is a substitute for suffering, but bereavement and grief are not equivalents which demand suffering. On the whole, the "why" of a funeral is to build a bridge between us, the living, and the silent totality in which most of mankind resides.

I do not expect the reader to recognize funerals as acts of responsibility, especially since all of us fear death to some degree and think of dying with the utmost reluctance. In fact some students of thanatology insist that our society is shot through with denials of death, and that funerals typify the plastic ceremony in which things are dressed up to be their exact opposite.

Do we really live in a death-denying society? Can there be a world without denial? Should death be abolished? In the presence of technologies that would perpetuate biological survival beyond any sensible reason, does it make sense to euphemize death? How does this justify the clan's values? In what respect would denial of death represent an act of responsibility?

It seems to me that a death-denying culture is a contradiction. More specifically, the ticking of a clock, the rhythms of day and night, the cycle of seasons, along with our newspapers, books, television, radio, and conversations—incessantly confront us with death and dying. Even the gods must die, some one once said. Shudder as one might, death will not go away. The Angel of Death has a standing appointment with everyone, which I am sure will be kept. Freud, of all people who should know better, once wrote that death has no representation among unconscious ideas. However, fear of death can be repressed as much as any other fear. I say that if there is no place in the unconscious for death, time, and contradictions, all of which permeate existence, then so much the worse for the unconscious. As human beings, our task is to bring inner life and external death together into a common reality, which we can realize as our very own.

It is a common fallacy that ours is a world of facts, there to be seen and handled, accepted or denied. Facts are objects, people, and things which are joined together in a latticework of theories and myths. Moreover, we are compelled to deal with symbols, those familiar and yet strange representations of acts and facts too complex to encompass by a single theory, myth, or observation. In everyday parlance, we are never quite certain whether we are talking about symbols, facts as simple self-evident, unquestioned theories, or even made-up stories. The everyday world is not quite as real or self-evident as we suppose. We dwell among invisibles and intangibles as much as in concrete facts. We determine what to do on the basis of an unknown future, based solely on what we desire and fear. Now, because no one has experienced death except vicariously, the fear of death is one of these invisible entities. We conjure with it, as if we were all magicians.

In society at large, the invisible, intangible, and imaginative help to determine the value and direction of what people do, feel, think, and are afraid of. There are beliefs and disbeliefs which direct us so inconspicuously that, like symbols, theories, and ordinary facts, we are defined by them. The notion of time, mortality, individuality, and so forth are examples of these directive beliefs, which may be called "suprafacts." Death may be a suprafact in just the same degree as it is a fact, a theory, and a symbol.

Whether this is a death-denying society is less a valid question than a popular platitude. At times, our intention is to live forever, as if we knew what to do with all that time. The funeral makes it very difficult to deny death. Ideally, of course, a funeral should help relieve the fear of death, at least by calling on us to reflect what fear of death means. The ideal funeral is not a vehicle for denial, but an instrument of personification. Implicit in the common phrase, "living up to our ideals and potential," is a belief that it is possible to make sense out of life and death, finding both suprafacts acceptable and appropriate. Unless death can be timely, acceptable, and consistent with what we have struggled for, it makes no sense to cope at all. We might as well deny it all, too. However, an authentic funeral should help us to grapple with the vulnerability found in life. The deceased who is honored at a funeral is neither a person nor a corpse, but an idealized personification of the clan's central objectives. Such personification is a suprafact.

A funeral compels us to face death, but grief is the certitude of death. Denial attentuates this perception: the funeral is neither good nor bad, but a necessary series of interactions which help realize death, a social reality, and the promise that we, too, shall die. The "why" of a funeral is found in custom, compassion, and the necessity of marking the honorific passage of someone essential to our support systems.

Our explorations into acute grief and the funeral will soon be covered over by the attrition of time. Nevertheless, there is no question but that, today and tomorrow, funerals will reflect and even direct our appreciation of the personhood of someone who dies within the structure and responsibility of the clan. I congratulate the authors and editors who will, in what now follows, clarify the subtleties of the social roles and personal experiences of the bereaved in relation to the funeral. It is not inconsistent with the spirit also to offer condolences and sympathy for an arduous task, well done.

CONTENTS

                                                              Page

Contributors v

Introduction—Why Is a Funeral—Avery D. Weisman ix

PART ONE—ACUTE GRIEF AND THE FUNERAL

Chapter

  1. Acute Grief: A Physician's Viewpoint—
     Robert G. Twycross 5
         The Use of Psychopharmacologic Agents 5
         Post-Bereavement Family Support Service 6
         Terminal Care and Acute Grief 9

  2. The First Three Steps Beyond the Grave—
     Ned H. Cassem 13
         Are These Rituals Hazardous to Health? 14
         Initial Quandries of Acute Grief 14
         The First Three Steps Beyond the Grave 15
         Recommendations 20

  3. The Traditional Funeral and Contemporary
     Society—Robert Fulton 23

  4. The Funeral and the Bereaved—Paul E. Irion 32

  5. Some Observations on Grief and the Funeral—
     Royal Keith 41

  6. The Sociology of the Mortuary: Religion, Sex,
     Age and Variables—Baheej Khleif 55
         Collection of Data 56
         Sample Description 57
         Findings 59
         Expressing Grief 72
         Summary Conclusions 78
         Appendix A: Questionnaire 79

  7. The Legal Aspects of Death—Erwin H. Greenberg 92

[xvii]

Chapter *Page*

  8. THE ROLE OF THE CEMETERY IN GRIEF EXPRESSION—
     John P. Danglade 98

PART TWO—THE FUNERAL AND THOSE WHO SERVE

  9. GRIEF, BEREAVEMENT AND MOURNING: THE REALITIES
     OF LOSS—Vanderlyn R. Pine 105
 10. SOCIAL MEANINGS OF THE FUNERAL—Vanderlyn R. Pine ...115
     DEATH, FUNERALS AND FUNERAL DIRECTORS 116
     FUNERARY SOCIAL BEHAVIOR 120
     FUNERALS AS SOCIAL MECHANISMS IN THE
      ACCEPTANCE OF DEATH 122
     CONCLUDING REMARKS 124
 11. EMPHASIS EMPATHY—Kermit Edison 126
 12. THE ADAPTIVE FUNERAL—William G. Hardy, Jr. 131
 13. THE HUMANIST SERVICE—Corliss Lamont 139
 14. THE ITALIAN FAMILY: HOW IT DEALS WITH GRIEF
     AND THE FUNERAL—Frank R. Galante 142
     THE LA POSTA 142
     FLORAL OFFERINGS OF SIGNIFICANCE 143
     THE FAMILY "COLLECTS" 144
 15. SOUTHWESTERN PERSPECTIVES ON THE RESOLUTION OF
     GRIEF—Edward J. Fitzgerald 145
 16. THE FUNERAL DIRECTOR: SERVING THE LIVING—
     Francis J. Gomez 151
     THE FUNERAL DIRECTOR AS AN INFORMANT 152
     THE FUNERAL DIRECTOR AS COUNSELOR 153
     THE FUNERAL DIRECTOR: SERVING THE LIVING 154
 17. GRIEF THERAPY—Gene S. Hutchens 155
     SOME INTRODUCTORY THOUGHTS 155
     A FUNERAL DIRECTOR DOES SOME RESEARCH 156
     METHODOLOGY 157
     CHANGES REVEALED 158
     ANECDOTAL REPORTS 158
     QUESTIONS AND TABULATIONS OF ANSWERS AND
      SOME COMMENTS 165

Chapter *Page*

18. Who Are We—What Are We—Why We Do
   What We Do—C. Stewart Hausmann 169
      Definition 169
      Who Are We 170
      What We Are 171
      Why We Do What We Do 171

19. The Death Anxiety of Those Who Work in
   Funeral Homes—Donald I. Templer, Carol F. Ruff
   and Joyce Ayers 174

20. The Clergy on the Firing Line—Regina Flesch 179
      Failure in Heart 182
      Failures in Mind 183
      Clerical Failure in Role 185

21. The Pastor's Problem With His Own Discomfort—
   Robert B. Reeves, Jr. 188

22. Acute Grief, Aesculapian Authority and the
   Clergyman—Steven A. Moss 191

23. Serving With Respect and Compassion—Vincent Fish ... 194

PART THREE—THE FUNERAL AND THOSE WHO SURVIVE

24. A View of Life and Death—Howard C. Raether and
   Robert C. Slater 203

25. In a Hospital Room—and After—Florence M. Hetzler ... 209

26. Loss and Grief in the Later Years of Life—
   James O. Carpenter 218
      The Process of Bereavement 219
      The Effects of Loss and Bereavement 221
      Society, The Aged and Grief 225
      Conclusions 228

27. Grief, The Funeral and The Friend—
   Jeannette R. Folta and Edith S. Deck 231
      Family Structure 232
      Human Relationships 233
      Grief 234
      Friend, Grief, Funerals 235

Chapter   *Page*

28. FUNERAL BEHAVIOR AND UNRESOLVED GRIEF—
John J. Schwab, Patricia B. Farris, Shirley J. Conroy
and Robert E. Markush 241
    METHOD 241
    RESULTS 242
    DISCUSSION 244
    APPENDIX A: GRIEF EVALUATION ITEMS 249

29. GRIEF, LOVE LOST, AND THE FUNERAL RITE—
Albert B. Hakim 249

30. I CAN'T BELIEVE IT YET, HOW CAN SHE?—
Ann S. Kliman 252

31. HELPING THE CHILD TO MOURN—Robert A. Furman 256
    INTRODUCTION 256
    ACUTE GRIEF 257
    THE FUNERAL 258
    SUMMARY 259

32. THE CHILD AND THE FUNERAL—Morris A. Wessel 260

33. THE SCHOOL AND THE FUNERAL—Robert G. Shadick 265
    A DOUBLE TABOO 265
    TABOO STIRS THE PARENTAL FEAR 266
    FUNERALS ARE NOT TABOO 267
    ACUTE GRIEF FOLLOWS THE FUNERAL 268
    GRIEF'S LASTING IMPACT 269
    THE SCHOOL'S RESPONSIBILITY 269

34. HELPING YOUNG CHILDREN TO COPE WITH ACUTE GRIEF:
A BIBLIOTHERAPY APPROACH—Joanne E. Bernstein 274

35. STUDENTS WITHOUT PARENTS: AN OPPORTUNITY
TO TALK—Marcelle Chenard 281

36. THE CONTINUITY OF LIFE—Wendy Veevers-Carter 285

Index 293

ACUTE GRIEF AND THE FUNERAL

PART ONE

ACUTE GRIEF AND
THE FUNERAL

CHAPTER 1

ACUTE GRIEF: A PHYSICIAN'S VIEWPOINT

ROBERT G. TWYCROSS

INTRODUCTION

A CUTE GRIEF IS characterized by recurrent episodes of severe anxiety and psychological pain during which the dead person is strongly missed and the survivor sobs or cries aloud for him. These "pangs of grief" begin within a few hours or days of bereavement and usually reach a peak of severity within five to fourteen days. Initially, they occur frequently and spontaneously. Parkes (1972) has written:

> Feelings of panic, a dry mouth and other indications of autonomic activity are particularly pronounced during pangs of grief. Add to these features deep sighing respiration, restless but aimless hyperactivity, difficulty in concentrating on anything but thoughts of loss, ruminations around the events leading up to the loss as well as loss of interest in any of the people or things that normally give pleasure or claim attention, and one begins to get a picture of this distressing phase of grief.

THE USE OF PSYCHOPHARMACOLOGIC AGENTS

In view of this catalogue of symptoms, it is not surprising that many people consult their doctor in the months after bereavement. Indeed, in the United Kingdom, where it is common for all members of a family to be cared for by a single practitioner within the National Health Service, a growing number of doctors regard visiting the newly bereaved as part of their routine. In this situation, what help should the doctor offer? In particular, to what extent should the use of psychopharmacologic agents be encouraged? Benjamin Rush, famous American physician and signatory of the Declaration of Independence, advised the prescription of "liberal doses of opium." Today, he would no doubt recommend equally liberal doses of barbiturates or benzodiazepine tranquilizers. Kübler-Ross (1973) has denounced this type of approach, suggesting instead that we should establish a "screaming room" where the unexpectedly bereaved could sit and cry and scream in the presence of an understanding listening nurse or minister. She believes that we could take care of these people with much less medication, thus enabling them to face the painful reality fully conscious and without feelings of shame or embarrassment. If, despite this sort of approach, sedation still appears necessary, it should be given, but in a dose that does not leave the bereaved person feeling drugged or drowsy. All too often, it has been the medical attendant's intolerance of the bereaved's expression of anguish that has led to the immediate offer of a sedative so as to "keep everything and everybody quiet and calm."

As yet, there is no scientific evidence comparing the therapeutic effect of a sympathetic listener with a doctor who does little more than provide what he considers to be a suitable prescription. Nor do we know whether tranquilizers and antidepressants reduce the pain of grief or merely postpone it. Despite the scientific uncertainty, I suggest that the total denial of psychopharmacologic support in bereavement is both shortsighted and inhumane. Take, for example, the woman who has nursed her husband at home, with little outside help, throughout his terminal illness. The last few nights or more may well have been virtually sleepless ones; she is totally exhausted with little or no mental and physical reserves with which to face her bereavement. The use of a bedtime hypnotic until, at least, after the funeral would seem to be reasonable. Other indications for the use of psychopharmacologic agents have been discussed by Wiener (1973). As always, of course, they should be used only as adjunct therapy and not as substitutes for human care.

POST-BEREAVEMENT FAMILY SUPPORT SERVICE

Several studies confirm the potential pathogenic effect of major bereavement in adult life (Parkes, 1965; Stein and Susser, 1969; Parkes, 1970; Birtchnell, 1970a, b, c). Because of these reports, a post-bereavement family support service was set up at St. Christopher's Hospice, London, some four years ago in an endeavor to reduce post-bereavement morbidity. First, it was necessary to identify those relatives at special risk and, then, to develop a service to reduce the incidence and degree of maladjustment. To this end, an eight-point questionnaire relating to the next-of-kin or "key person" was introduced based on the results of Parkes' Harvard Bereavement Study (Parkes, in preparation). It was hoped that if completed by a member of the nursing staff shortly after a patient's death, it would be possible to predict the key person's state a year or so later. The eight questions were supplied with "multiple-choice" answers which were scored from either 1 to 5 or 1 to 6. By adding the results together, an overall "predictive score" is arrived at. Each key person is then allocated to one of the following groups:

A. Imperative Need

These individuals are felt to be in great need of help, so much so that it would be unethical to withhold it. In practice, this means all those who have a high score on the eighth question: "How will key person cope?" This is, in effect, an intuitive assessment of the possible outcome.

B. High Risk

These individuals have a predictive score of 18 or more and, unless thought to be antagonistic to follow-up, are randomly allocated either to an "experimental" or a "control" group, the control group being necessary for an objective assessment of the service.

C. Low Risk

Those individuals with a predictive score of less than 18.

Follow-up visits are then arranged for the whole of Group A and the experimental half of Group B. The selection of the person to make the follow-up visit is discussed and, where possible, the member of staff best known to the key person visits approximately two weeks after bereavement. Help is given whenever possible and further visits arranged as considered necessary. Each month, the staff "visitors" meet Dr. Parkes, the social psychiatrist directing the project, to discuss any problems that have arisen, to plan further support, and to consider ways of improving the service.

More than 1,500 questionnaires have now been completed. The distribution of the key persons is as follows:

Group A.	82	(6.0%)
Group B.	288	(19.0%)
Group C.	1,145	(75.0%)

Of these, 227 (15%) have been visited, usually at least twice: that is, all Group A and the experimental half of Group B. With very few exceptions, the visitors have been welcomed by the respondents and have been pleased with the results of their visits. Visitors see their main roles as:

1. Providing continuity of contact with an understanding person, that is, someone with whom feelings about the bereavement can be expressed.
2. Serving as a link to other forms of specialized help.
3. Assessing the risks of suicides among the bereaved.

In order to evaluate the benefit of this service, some 40 to 50 key persons from each group are being visited by an interviewer from the research unit, 18 to 24 months after bereavement. The questions then deal with problems faced and help offered since bereavement, including any contact with St. Christopher's, and the key person's attitude to each source of help. The second half of the interview is a shortened version of the "Health Questionnaire" used to measure "outcome" in the Harvard Bereavement Study (Parkes and Brown, 1972). So far, 104 respondents have been approached by the research interviewer, 25 refused an interview, 18 could not be located and five had died; the other 56 were interviewed for the project and the results are summarized in Figure 1-1. It is evident that the predictive score is not a highly reliable indicator of outcome 21 months after bereavement in that high risk survivors are scattered fairly evenly along the "y" axis.

However, the important practical question is not the correlation between predictive score and outcome but with the reliability of the predictive questionnaire as a means of screening out a population which will include those with a poor outcome. We must ask, therefore, what proportion of the respondents with poor outcome were identified as "high risk" cases and what proportion were incorrectly classified as "low risk." Taking a predictive score of 18 as our cut-off point for a "high

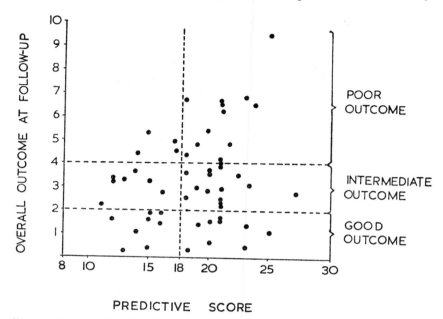

Figure 1-1. Relationship of Predictive Score to outcome after 18 to 24 months: results from fifty-six interviews.

risk" case, we find that 13 out of 17 (77%) of the poor outcome group were correctly designated as "high risk" and four (23%) as "low risk."

Further evidence for the predictive validity of the questionnaire relates to four respondents who committed suicide within two years after the death of their spouses. All four were found to have scored 18 or more on the predictive questionnaire. Modifications to the questionnaire are being made following a multivariate analysis of the findings and it is hoped that we shall eventually have a much sharper predictive instrument than the one in current use. It is still too early to compare outcome in the high risk "experimental" and the high risk "control" groups.

TERMINAL CARE AND ACUTE GRIEF

However helpful the family support service may prove to be, there is little doubt that a high standard of terminal care not only benefits the patient but also the relatives in their bereavement.

"I am very grateful for all you did for my mother. Although I am still very sad over her death, I get some comfort from the fact that she was in the very best place possible."

"We loved our sister and the knowledge of the loving care she received during her last dreadful illness will help sustain us in our grief."

"You have proved by the peace with which you helped Doug on his way, that death is not a thing to be feared. It gave us great comfort in our loss to know this."

"Since my husband died last week, my mind has been very confused. I miss him dreadfully and mixed with a certain guilty relief is an absolute horror at the disease and what it did to him. . . . The calm love you have shown us both over the past months has filled me with gratitude."

These letters emphasize particularly that good terminal care is not, nor could ever be, a means of erasing grief. The grief is still there, still hurts, still has to be coped with and worked through. Yet, the memory of a dignified, peaceful death brings a tremendous "plus" factor into the total situation. What do I mean by good terminal care? First, I mean the kind of care in which every effort is made to overcome and keep at bay symptoms such as pain, nausea, constipation, anorexia and breathlessness. Many of our patients require a narcotic analgesic regularly, every four hours, usually in association with other preparations. Their use, within the context of total patient care, has been well documented in recent years (Saunders, 1967; Lamerton, 1973). I would emphasize, however, that it is possible for a patient to be free from pain and also fully alert when receiving drugs of this nature.

Second, I mean the kind of care in which a patient is not isolated and enclosed in a mesh of negative thinking. Instead, the patient is respected as an individual, allowed to talk about his illness, allowed to work through to a positive acceptance of his death, allowed to express his fears and anxieties concerning not so much his death, but the manner of his dying. Will it be painful? Will I suffocate? How long will it be?

I also mean the kind of care in which the family members are seen as part of the "treatment unit": they, too, need to work through stages of denial, anger and depression to a positive acceptance of the inevitable. Until they do, they can adversely affect the patient by maintaining and transferring unhelpful or negative attitudes. It is important to encourage them to continue to do things for the patient such as tidying pillows, assisting, if necessary, at mealtimes and joining in the activities that are arranged from time to time. In this connection, it is important for the staff not to "take" the patient from the family, not to become possessive and exclusive. To this end, it is imperative to have liberal visiting hours and to do away with restrictions such as "only two visitors to a patient" or "no children under 12."

About three years ago, a police sergeant, aged 39, was admitted to St. Christopher's with motor neurone disease. He was an inpatient for about two years and from time to time discussed his attitude to illness with one of the doctors. He disliked phrases such as terminal or catastrophic illness; instead, he preferred "bringing-together illness." When asked if he always saw this "bringing-together" happen, he replied, "Yes, I am a trained observer and I've been here for 18 months. Patient and family, patient and staff, patient and patient—yes, it does happen" (Saunders, 1973).

Because it takes time to help both patients and relatives reach the point where the illness can truly be called a "bringing-together illness," we do not like having "bed and breakfast" patients, that is, patients who come in one day and die the next. However, since prognostication is an art and not a science, we shall always have a certain number of these extremely short-stay patients. But even here there is quite a lot one can do, not least to assuage the guilt implied in statements such as "If we'd known it was going to be so short, we'd have kept him at home."

CONCLUSIONS

1. Psychopharmacologic agents have a definite, though limited, place in the management of acute grief.
2. Bereavement bears many similarities to an illness: it is certainly a state of ill health. A sensitive and reliable method for predicting the high risk survivor is needed if we are to make the best use of our resources.
3. Meanwhile, it is important to develop a positive, almost aggressive approach to the problems of terminal illness in order to help not only the patient to die with dignity and in peace but also to

give those who will be left behind the best possible support as they work through their grief.

REFERENCES

Birtchnell, J.: Recent parent death and mental illness. *Br J Psychiatry, 116*: 289, 1970a.

———: Depression in relation to early and recent parental death. *Br J Psychiatry, 116*:299, 1970b.

———: The relationship between attempted suicide, depression and parental death. *Br J Psychiatry, 116*:307, 1970c.

Kübler-Ross, E.: On the use of psychopharmacologic agents for the dying patient and the bereaved. In Goldberg, I. K., Malitz, S., and Kutscher, A. H., (eds.): *Psychopharmacologic Agents for the Terminally Ill and Bereaved.* New York, Columbia U Pr, 1973.

Lamerton, R. C.: *Care of the Dying.* London, Priory Press, 1973.

Parkes, C. M.: Bereavement and mental illness. *Br J Med Psychol, 38*:1, 1965.

———: The psychosomatic effects of bereavement. In Hill, O. W., (ed.): *Modern Trends in Psychosomatic Medicine—2.* London, Butterworth, 1970.

———: *Bereavement: Studies of Grief in Adult Life.* London, Tavistock Publications, 1972.

———: Determinants of outcome after bereavement (in preparation).

Parkes, C. M., and Brown, R. J.: Health after bereavement: a controlled study of young Boston widows and widowers. *Psychosom Med, 34*:449, 1972.

Saunders, C.: *The Management of Terminal Illness.* London, Hospital Medicine Publications, 1967.

———: A death in the family: a professional view. *Br Med J, 1*:30, 1973.

Stein, Z., and Susser, M.: Widowhood and mental illness. *Br J Prev Soc Med, 23*:106, 1969.

Wiener, A.: The use of psychopharmacologic agents in the management of the bereaved. In Goldberg, I. K., Malitz, S., and Kutscher, A. H., (eds.): *Psychopharmacologic Agents for the Terminally Ill and Bereaved.* New York, Columbia U Pr, 1973.

CHAPTER 2

THE FIRST THREE STEPS BEYOND THE GRAVE

Ned H. Cassem

WHAT IS THE USE of perpetuating wakes, funerals and burials? Are they not cruel and clumsy parodies more calculated to shatter than to console the bereaved? Perhaps as many as half of all the persons in our contemporary society have strong negative feelings toward one or all of these rites for the dead. Those opposing such rites are likely to denounce them as traumatic, morbid, terrifying or even sadistic occasions which they themselves avoid and would like to see stopped. Of the three, the wake is the most criticized and the funeral the least. Many persons, in fact, particularly with more current trends, never attend a burial service in which the body is actually placed in the ground.

Negative feelings toward these rituals have found recent public support in the form of Memorial Societies, which offer the ostensible service of avoiding elaborate funeral arrangements. Often the clearer purpose is to get the dead person's remains out of sight (and therefore out of mind) as quickly as possible. In addition, for those who would diminish ceremonials of mourning, there are even legal aids. Civil authorities in some quarters are doing their part to reduce rituals after death. Recently, in certain cities of Ontario, the funeral procession from church to cemetery has been forbidden by law. Whether the reduction of traffic jams was relevant to the needs of the bereaved was apparently not considered. At the time of this writing, any bereaved persons in Menominee, Michigan who wish a graveside service for the dead member of their family must get clearance of the mayor—clearance that in no way can be routinely counted upon.

I view these trends as ominous. However, it is not enough merely to say that wakes, funerals and burials should be defended and continued as they stand. True, these rituals are routinely and irresponsibly under-emphasized to the detriment of the bereaved. Failure to face and to participate in these ritual steps is a serious mental health hazard for those who have just sustained the loss of a loved person. Much as this underemphasis fits in with "the American way of not dying" (Paul Ramsey's phrase), it deprives mourners of the social context best suited for the integration of loss.

ARE THESE RITUALS HAZARDOUS TO HEALTH?

Loss itself is a major health hazard. In a survey of press reports of sudden death during psychological stress, George Engel (1971) found that loss was the precipitant in 59 percent of the cases. Few would contest that the work of mourning is itself so difficult that some persons never recover from it. The specific question here, however, is whether there are reported instances of sudden death during any of the ritual ceremonies described, namely, wakes, funerals or burials. In his survey of 170 news items reporting sudden death, Engel reported no incidence of sudden death at any of these rituals. In a large systematic survey of sudden death in a population of 44,000, Greene (1972) reported 26 deaths, but none of them occurred during these rites. The only recorded instances I was able to find were those reported by W. Dewi Rees (1972) who reported two such deaths in his extensive experience, one at a funeral and the other at the grave. Therefore, one cannot say that there is no risk to health at wakes, funerals and burials, but apparently these are not the most dangerous and vulnerable times following the death of a loved one. Because most of the cases of psychological morbidity following loss indict unresolved grief as the cause, it is still essential to examine the role of early rituals in getting the process of mourning started correctly.

INITIAL QUANDARIES OF ACUTE GRIEF

Early stages of mourning can be subdivided many ways, but all must include shock and denial. First of all, there is a sense of numbness that occurs even when the death is expected. In the majority of deaths, a sense of confusion pervades the life of the bereaved. During this time, emotions are well below their peak and the mourner may feel in a daze. Often there is a sense, as there is when one is in severe danger, of "going on automatic." In fact, Parkes (1972) gives evidence that the peak of the mourning period probably comes sometime during the second week (p. 159). This, of course, is after the wake, funeral and burial have ended. Because of the confusional state of the acutely bereaved, which is part of grief itself, some ritual seems almost necessary to help these bereaved persons negotiate the earliest period of their grief. In such a way, they could retain a sense that what they are doing is at least appropriate. Ritual, after all, is one of society's ways of sharing communal responsibility for one of its members during a life crisis.

Denial after bereavement can never be underestimated. It has been my practice with the families of hospitalized patients who die to ask whether the bereaved would like to see the body before it is taken to the morgue. About two-thirds say they would like to. Among those who have seen the body, there have still been many who found it extremely difficult to believe the person had really died. One 64-year-old widow, two years after her husband's death, said, "If I hadn't seen him myself in the recovery room [where the final resuscitation effort took place], I don't think I would believe that he's dead." In his extensive studies with the bereaved, Parkes (1972) reported several anecdotes of similar inability to believe the dead person gone. For some widows, viewing their husband's lifeless body forced them to believe him dead, while for others it was the funeral service that "brought home" the reality (p. 65). Those who have not been bereaved cannot conceptualize how extreme the sense of unreality may become during the time of acute grief. Both confusion and denial enter into this. One of the most important functions of wakes, funerals and burials is not to call to mind for the bereaved that a reality is occurring or has occurred, but to provide crucial opportunities for reality testing to take place during the time of acute grief.

THE FIRST THREE STEPS BEYOND THE GRAVE

Wakes, funerals and burials are clearly for the living, not the dead. What then are some of the advantages to be derived from them? The following is a list of benefits that have accrued from some or all of these services to the bereaved.

During the time between death and the funeral, the body ordinarily resides in the funeral home. According to the customs of each family, special arrangements, such as wakes, are made in which the bereaved are visited by other members of their community. Some persons object to these rituals (like wakes) because of the open casket. Parkes (1972) reported that of his Boston widows and widowers one-half of the woman and one-fourth of the men were upset by viewing the corpse, even though they were not critical of the funeral director (p. 157). Others dislike wakes for their awkwardness and the manifest inadequacy of words on such occasions. Some fear them because they fear all circumstances in which strong emotion is likely to be expressed. Perhaps the most telling criticism of wakes is aimed at their stereotyped qualities, with expressions of condolence somehow ringing hollow in the ears of the bereaved.

A living memorial to the dead person receives substantial architectural contributions during the time of wake and funeral. Many family members have told me that the most memorable parts of the wake were the stories recounted about the dead person by his or her old friends. Many of these had not been known to some or all family members. One young woman who regarded her alcoholic bartender father as a pathetic failure in life reported that she was amazed at the number of men who came to pay respects at the wake. Moreover, she learned of many acts of generosity and kindness her father had done for them during the time they knew him. Because her parents had been separated for many years, these anecdotes were extremely helpful in filling out her memories of her father.

The tributes paid to the dead person during the time of wake or funeral are worthwhile not only in emphasizing the worth of the person who died but also establishing that he or she is worth the pain and stress of grieving, which the mourners now acutely feel. Parkes also found this to be important.

Family units should be drawn closer together during these rituals (although, of course, this does not always happen). The families in which it does not happen are those in which the family bonds are already defective. The effects of funeral rituals on increasing family unity throughout many different cultures in the world have been commented on by Mandelbaum (1959), who would also see this as an important function of rituals for the living following death.

The re-emphasis of the social network of support surrounding the family emerges at the time of death and can often be strongly expressed in wakes and funerals. Whether they like these rituals or not, persons are often impressed by and remember who shows up at the wake or funeral of their spouse or family member. Despite just criticism about the inadequacy of words during these times, presences are remembered more strongly than words. Genuine concern, moist eyes, or the touch of a hand and caring gestures are remembered better by the bereaved than specific words spoken. Those who care have ways of showing it. Perhaps wakes and funeral services should be viewed as settings in which the more caring persons of communities can be allowed to exhibit their abilities and healing power in this regard.

Rituals, while permitting expressions of sorrow, also may set some limits on grieving or provide legitimate outlets for expressing positive feeling as well. When a person has a ritual to perform during the wake, such as the saying of special prayers shared by all, he is momentarily spared some of the little agonies of repeated individual encounters at wakes. Rituals are meant to provide a sense of solidarity for the group that performs them together. Unfortunately, rituals are often ridiculed or resented, a convenient defense against responsible sharing of a painful mourning process. Rather than denouncing the defects, we could expend energy more constructively by searching for methods of supporting or modulating the sorrow. The custom of the old Irish wakes of providing whisky for those who came served many a useful purpose. Mandelbaum (1959) recounts the customs of the Roman Catholic people of Barra, the southernmost island of the Scottish Outer Hebrides. For them, condolences first come from men who meet at a specially prepared bar. Later, watchers stay with the coffin throughout the night. Neither was alcohol abused nor were the topics of conversation morbid, and the men talk through the night about subjects from seafaring to sheep raising. When dawn comes, the coffin is carried in procession to the chapel, with every man of the community taking his turn as a pallbearer. Having something to *do* that is helpful must be a welcome relief from merely standing by helpless. Mandelbaum also reported that the Kota, natives of the Nilgiri Hills in southern India, permit strong expressions of grief for the mourners of the dead, but also provide tribal dancing which serves to mollify and to some extent limit the expressions of grief. Some funeral homes still provide a side room where certain visitors at the wake are invited for a drink and from time to time these visitors will either bring coffee for members of the family or get them to step away from the parlor to the room to sit down. Friends of the family could be encouraged to bake loaves of bread for these "comfort stations," bring one bottle of wine or make some other contribution which would make them feel helpful to the bereaved. Such customs and arrangements should ideally arise from the community churches.

Rituals must underline the reality that the object is lost. The difficulties which persons have in acknowledging this simple fact have been mentioned above. Because only those who have no experience with bereavement fail to see the importance of this, it is crucial that the bereaved be given not only the initial opportunity to view the body, but a chance to change their view. Filing by the casket, a spot to kneel for prayer near the casket, going with the casket to the grave, witnessing the descent of the casket into the grave—all underline and encourage the essence of these rituals, which is saying farewell to the deceased.

Factions which exist in families or communities may be partially healed in the working out of the ceremonies themselves. Since funerals and wakes are for the living, efforts to make them as helpful as possible for all members of the family can be extremely beneficial. Unfortunately, organized religions may allow little or no individual departures from or variation on themes of funeral or burial rituals, or families and their clergy may not be responsible enough to undertake these mutual efforts. A clergyman may find, for example, that a family has been severely split along conservative and liberal lines of religious tradition. The funeral service, depending on the willingness of the family members, can be helpful in resolving some of these tensions provided deliberate attention is given to the problem during the planning.

The funeral is a rite of passage. The dead person has affected the lives of many others. The funeral rite should therefore be designed to permit those persons to review and reintegrate the meaning of the dead person in their lives. As Weisman (1972) points out, people come literally to pay their respects, to undo guilt and hostility, to put in perspective. To some extent, attending funeral or similar rituals gives those who have known the deceased person a way of formally acknowledging that he or she had some impact on their lives. For some persons, attending a funeral may be viewed as indeed paying off a debt to the dead person. In short, one comes to say goodbye. This may be of no value whatsoever to the family. In fact, they may never know some of the people who attended the wakes and funerals of their loved ones. But the funeral service itself provides them a crucial occasion in which they can get on with their work of mourning.

Mourning rituals extend far beyond the individual whom they grieve. Recently, a young girl whose right arm had been amputated after the discovery of an osteogenic sarcoma told me that she began to cry bitterly at the funeral of her grandfather, only to find herself unable to stop. Surprised because she had really not known her grandfather so well, she said it suddenly became clear she was weeping for her lost arm. She felt unable to do this at home because her tears made her parents so sad. "It felt so good to have an excuse to cry," she said. Mourning rituals are just that—an occasion to cry, a chance to continue the unfinished business of grieving which all of us have.

Seeing the dead person to the final resting place, whether it be the depository of body or ashes, can provide both closure to the rituals and the memorial to a death whose reality will again come into question as soon as the day of burial has passed. Parkes described how most widows in his study like to visit their husbands' graves and "the almost uncanny attraction that drew them to the cemetery" (p. 51). In northern states where the ground is frozen in winter, bodies are placed in a burial vault and buried in the spring, sometimes with another burial service. Because the work of grieving is slow, this can provide another ideal opportunity for a modest ritual. In the hands of a clergyman highly skilled in and sensitive to the needs of bereaved persons, such as Edgar Jackson (1974, Personal Communication), these "second burials" can be extremely beneficial rituals for the family. Graves and other resting places of the dead (like the Ganges River) are important anchor points in the reality of our lives. To the extent that we can mourn the part of ourselves which lies buried there, we can reaffirm and build upon the living part of us forged and tempered by the love of the person we have lost.

P. Rosenblatt (1975), in a review of tribal customs during grief and mourning in seventy-eight societies all over the world, concluded that the overt expression of anger and overt physical attacks following a death were less common in societies where ritualists dealt with the body up to and during burial. It is difficult to draw any conclusions from this finding that are applicable to our own culture, save perhaps presenting a caution to those who would do away with the rituals we already have. We do know that in the majority of murders committed in this country the murderer is closely related to the victim. It is tempting to speculate, in a society which works so hard at denying the reality of loss and death and shows itself so inept in sustaining those in mourning, that a surplus of aggressive behavior may represent displaced or misguided elements of unresolved loss.

RECOMMENDATIONS

Extensive review of cultural customs at the time of death have shown that it is rare for an adult death not to be dealt with ceremonially (Rosenblatt, 1975). Moreover, Mandelbaum's review of several cultures suggests a direct relationship between the extensiveness of the ritual and the extent to which the culture fears death or is haunted by the spirits of their dead. Among a tribe like the Kota, where in addition to an individual funeral a second large community funeral is held, the spirits of the dead never return to haunt or frighten the tribe. By contrast, the Hopi Indians, whose rites are designed to minimize death and get the burial over with as quickly as possible, are a tribe haunted by the spirits of their dead. Those who would do away with the chief rituals following death such as wakes, funerals and burials will pay the price of a culture with even more juvenile death-denying ways, haunted by unresolved guilt, pent up anger and half-finished relationships.

One of the major problems in our society is that ritual itself became taboo two or three decades ago. Mindless superstition became the target of science while mindless irrelevancy became the target of religion. Scientists by and large have attacked beliefs in immortality while failing to look deeper into the strong needs men have to mourn their dead. Humanitarians and religious leaders have attacked funeral customs on the grounds of excessive cost for the bereaved or their tendency to glamorize and deny death. Religious customs surrounding wakes, funerals and burials have been severely criticized because they stress ritual to the exclusion of the individual. In some Catholic churches, for example, the homily preached at the funeral mass by custom never mentions the person who has died. Overhearing the criticism of funeral directors, one sometimes hears the suggestion that elimination of wakes, funerals and burials would somehow solve the problem of mourning. It is probably more correct that these criticisms themselves are often masks for the weak, deluded plea that loss does not or should not occur at all.

Death is a threat that can smash family structures and disrupt community networks. As the most powerful of all losses it poses the greatest threat to individual maturity and the ability to integrate loss (Cassem, 1975). The eleven advantages set forth in the preceding section should be viewed as goals or achievements that should be worked at whenever someone dies. They are goals to be striven for commonly, by immediate family, clergy, community, and friends. While it is true that slavish conformity to ritual can dehumanize by robbing mourners of any personal sense of the services, it is also obvious that the very standardization of the essence of the ritual is a necessary reassurance to mourners as well. There should be no ritual which does not permit and encourage personalization. The effort at bringing about the union of personalized with familiar ritual elements that surround wakes, funerals and burials is itself part of the healing process for mourners during acute grief.

The importance of these rituals cannot be underestimated because they are the primary catalysts of acute grief. It seems to be a consensus among investigators of grief and mourning that the early defects in grieving are the most serious ones. Rituals which permit and encourage these expressions are therefore essential to the culture. The defects that occur early are not only those of the mourner himself but of those members of his family or community who for various reasons were unable to provide him with the support required during the initial intense phase of mourning. Attention to one's responsibilities for mourners during the acute phase of grief is a means for promoting their emotional growth as well as one's own. Mourning is a task much larger than most persons (perhaps fortunately) suspect. The beginning must be proportionate.

REFERENCES

Cassem, N. H.: Bereavement as indispensable for growth. In Schoenberg, B., Gerber, I., Wiener, A., Kutscher, A. H., Peretz, D., and Carr, A. C., (eds.): *Bereavement: Its Psychosocial Aspects.* New York, Columbia U Pr, 1975.

Engel, G. L.: Sudden and rapid death during psychological stress. *Ann Intern Med, 74*:771, 1971.

Greene, W. A., Goldstein, S., and Moss, A. J.: Psychosocial aspects of sudden death. *Arch Intern Med, 129*:725, 1972.

Mandelbaum, D. G.: Social uses of funeral rites. In Feifel, H., (ed.): *The Meaning of Death.* New York, McGraw-Hill, 1959.

Parkes, C. M.: *Bereavement.* New York, Intl Univers Pr, 1972.

Rees, W. D.: Bereavement and illness. In Schoenberg, B., Carr, A. C., Peretz, D., and Kutscher, A. H., (eds.): *Psychosocial Aspects of Terminal Care.* New York, Columbia U Pr, 1972.

Rosenblatt, P. C.: Uses of ethnography in understanding grief and mourning. In Schoenberg, B., Gerber, I., Wiener, A., Kutscher, A. H., Peretz, D., and Carr, A. C., (eds.): *Bereavement: Its Psychosocial Aspects.* New York, Columbia U Press, 1975.

Weisman, A. D.. *On Dying and Denying.* New York, Behavioral Publications, 1972.

CHAPTER 3

THE TRADITIONAL FUNERAL AND CONTEMPORARY SOCIETY

ROBERT FULTON

DOES THE FUNERAL meet the needs of our society; does the funeral meet the needs of our citizens? These are not new questions, yet they are worth pursuing still.

Sixty thousand years ago, if recent archeological discoveries at Shanidar, Iraq, are to be believed, man buried his dead with ceremony. He did so in a particular way and presumably for very specific reasons, either ideological or religious, given the manner of burial recorded. We must ask ourselves: are the practices that Neanderthal man saw fit to observe following a death some 600 centuries back still relevant and meaningful for contemporary man?

Herodotus commented upon the Egyptian funeral 25 centuries ago in his *Histories*. He reported that there were different types of funerals available to the Egyptian citizen, much as there are today; there were funerals for the wealthy, for the middle classes, and for the poor. Funerals were advertised by means of a sign hung from the doorways of the "houses of life" indicating the style of funeral that could be purchased for a particular price. It should be noted in passing that even at that time Herodotus commented on the high cost of dying and raised the question whether it was reasonable or practical for Egyptian citizens to engage in such rites and ceremonies.

There is evidence to suggest that throughout the entire period of ancient Egyptian history, from the first dynasty of Menes in 4400 BC to the advent of Mohammedism in the 7th Century AD, that the body was treated more or less in the same fashion; that is, embalmed and meticulously prepared for burial. It has been estimated that over four hundred million Egyptians were buried in accordance with this custom. The question remains: does embalming and burial of the body mean to us today what it meant to the ancient Egyptians?

Van Gennep, the Swiss anthropologist, has stated that of all of the rituals and ceremonies that he investigated, he considered the funeral to be the most significant for mankind, both anthropologically and historically. Moreover, he further observed that such rites were generally the most elaborate (Van Gennep, 1961).

Malinowski (1954) believed that the funeral served the individual in a very peculiar way also, apart from the religious premises that provide the philosophical support for individual participation in funerary rites. It was his contention that the funeral served to preserve the integrity of the individual's psyche by helping to keep him psychologically sound in the face of death and loss.

Durkheim (1954) and Evans-Pritchard (1965) have also argued that the funeral is an important social event. They perceived mortuary rites as preserving the structure of society by allowing its members to see that even in the fact of the devastation that death may have wreaked upon it, the society itself was still viable. The incorporation of the dead into the "world of the dead" was in fact, they believed, a vital act of social rejuvenation.

David Mandelbaum (1959) has added another dimension to the discussion of mortuary rites. He proposes that rites and ceremonies associated with death be understood in the same light as other rites and ceremonies that are involved in transition and change. He believes they can be more clearly understood if we view them from the perspective of their "latent" as well as "manifest" functions.

The funeral is primarily a ritual that allows us to dispose of a dead human body. There are, however, "latent" functions of a funeral that are not readily perceived. The supportive gathering of others, for instance, gives reassurance that order has been preserved while it provides an important vehicle for the survivors to articulate and dramatize their new as well as traditional roles and relationships within the family and community. The procession, the burial, the sharing of food, as well as the mourning and keening, tell us, dramatically, not only that a death has occurred, but also that the community lives.

But Mandelbaum would caution us that the funeral can also be dysfunctional. He observed that in Java the migration of certain rural groups to an urban environment had a negative rather than a benign effect upon the functional efficacy of their traditional funeral practices. Mandelbaum points out, however, that not all occasions where conflict results are necessarily dysfunctional experiences. He reports that at every funeral he observed among the Kotas of India certain members would be chased away, and prevented from showing their respect to the deceased. A fight would ensue and only after the expression of much hard feeling would a third group intervene and resolve the conflict between the two contesting parties. Such behavior among the Kotas, he informs us, is institutionalized; it is organized conflict and as such it is not necessarily a dysfunctional aspect of these particular ceremonies. To the contrary, he believes they serve to reinforce social bonds and the vitality of the group. Essentially he says they are "rituals of rebellion," and as such are an integral and important part of the funeral ceremony.

Some five years ago, the Minister of Defense for Kenya, Mr. Tom Mboya, was assassinated. His death resulted in the subsequent deaths of more than a dozen fellow citizens among the Luo and Kikuyu tribes of that nation, and the destruction of hundreds of thousands of dollars worth of property. The English journal, *The Economist*, reported at the time that never in the history of Nairobi had there been such disturbance and loss of life as that which followed the death of Mr. Mboya.

In Kenya, it is a tribal obligation to see that the deceased is returned to his village and buried on his father's land with only members of the tribal community in attendance. Mr. Mboya was killed by a member of the Kikuyu tribe. The Kikuyu were excluded from taking part in his funeral not only by virtue of the fact that they had been held responsible for his death, but also because it is traditional for the tribes to exclude all but their own. There is the possibility therefore that when Jomo Kenyatta, the present prime minister of Kenya, dies there will be civil strife in Kenya, strife of such magnitude that the national aspirations of Kanya may well be threatened. Mr. Kenyatta is a Kikuyu. It is possible that his mourners will exclude the Luo, who represent the second strongest political party as well as the second strongest tribal group in Kenya, from participation in the ceremonies. Indeed they may hold the Luo responsible for the death itself. If the national state of Kenya survives his death, it will be only because of the statesmanship of the Kikuyu and the intrinsic reasonableness of the Luo in recognizing that the state must take precedence over tribal ambitions and traditions.

If we can turn for a moment to the United States and review its history as it relates to the death of national figures, I think we can see a parallel that is important for us to consider as well as introduce another dimension to the discussion. I have moved from the point of asserting that the funeral can be a significant and functional activity for the individual and society to the observation that it also has the potential to jeopardize the integrity and solidarity of a community or national group. The funeral also has the power, I believe, to heal national wounds.

Recall if you will the state funeral that was held for President Kennedy. A montage of images of that funeral continue to have the power to stir the emotions and to remind us again of that tragic time: Mrs. Jacqueline Kennedy kneeling at the side of her husband's flag-draped casket with her daughter Caroline; John, the President's son, standing in brave salute; the solemn procession down Pennsylvania Avenue; the heavy casket borne gracefully and respectfully by both black and white members of the Armed Services; a spirited black horse following a casket laden caisson pulled by six matched greys.

We should remember too that the leaders of the entire allied world were also in attendance and took part in the funeral procession. When we reflect upon that fact, we can appreciate better what anthropologists mean when they say that the funeral is functional to society, because in one afternoon President Kennedy's funeral declared in effect that there was again order in America; that there was not a rightist take-over or a Communist plot that was going to destroy this country. It declared symbolically that the nation was united and prepared to go on despite the tragic death of the president.

The funeral of President Kennedy was followed in a few short years by the funerals of his brother, Senator Robert Kennedy, and that of Dr. Martin Luther King. As before, these deaths threatened social and political disruption throughout the nation. In the funeral of Dr. King, mules and a farm cart took the place of grey horses and a caisson but in essence the meaning was the same. The funeral declared to the world that Dr. King was dead. But most importantly it also reaffirmed those principles by which he had lived.

Recall the fact that there were white faces as well as black following those mules in Atlanta. How different was Dr. Martin Luther King's funeral from the funeral of Mr. Tom Mboya, and how different our society might be today if we had engaged in the same kind of behavior that was observed in Kenya. If the leaders of the Southern Christian Movement had said, "If a white man has killed Dr. King, the principal spokesman for nonviolence and racial harmony in this country, what hope is there ever for whites and blacks to live in peace? If this is their way of dealing with us, then to hell with them."

The peaceful association of white and black man in this country is more possible today by virtue of the fact that Dr. King's survivors saw, in his funeral, an opportunity to bind the wound that his death had caused to the body politic.

The funeral, then, is a functional or a dysfunctional activity depending upon place and circumstance. In the case of Kenya, I am tempted to predict that the funeral for President Kenyatta is going to do the state terrible mischief, given Kikuyu philosophy and tribal tradition. But for America, I would contend the recent national funerals have been functional with respect to the social order.

Thirty-nine surveys were conducted following the funeral of President Kennedy. They concluded that the American public responded to the funeral of President Kennedy in a way that was most personal and which followed a well-defined pattern of grief familiar to medical practice. In general, the studies reported that the people mourned the death of President Kennedy. They mourned him as Lindemann (1944) has described the process of mourning for people who have lost a significant relative or friend. I would conclude that the funeral for President Kennedy and those for Senator Kennedy and Dr. King were functional in that they served the formal needs of our society at the same time as they provided a vehicle for the utterance of private grief.

But we need to ask: because a funeral is functional at one level, need it be functional at another level? The answer, I believe, is no.

We have in our society a group of people who, increasingly, in the last few years, have expressed concern and criticism over the contemporary American funeral. I interviewed some of these people a few years back and, for the most part, it can be said that those who are most concerned about the American funeral are generally middle or upper-middle class in terms of their life style, better educated than most, nontraditional in their religious affiliation or profess no religious commitment whatsoever. These people do not accept the funeral for anything more than what they perceive it to have been since the days of Shanidar, namely, a ritual that is both pagan and ostentatious.

Yet, from the time of Shanidar to the present, we *have* engaged in a set of practices—both East and West—that expresses a belief in an afterlife, in a "world of the dead." The belief in immortality and its corollary belief in a world of the dead have meant, however, that the primary focus of the funeral has been that of a rite of incorporation, that is, a concern for the "physical" problem of transporting the deceased, with all of his attributes, privileges, rights and effects, into the "next" world, whole and complete.

Today such beliefs and practices are contrary to the philosophical and ideological commitment of certain groups of people in American society. Many people today do not believe in a life after death, they do not believe in a "world of the dead," and they do not believe that it is necessary or felicitous to consume the resources of the living for the doubtful benefit it may have for the dead. To the contrary, for many persons today the most desirable procedure is also the simplest—one that involves as little material expense as possible and as few people in attendance as are necessary to dispose of the corpse. For a growing number of persons this means immediate disposition of the body with no public ceremony or mourners in attendance.

But Van Gennep, Evans-Pritchard, Durkheim and other anthropologists have recognized that there are important aspects of the funeral other than the symbolic expression of a theological belief in immortality or the dramaturgical incorporation of the dead. I think it is important for us to consider what these aspects are and what their place and function may be for our contemporary world.

The funeral, besides being historically a rite of incorporation, is also a rite of integration as well as a rite of separation. The funerals of

President Kennedy, Dr. Martin Luther King and Senator Kennedy, and that of Mr. Mboya, were rites of integration, for their dramaturgy declared that the world goes on, that man lives, that the social order prevails and that we continue to have faith in the justice and mercy of God or whomever we choose to believe to be looking after us —albeit somewhat negligently—these days. But it is a drama that tells us that we have lost someone through death. As such, it focuses attention upon the survivors and to the degree that it does so it is a rite of separation as well.

The real question for us today is: if the funeral is a rite of integration and separation, is it functional? Is it worth the time and effort expended upon it? That is the question, and that is what I tried to find out in a study recently conducted at the University of Minnesota. Five hundred and sixty-five widows and widowers from the Twin-Cities area of Minneapolis-St. Paul were interviewed, and briefly, what I found was this: the people who participated in what would be termed a "traditional" funeral, i.e. who viewed the body and who involved their friends and relatives in the ceremony, reported having fewer adjustment problems than those who did not. Further, the respondents reported a more positive recall of the deceased, and reported closer ties and warmer relationships with their relatives. The funeral for these respondents seemed to have brought the surviving family members close together; there was reported a greater sense of urgency with respect to being kind and considerate of other survivors.

When we compared the respondents who had less than the traditional funeral, i.e. those who did not view the body or had arranged immediate disposition of the remains (setting aside the Jewish respondents who traditionally do not view), we found that those who had requested no viewing and/or immediate disposition of the body reported experiencing the greatest hostility following the death, the greatest increase in the consumption of alcohol, tranquilizers and sedatives, the greatest increase in tension and anxiety, the lowest positive recall of the deceased, and, in general, particularly among the male respondents, greater problems in adjustment to the death.

The male respondents also chose cremation more often as the method of disposition for their spouses, and reported fewer services in which the body was viewed, and, concomitantly, more instances of immediate disposition of the body. In terms of male-female responses, it is of interest to note the difference between the reactions to, and disposition of, the body. Wives treated their husband's body traditionally, i.e. they arranged for an earth burial, while husbands, particularly those reporting a professional occupation, had their wives' bodies cremated in a significantly greater number of instances. They also reported having the least positive recall of the deceased of any of the groups studied and the greatest difficulty in adjusting to their loss.

The study is partial and incomplete and there is still much to be done, but I would say in response to the question, "Is the modern contemporary funeral functional?" that these people who are looking for alternate ways do not appear to have found any to be particularly functional for them. On the other hand, those people who observed the practices generally associated with the traditional funeral reported a better post-death adjustment.

I think our study shows the contemporary funeral to be functional to the extent that it recognizes the separation and integration issues associated with a death. And I would argue that, given our new-found understanding of the social and psychological dimension of loss and grief, we should put greater emphasis upon the funeral as a rite of separation and integration and less upon the funeral as a rite of incorporation. To do so is not only to recognize the social and clinical values associated with such an orientation, but also to recognize the decreasing relevancy of the funeral for a great number of people as a rite of incorporation. I would think that in appreciating this subtle but nevertheless significant shift in emphasis, we will do ourselves and our fellow men a great service.

REFERENCES

Durkheim, E.: *The Elementary Forms of Religious Life,* translated by J. W. Swaine. London, Allen and Unwin, 1954.

Evans-Pritchard, E. E.: *Theories of Primitive Religion.* Oxford, Clarendon, 1965.

Lindemann, E.: Symptomatology and management of acute grief. *Am J Psychiatry, 101*: 141, 1944.

Malinowski, B.: *Magic, Science and Religion.* New York, Doubleday, 1954.

Mandelbaum, D.: Social uses of funeral rites. In Feifel, H., (ed.): *The Meaning of Death.* New York, McGraw-Hill, 1959.

Van Gennep, A.: *The Rites of Passage,* translated by M. B. Vizedom and G. L. Caffee, Chicago, U of Chicago Pr, 1961.

CHAPTER 4

THE FUNERAL AND THE BEREAVED

PAUL E. IRION

THE LITERATURE of cultural anthropology indicates that nearly every culture has developed some sort of ceremonialized patterns for marking the death of a member of that society. Such ceremonies seem to have two major functions: to separate the body of the deceased from the community of the living and to assist the mourners in adjustment to their loss.

It is my intention to describe in some detail, according to our psychological understanding, the major needs of the bereaved and then to point ways in which the funeral, rightly understood and conducted, can meet those needs.

The funeral is part of a process in which the mourner restructures his life without the presence of the person who has died. This process recognizes changes in the status of both the deceased and the mourners. It is obvious that the deceased has changed because he has died and is no longer a part of the aspect of existence which we call life. The mourner has changed because his life is now lived without the relationship to the deceased as he has known it. There is movement along a continuum from a relationship of presence (i.e. living, interactive, responsive relationship) to a relationship of memory.

The funeral also is part of a pattern through which the mourners interact with the social groups of which they are a part. In its optimum expression the funeral is a social event in which mourners are surrounded by a group which shares something of their loss and joins them in marking the end of the relationship of presence with dignity.

Then follows a period of transition during which life is reorganized without the deceased. When this transition is completed, there is reunion or reincorporation of the mourners into normal social relationships with the group. This process is much more apparent in a society which observes formal mourning periods. Modern American social practices no longer follow such a pattern. Within a day or two following the funeral, most behavior unique to mourning is abandoned. Individuals have little or no social guidance for the reorganization of life without the deceased. This means that the brief period, in which the funeral is one of the major focuses, is extremely important because it contains a condensation of experiences which were formerly prolonged. If one views mourning as a painful, abnormal experience, this brevity is cause for rejoicing. If one sees mourning as a therapeutic process which inevitably requires time, there must be concern that the brief period allotted be utilized with maximum effectiveness. A part of the vital function of the funeral is to assist in all three of the phases in the rite of passage of the mourners (to use van Gennep's term [1961]) during these days: the separation or isolation, the transition to life without the deceased, and reunion with the group.

Loss which comes through the death of a significant other produces in mourners psychological needs that can be met in the funeral. Lindemann (quoted in Jackson, 1963), who pioneered the modern psychiatric understanding of grief, stated: "The funeral service is psychologically necessary in order to give the opportunity for 'grief work.' The bereaved must be given the capacity to work through his grief if he is to come out of the situation emotionally sound. Finally, we need to see to it that those whom we serve are left with comforting memories. Some will argue this point. I think, however, it is psychologically sound." The funeral is an integral part of the series of experiences through which persons pass in the course of bereavement.

The funeral has several fundamental psychological functions: to increase the acceptance of the loss, to sanction and encourage the expression of one's feelings toward the reality in which one finds himself, and to participate in the process of working through these feelings.

The funeral is helpful psychologically by enabling mourners to confront realistically the crisis of loss. Anthropological studies indicate that there is some basis for assuming that one of the points of origin for the funeral was the need to cope with the reality of death. A mourner who is unwilling or unable to face the fact of death encounters difficulty in coping with the loss. The person who accepts as reality that death has taken place is aided because there is then a reasonable explanation for the profound feelings which sweep over him in bereavement. He knows why life seems so empty, why he seems to be resentful of other people whose lives are untouched, why he wants to pull away from contact with others. But even more important, the individual is motivated to begin the painful process of mourning, the process of reorganizing life without the presence of the deceased.

The funeral underscores the reality of the bereavement situation as it offers realistic interpretation of what has taken place. It provides a kind of consensual validation because the mourner is joined by others in the group who are experiencing a similar loss. The separation from the body of the deceased by burial or cremation affirms further that the relationship as it has been known has really been severed.

Acceptance of reality demands a response which is seen in the various feelings evoked by bereavement. Each individual response is unique, but all have in common the need for expression. This ventilation of feelings of the bereaved serves a variety of purposes. It is a healthful catharsis, giving release to pent-up feelings, making available for more constructive use energy which has been devoted to denying or avoiding such strong feelings. The need for catharsis is followed by the need for developing insight. While catharsis is helpful, its healing capacity is limited without a growing awareness of the nature of the feelings that are released and some understanding of their origin. Although the funeral itself will very probably not be an occasion for such insight, it can be an event in which catharsis is enabled, opening the way for the development of insight.

Another psychological value of the funeral is seen in the way in which it supports the process of remembering the deceased. Freud's (1959) early discussion of mourning begins to illuminate this task. "Reality passes its verdict—that the object no longer exists—upon each single one of the memories and hopes through which the libido was attached to the lost object, and the ego, confronted as it were with the decision whether it will share this fate, is persuaded by the sum of its narcissistic satisfaction in being alive to sever its attachment to the nonexistent object." Lindemann's research built on this foundation and pointed to the necessity for "learning to live with memories of the deceased." This is a matter of delicate balance. It would not be healthful for the mourner to try to recall the deceased from the dead by his memories, trying neurotically to perpetuate the relationship through illusion. Neither would it be healthful to seek to extinguish all memory of the deceased because of the painfulness of such recall. The deceased must be remembered in a context of finality as one who has lived *and died*. The remembrances are a point of contact with the life of the deceased which are radically different from the relationship of presence during life.

The funeral itself is only one part, sometimes even a small part, in the whole psychological process of meeting bereavement. Yet, because of its public nature it is extremely important. It represents the response of the community or the church to the emotional experiences of the mourners. Thus, it cannot be regarded as either irrelevant or contradictory to the psychological processes of acceptance, release, expression and assimilation that enable the mourner to endure and overcome the tremendous disorganization of his life which has taken place.

Form follows function. Design must, therefore, be related to usefulness and efficiency. But, even more, design seeks to integrate usefulness and beauty. The designer's problem is to find forms which meet diverse and complicated needs.

Several assumptions are basic to this effort to lay out an effective form for the funeral. First, the rationale of the funeral is fundamentally sound. I believe that the psychological, social and religious principles for helping those who are bereaved are well enough established to enable us to describe with some adequacy the function of the funeral. Rightly understood and conducted, the funeral has the potentiality for providing the form by which these functions are fulfilled.

Second, elements of the funeral practice of many ages, including our own, have not followed this rationale. It is undeniable that some forms have developed which have not been related to the major purposes of the funeral, or which may represent minor functions that disregard or even contradict more significant function.

A third assumption is that the existence of forms which do not follow the real function of the funeral has only damaged, but not destroyed, the validity of the funeral. I cannot share the view of some that the funeral is anachronistic and should be discarded. I believe that full value can be reclaimed for the funeral by bringing together function and form.

What, then, are the functions the funeral can fulfill for those in acute grief?

One of the functions of the funeral is to provide a framework of supportive relationship for mourners. This support is operative on two rather different levels: the support of religious or philosophical meanings and the support of a concerned group of family and friends.

As thoughtful man confronts death, he is driven by age-old questions. What is death? What happens when a person dies? What causes death? Is there any justice in death? It is not only the meaning of death in general that is being probed, but mourners also struggle to fit the death of a loved one into their total picture of existence. The religions of the world and various philosophies of life have sought to provide some answers, hypotheses, articles of faith. The major goal is to support the mourners with a context of meaning which will be helpful in working through some of the intellectual problems associated with bereavement.

Since bereavement is a shared experience, the group (family, congregation, neighborhood) stands ready to support each of its members, particularly those who are most deeply involved in this individual loss. One of the ways in which the group fulfills this function is by just standing by to sustain the mourners until they have sufficient strength to assimilate their loss. Not only is this done through thoughtful gift-giving, flowers, memorials, food, favors, it is also done through attendance at the funeral. Here family and friends gather for the public occasion in which a life is commemorated, common meanings for death are affirmed and there is separation from the body of the deceased. On most occasions these are painful experiences for mourners and they are sustained by the presence of others in an act of community.

The funeral fulfills the function of providing supportive relationship most adequately when maximum participation by the community is enabled. This means that it is best when the funeral can be so arranged that a maximum number of the community can be present and participating. It also means that those in attendance should be participants rather than merely observers. Opportunity should be provided for readings in unison or, where possible, for some of those in attendance to speak of the loss which is shared by all. The public, corporate dimension of the funeral can be an effective channel for supporting those who have sustained the heaviest loss.

A second major function of the funeral grows out of the need for reenforcing the reality of death. The funeral is a means for enabling the individual to acknowledge his loss in a public setting. Not only does it provide a way of dramatizing the loss and what it means to the individual, it also, as we have said, affords a supportive relational framework in which the weight of reality can be tolerated and the painful process of reorientation begun.

To follow this function, it is necessary that the form of the funeral have a note of authenticity. It would probably be naive to insist that everything appear exactly as it really is. Life is just not lived that way. However, it is possible to strive to reduce to a minimum the disguises of reality and to work toward full recognition that disguises are involved. It would probably be expecting too much to propose the removal of all the accoutrements of the funeral that are provided to make it more aesthetically pleasing: the cosmetics provided to make the corpse more presentable, the simple flowers which relieve the starkness of the occasion, the artificial turf covering the excavated grave. Such things do damage only when they are taken seriously, when they complete the illusion of unreality, when they participate in a grand disguise of death as life. If that is their purpose, they should be resisted.

The funeral should not lend itself to any *serious* attempt to disguise reality. In a way, what is required here is what Kierkegaard called humor. This he defined as the capacity to see inadequacies and imperfections in something and still to maintain the capacity to hold it in high regard. Applied to the reality of the funeral, this would mean that one could see the imperfections manifested by the efforts made to approve appearances: removing the pallor of the corpse, of covering a pile of dirt. But such minor embellishments must *never* be used to hide the fact that death has occurred, that relationships have been severed, that a new focus for life must be found by the bereaved.

There should be no effort to disguise the fact that we are dealing with the *dead* body of a loved one, with an open grave. Careful evaluation must be made to see whether practices are merely minor aesthetic touches or major attempts to deny the reality of death. Probably the central point in this whole issue is the corpse, the body of the deceased. On the one hand, it often has been regarded as a means for creating the illusion of life instead of facing the reality of death. It has been regarded as asleep rather than dead, it has been treated to give the illusion of imperishability, it has been the object of feelings which will not admit that death has changed relationships. So there have been proposals, many of them thoughtful, that getting rid of the body from the funeral entirely would avoid these illusions.

But one can also argue that, surrounded by the proper meanings, the presence of the dead body can be a significant means for reenforcing the reality of death and loss. If we have regard for the wholeness of man, his body, now dead, cannot be sloughed off unthinkingly. It provides tangibility, a physical object, which all the mourners see and consensually validates the fact of death.

Another function of the funeral is to make possible the acknowledgment and expression of the mourners' feelings. A mourner needs to be freed to release the great variety of feelings which may be welling up in him. Some of these feelings may well be verbalized or acted out in the funeral. Of course, not all feelings will emerge fully at the time of the funeral. But it is one of the functions of the funeral to provide a pattern of freedom and acceptance which will permit the emergence and assimilation of feelings as the mourning process goes on.

One can see the funeral as a means of creating a climate of acceptance within which the feelings that a person already has within him can be recognized and accepted. The content of the funeral should convey understanding of the feelings of the mourners, e.g. the sorrow which accompanies many deaths, the pain of separation. It is important not to dictate what feelings the mourner should be having.

Too often in the past one of the important criteria for judging elements of the funeral was: will it cause an expression of feelings? On this basis some funerals have been made coldly impersonal because references to the deceased brought tears to the eyes of mourners. Others have proposed eliminating the body of the deceasd from the funeral because it becomes a focus for the feelings of the bereaved. Still others want the funeral to be very brief, to the point of being perfunctory, as a way of reducing the emotional involvement of the mourners.

It is more helpful for the funeral to permit and even encourage the mourners to accept their feelings toward their situation, toward the deceased and toward themselves. The funeral can affirm the willingness of the community to understand and accept the feelings of the mourners. So any effort to screen the bereaved family from the community, to privatize the funeral, carries the implication that this community is unable or unwilling to accept and share in the expression of the mourners' feelings.

One other function of the funeral is to mark a fitting conclusion of the life of the one who has died. It may be thought of as a ritual of separation. There is a sense in which the radical discontinuity of death from life makes itself felt in sensing the ending of the relationship as it has been known.

There are a number of ways in which the funeral can accomplish this purpose. The realistic way in which the funeral faces death is involved. Realism is supported by the presence of the body of the dead and the separation from the body. It is sustained by a disavowal of the goal of long-term preservation. It is supported by the practice of concluding the funeral by disposing of the body of the deceased, whether by burial or cremation.

Death should be portrayed in terms of *both* the continuity and discontinuity it involves. To overbalance either of these poles renders the funeral less effective in carrying out this function. If the funeral rests solely on the theme of existence after death, as resurrection, social immortality or the ongoingness of the life-process, the finality of death from the standpoint of human experience may be regarded as illusory. The funeral is not designed to affirm that death has no effect upon man, that death is circumvented rather than endured.

The function of fittingly marking the conclusion of life also involves ways in which honor and respect can be shown for the one who has died. This does not mean an extravagant display of esteem by planning an unduly lavish funeral or through expansive memorials. This is no effort to deify the dead. Rather it is a recognition that death is an intensely personal thing. A person has died. Man's death is as distinctly individual and personal as his life. To pay no attention to his demise is a depersonalizing measure, just as much as it is to pay no attention to his living. Sophocles in his *Antigone* bore ancient witness to this fact. In a real way, marking the death of a person is a means of testifying to the worthwhileness of his living.

Obviously, it is clear that I regard the funeral as a valuable experience when it is rightly understood and conducted. I am not oblivious to some of its present shortcomings, but I am unwilling to accept the thesis that the funeral no longer can fulfill useful functions. There are elements of the funeral which have brought value to individuals and groups for many centuries. It can be shown that, even though some of the values may have been obscured by some contemporary patterns, the values persist and can be restored to full effectiveness.

REFERENCES

Freud, S.: Mourning and melancholia. *Collected Papers.* New York, Basic Books, 1959, vol. IV.

Jackson, E.: *For the Living.* New York, Channel Pr, 1963.

Lindemann, E.: Symptomatology and management of acute grief. *Am J Psychiatry, 101*:141, 1944.

Van Gennep, A.: *The Rites of Passage.* Chicago, U of Chicago Pr, 1961.

CHAPTER 5

SOME OBSERVATIONS ON GRIEF AND THE FUNERAL

ROYAL KEITH

"GRIEF: MENTAL SUFFERING from bereavement; remorse or the like or cause of it." How abstractly, coldly, and impersonally does the dictionary define one of the most universal and poignant emotions of the human condition. Feelings of grief can be caused by a number of events in a person's life which result in loss or separation: divorce; loss of money, income, or job; loss of physical health; loss of freedom; and so forth. Perhaps the most severe of all feelings of grief are those accompanying a loss experienced because of a death.

Edmund Spenser said, "Great grief will not be tould, and can more easily be thought than said." Throughout recorded history man in all walks of life—from artists to philosophers, from poets to theologians—has grappled with not only the abstract concept of the meaning of death, but just as significantly with the impact of death on those who survive. It is they, the survivors, who must reckon with the awesome feelings of grief and sorrow.

Individuals do not receive much practice, training, or rehearsing for coping with these feelings. But in a lifetime, each person will be the survivor of many deaths which affect him in varying degrees. Before some observations are made, it is important to describe these variations of the grief experience.

When death occurs, it is possible to distinguish at least three groups of survivors who have varying degrees of needs and emotional responses to that death . To illustrate this concept let us use a hypothetical example. A thirty-five year-old man is killed in an auto accident. He has a wife, two teenage children, parents and two brothers. They would show all the symptoms of acute grief that have been described in the literature: the sense of irretrievable loss, somatic distress, disorientation, denial feelings, hostility, etc. (Lindemann, 1965; Jackson, 1961). They would be the primary survivors of his death.

The young man has several intimate friends with whom he shared much of life's experiences and the closeness of human companionship. They would show some of the signs of acute grief, including the feelings of denial, irretrievable loss, and possibly hostility, but probably would not have the feelings of disorientation and physical symptomatology of the primary survivors. For them life would still go on normally after some grief work has been accomplished. These friends would be the secondary survivors of his death.

The young man has been an active member of his community and has many social and business acquaintances. They would probably suffer none of the feelings of acute grief, with the possible exception of feelings of denial. They would experience a personalized feeling of transference of that death situation into their own life experience. In addition, they would feel the generalized sense of loss expressed by John Donne: "Any man's death diminishes me, because I am involved in Mankinde." They would be the tertiary survivors of that death.

Obviously, this general definition of primary, secondary and tertiary survivors is not uniformly applicable to all situations. In each grief situation, there may be different responses, i.e. a brother who was remote from the dead brother may be a tertiary survivor, an extremely close friend may have all the responses of a primary survivor. However, for the purposes of this discussion, these rather artificial delineations can be meaningful.

As has been mentioned above, it is fortunate that none of us are required to play the role of a primary survivor of a death frequently. Less infrequent will be the occasions when we will be the secondary survivors of a death. But, particularly as we grow older, we will be the tertiary survivors of a death. When we view the grief experience in this context, its universality becomes glaring and its occurrence begins to become a common experience in all lives.

It is not surprising then that man has devised "an organized, purposeful, flexible, time-limited, group centered response to death" in order to cope with these multiple reactions he must experience (Lamers,

1969). Most cultures have worked out a ceremonious disposition of the dead to help the survivors work through their grief. Among the reasons for this ceremonious disposition or funerary behavior are the need for religious and social support, the need for reality, the need for expression of sorrow, and the need for new relationships (Irion, 1956).

In developing ceremonious disposition of the dead, man has attempted to meet the plethora of needs of the multiple survivors of a death. It is not the author's intent to judge whether these practices have historically accomplished their purpose, i.e. to assist the primary, secondary and tertiary survivors through the grief experience. Rather, these practices must be examined as they relate to modern man's needs in the death crisis in a depersonalized, technological, and mobile society. We should evaluate our practices as they relate to all the survivors of a death: primary, secondary, and tertiary. Some observations can be made at this point which may help us in our evaluation and examination.

First, the survivors of a death have very real needs which must be met (Irion, 1956). These needs are psychological: the need to work through the grief emotion, to accept the fact that death occurred, and to work out new patterns of behavior; sociological: the need for human companionship and support; theological: the need to understand the meaning of death and life in a religious and/or spiritual context; and physical: the need to work through and acknowledge what Lindemann refers to as a "syndrome with somatic symptomatology (Lindemann, 1965). None of these needs can be ignored or avoided without the possibility of harmful consequences. For the mental and physical well-being of the survivor of a death, these needs must be faced realistically; society, in its supportive procedures for the survivors, must hold these needs as paramount in importance.

Secondly, it has been mentioned that in most human cultures there are rites and ceremonies when death occurs. There is no evidence to suggest that modern man needs ritual less than earlier man during major life events. On the contrary, the evidence is building that man may need ritual more than ever before. Alvin Toffler in *Future Shock* states, "In an accelerative society the need may well be for the preservation of certain continuities. Ritual provided an important change-buffer. Certain repeated ceremonial forms—rituals surrounding birth, death, puberty, marriage and so on—helped individuals in primitive societies to reestablish equilibrium after some major adaptive event had taken place." He goes on to say that today's society ". . . may even need to manufacture ritual" (Toffler, 1970).

In *Twentieth Century Faith, Hope and Survival,* Margaret Mead describes the essence of ritual as the "ability of the known form to reinvoke past emotion, to bind the individual to his own past experience, and to bring the members of the group together in a shared experience." She goes on to state that "Ritual also gives people access to intensity of feelings at times when responsiveness is muted." It appears that in a depersonalized, technological, and mobile society such as ours that the need for shared experience through ritual may be greater, not less, than the past.

But there is a certain paradox here. Mead states: "Contemporary American celebrations suffer from our objections to anything we can classify as ritualistic, repetitive, or even familiar." Dr. Robert Kastenbaum seems to touch on the same point when he states: "The orientation of the healthy person toward the prospects of his own death, the orientation of the dying person, the orientation toward funerary practices—these are among the situations which now require decisions by the individual. Death, in this sense, has become decontextualized. There is not the reliable, heavily reinforced social fabric that enabled the ancient Egyptian, for example, to know that he was doing the right thing in the right way" (Kastenbaum and Aisenberg, 1972). At a time when it is apparent that man needs stabilizing human behavior patterns in response to death, it is ironical that there are efforts to de-ritualize and "de-contextualize" our responses to death. As Geoffrey Gorer states, "we must give back to death—natural death—its parade and publicity, readmit grief and mourning" (Gorer, 1965).

A third observation is that each survivor of a death is going through a uniquely individualistic experience. The Book of Lamentations records: "Is it nothing to you, all ye that pass by? Behold, and see if there be any sorrow like unto my sorrow." Although we can observe similarities of grief reactions, it should always be remembered that each man's grief is indeed unique to him. As psychiatrist William M. Lamers has observed: "For unless we appreciate the fact that human behavior has infinite depth, variety, and sequence we will continue to deal with people in a stereotyped manner. Only if we gain understanding of the forces and reasons underlying behavior will we be able to appreciate the wide variety of reactions to loss" (Lamers, 1965).

The form of response each person uses in an acute grief crisis should reflect his individual reaction to the loss and/or the individuality of the person who died. The pattern of this behavioral response should include, at least within a broad framework, Mead's "known form," Toffler's "repeated ceremonial forms," and Kastenbaum's "heavily reinforced social fabric." But to adhere strictly and exclusively to a routinized, stereotyped, or "doing it as it's been done before" ritual or ceremony may possibly be dysfunctional to the primary survivors of the death. In other words, routinized or stereotyped ritual may be beneficial to some, but it certainly is not mandatory for all survivors to achieve healthy and stable response and behavior patterns during their grief crisis. Certain fundamental elements of funeralization should be present to provide its basic benefits. These elements include the opportunity to face the reality of death, the opportunity for social support, the opportunity for religious support, the opportunity for the expression of emotion, and the disposition of the body (Irion, 1956). All these elements can be present, but at the same time there must be the opportunity for the survivors to express their individualism and uniqueness. It is incumbent on those who serve and counsel the survivors to encourage them to express their individuality, but to do so within the affirmatively flexible perimeter of ritual.

The individuality of the grief response can be further illustrated in Lindemann's concept of "anticipatory grief" (Lindemann, 1965). Dr. Robert Fulton and Julie Fulton have stated: "For many people today the death of an elderly relative occasions only the barest acknowledgment, and such a death might properly be designated as a 'low grief' death." The low grief response is due to the fact that . . . "the family members are so concerned with their adjustment in the face of the potential loss that they slowly experience all the phases of normal grief as they cope with the illness or endure the separation prior to the death" (Fulton and Fulton, 1970). This phenomenon is anticipatory grief. For our consideration of the individuality of the grief response, it is important to observe here that not all the primary survivors have the opportunity to experience anticipatory grief. In our mobile society, it is frequent that some of the primary survivors live apart from the location of the dying person. Although the primary survivors who are continually confronted with the dying patient may experience anticipatory grief, those primary survivors who are remote in distance will not experience the same grief reactions. In effect, although they expect the death, they do not anticipate the grief. When the death does occur, they have most, if not all, of their grief work yet to do. This observation again points out the wide diversity of needs and reactions to death, even among the primary survivors of the same death.

A fourth observation is that the survivors of a death, particularly the primary survivors, are in a situation where multiple decisions are to be made, yet the impact of grief makes it a most difficult time to be making decisions. It has been suggested by some that the way to circumvent this dilemma is to make the decisions before the death occurs, when rational decision making is more feasible. It is generally agreed and increasingly accepted by our society that death should not be a taboo subject. As Dr. Avery Weisman observes: "The bereavement process may be facilitated by an early discussion with and among the potential survivors" (Weisman, 1972). Although the facing of death and the discussion of death before the event can develop a healthy mental attitude about death, there is substantial evidence developing that specific decisions made a priori can be detrimental to the grief process of the survivors when the death does occur.

An example may help to illustrate this point. The young parents of a three-year-old girl who died of cystic fibrosis had discussed prior to the death the fact that they did not wish to view the body after their child had died. Arrangements were made to dispose of the body immediately, with a memorial service to be held at their church two days later. A few minutes before the service, the mother arrived at the funeral home requesting to see the body. After viewing her daughter, the mother conceded that although she thought she had adjusted to the grief experience during the dying process, she could not face the fact that her daughter was really dead. She later indicated that the service had more meaning for her as she was fully aware that it related to her daughter's death, which she could have denied had she not seen the dead body. A firm decision a priori had to be rescinded because of feelings unanticipated when the decision was made. This woman was fortunate. Usually in the acute grief experience, "What is done cannot be changed, what is not done will ever remain so" (Raether, 1971).

A fifth observation can be made which closely relates to the above. Because of the difficulty of decision making, the susceptibility of the primary survivors to influence and suggestions by others frequently results in inadequate and sometimes harmful advice. In the example given above, the advice not to "view the corpse" had been read in an article by these parents. Frequently advice is given by well meaning friends and other family members who are not suffering from acute grief. Because their thinking is clear, at least as it relates to their own personal reactions and desired responses to grief, they can advise and influence without realizing that their feelings and suggested responses are not the same as those of the primary survivors. "I know that your mother wanted to be buried back in her home state." "Nothing is too good for your mother." "Vocal music will just drag the funeral out." However, unknown to the friends giving this advice is that intervening years have severed all ties with the home state, the family is undergoing economic hardship because of the long illness, and the singing of a granddaughter had meant a great deal to her grandmother and to the primary survivors. Although well-intentioned, the advice given, if followed, could have harmful effects on the primary survivors at a later time.

Shakespeare observed, "Every one can master a grief but he that has it." Often advice that is given by secondary and tertiary survivors of a death is transference of their own wishes, desires, and responses as if they were the primary survivors. Since they are not directly experiencing the wide range of emotions of acute grief, they are able to intellectualize and rationalize their reactions without understanding the difference between their feelings and needs and those of the primary survivors.

In some instances these rather general observations about the survivors of a death and their grief responses pose challenges for further research, and in other instances they pose dilemmas that must be resolved regarding our reactions as survivors of a death. Let us propose here some rather tentative suggestions, hypotheses and challenges relating to these observations.

First, we have observed that at few times in our lives will we be the primary survivors of a death. However, we will frequently be involved as secondary and tertiary survivors. With the exception of exhaustive study and perhaps painful introspection, there is no procedure whereby an individual can prepare himself or condition himself for the eventual role as a primary survivor. It is suggested here that a person can gain much insight into this role because he is a frequent secondary or tertiary survivor. To some extent, the secondary or tertiary roles a person plays become the only rehearsal stage or practice field for the inevitable role of acute grief. If this suggested concept is valid, then trends toward privatization of funerary behavior for only the primary survivors may be depriving many people of preparation for their own acute grief experiences. It would appear that this suggested concept and hypothesis requires further research.

The privatization or the lack of funerary activity by the primary survivors may have other detrimental consequences. Those we traditionally assume to be the primary survivors may not be the survivors with the most acute grief needs. This could occur for several reasons, including but not limited to: 1. the primary survivors have worked through their loss with the phenomenon of anticipatory grief, which has been examined elsewhere in this paper; 2. they have intellectualized or rationalized the loss to the extent they feel they have no need for social, emotional, or religious support; 3. exaggerated forms of denial may prevent the primary survivors' acknowledgment of the death in any way, including funerary behavior. Many times when this occurs, however, there are secondary or tertiary survivors who do have acute grief needs. They may include a favorite grandson of the deceased, a close friend of the deceased, or, in the instance of our elderly, a close acquaintance from late in life at a retirement home. Insofar as needs are concerned, they become the primary survivors, but they seldom have the opportunity to make the decisions regarding funeralization. This situation is growing in frequency and poses many problems, most important of which is: Who or what will meet the acute grief needs of secondary and tertiary survivors when funerary behavior is denied them?

Secondly, the multiple needs and the plethora of decisions of the primary survivors demand that society provide them with reliable experts in grief. As Lindemann has observed, "There is . . . a painful lack of capacity to initiate and maintain organized patterns of activity. This loss leads to a strong dependency on anyone who will stimulate the bereaved to activity and serve as the initiating agent" (Lindemann, 1965). It has already been observed that relying on the advice of friends who are non experts in the crisis of grief can potentially have detrimental effects.

Most frequently the primary survivors turn for help and advice to those who Kastenbaum refers to as the "Professionals in our death system," funeral directors, physicians, nurses, clergy, and mental health specialists. Kastenbaum observes that these professionals have not given "the participants in the death situation . . . effective answers and emotional support" (Kastenbaum and Aisenberg, 1972). The physicians and nurses, although involved in the dying process, frequently opt out of the system when the death actually occurs. " 'Conspicuous by his absence' is a fairly accurate appraisal of the role of the mental health expert in our culture's death system" (Kastenbaum and Aisenberg, 1972). Most would agree with Kastenbaum's statement that the minister "represents perhaps our most ancient and traditional resource in the death system." The minister in the death system has been examined, and sometimes criticized, in depth in other writings such as Fulton's study in 1959. Suffice it to say here that there are encouraging signs that the clergy are increasing their effectiveness through enlarged seminary and practical seminar training in grief reactions and needs. However, some statistics are showing that nearly 60 percent of the American people have no strong church ties. This suggests that it will be unlikely that the clergy can fill the total role as the expert in our death system. Even within their church community, many clergy wish to confine their role to the affirmation of faith as the vehicle in the resolution of grief.

This leaves the funeral director to fill a significant portion of this critical role in our society, and herein lies the seed for great controversy. It can be argued that the funeral director, almost by default, is already filling this role in contemporary American society. However, objections on two fronts are raised by Ruth Harmer, Jessica Mitford, and others to this evolution of the funeral director as one of the key supportive persons in our death system (Mitford, 1963; Harmer, 1963). First, he has had no specialized training, beyond experience, to qualify for this role, and second, his objectivity as a grief expert is limited by economic motivation. These objections deserve to be examined.

Fulton showed in a study that the general public is looking to the funeral director not only for his physical administrative function, but also as a source of emotional comfort and support during their grief crises (Fulton, 1965). This reliance on the funeral director has had some positive stimulative results. In the past ten years there has been a marked increase in attendance at professional conferences and grief seminars by funeral directors desiring to supplement their knowledge. Curriculum in grief psychology has been expanded and improved at the colleges of mortuary science.

The "in service experience"—the funeral director is the only death system professional who is solely involved with the grief crisis—should not be discounted as a source of knowledge and expertise in assisting the survivors of a death. Documentation of this knowledge is indicated in a study of childhood leukemia by the Langley Porter Neuropsychiatric Institute (Binger, et al., 1969). The authors report the findings of interviews with twenty families of children who died of leukemia and report that 15 families expressed positive feelings toward the funeral director for services he rendered during their grief crisis. The authors conclude that the funeral director's experience with grief reactions provides help to grieving families. The challenge still exists, however, for the funeral director and the student of funeral service to increase and supplement their knowledge and experience to qualify for the role placed on them. Even though some in our society object, including some funeral directors, the fact is that the funeral director is increasingly looked to as *the* key supportive person. This places a substantial responsibility on him to be qualified for that role. The signs are encouraging today that he is working toward that goal.

Society, then, is recognizing the funeral director as one of the key supportive persons in the death system as he demonstrates that his primary concern in a death crisis is the survivors' physical, emotional, and social adaptation to that crisis. This recognition makes it even more imperative that the economic motivation issue be examined. Obviously, the funeral director does have financial considerations. "The funeral director's 'product'. . . is the funeral which is a most complex admixture of service, facilities, equipment and merchandise. It is a thing of infinite variation, related to individual human beings and influenced by a multiplicity of religious, social and psychological customs and traditions" (Bustard, 1971).

The funeral director is not unique in this sense. Other professionals have a similar "admixture" as they deal with the various forms of grief: doctors, lawyers, ministers, hospital administrators, etc. However, the funeral director's financial consideration does include a unique element. Many professionals practice out of tax supported or otherwise public supported buildings while the funeral director must provide his own facility. This factor obviously contributes to the economic concerns of the funeral director. In addition, the funeral director sometimes has the obligation to provide his facility to those either unable or unwilling to compensate him for its use.

To fulfill this obligation, and to avoid the alleged "high cost of dying" criticism, the funeral director has a "social responsibility to make available a wide range of prices to accommodate all of the families . . ." he serves (Nichols, 1971). By offering this wide range of prices he considers the financial concerns of the primary survivors and also considers their personal desires, wishes, and needs (or lack of them) in regards to funeralization. Again, there are positive signs that this policy is becoming the norm. The Code of Professional Practices of the National Funeral Directors Association states: "(the funeral director) . . . shall provide the necessary services and merchandise in keeping with the wishes and finances of the family" (1965). In a Statement of Policy, it is further stated by the National Funeral Directors Association: "There are some people who feel that their needs are not met by a funeral, and they may seek an alternate method of final disposition. After counselling, if a less-than-total funeral is desired, it should be available from the funeral director with his charges adjusted accordingly" (1973). As the public sees these expressions of professional philosophy in practice by funeral directors, the stigma of economic motivation is largely removed.

To further dispel this objection, it is the responsibility of the funeral director to look critically at his costs. He may then come to the realization that the personal supportive services he provides are on a higher value scale than the building he occupies, the cars he provides, or the advertising for which he pays. In the opinion of this writer, the public is increasingly accepting and valuing the funeral director as a key supportive person in the death crisis because his professional expertise is outweighing his economic concerns. This evolution is a positive one for the survivors as they seek help and advice during their grief crisis.

Thirdly, in close relation to the above, there is a critical need for qualitative measurement of the benefits of funerary procedure practiced in the United States today. Is the funeral ceremony as we know it today necessary and helpful? Is it helpful to view the dead body? Should the funeral be public? Should the body be present at the funeral? In effect, is value received for the funerary expenditure? The preponderance of *expert* opinion to date, including that of psychiatrists, sociologists, psychologists, clergy, and funeral directors, is in the affirmative to all these questions. Yet the questions persist and, with the absence of empirical findings, the public remains confused and uncertain in their grief crises. In the meantime, literature suggesting a negative response to these questions is widely read and sometimes followed. The potential for emotional harm can be avoided only if those within the death system begin to give to the public substantiated findings on the most meaningful procedures and responses of survivors when death occurs.

Finally, the only formalized societal response to death and the survivors is during the funerary period lasting two to six days after a death. Society accompanies the primary survivors in this all-important first step toward the recognition and the resolution of their grief, but then, in effect, abandons them. We know, however, that the acute grief symptoms last beyond this period. Gorer states: "During this period (six to twelve weeks) the mourner is in more need of social support and assistance than at any time since infancy and early childhood; and at the moment our society is signally failing to give this support and assistance. The cost of this failure in misery, loneliness, despair and maladaptive behavior is very high" (Gorer, 1965). Dr. Elisabeth Kübler-Ross, Dr. Richard Kalish, and others have shown us how society avoids and shuns the dying patient (Kübler-Ross, 1969;

Kalish, 1966). It is just as evident that we avoid and shun the primary survivors, at least after our encounter with them during the funerary period. With a few notable exceptions, such as the Widow-to-Widow Program of Dr. Phyllis Silverman (Harvard Medical School), there have been few efforts to develop supportive systems after the funerary activity for the recently bereaved. Even the professionals in the death system have abdicated their roles in this critical period. It is incumbent on them, particularly the minister, funeral director, and mental health specialist, to concentrate their efforts and research on this post funeral period which is so difficult for the primary survivors of a death. Hopefully, this effort and research will produce meaningful resources with which all of society can help meet the needs of the survivors weeks and months following the death.

Meanwhile, we must be aware of the stimulating questions asked by Kastenbaum: "Will it become increasingly the case that virtually no notice will be taken of death (and the dead) except for those few individuals deemed especially prominent? Perhaps, however, grief would become interminable and exert a pervasive influence over thought and behavior. This could be a consequence of lacking palpable proof of death and the opportunity for the survivors to traverse a vicarious rite of passage. Can we truly banish the dead without offending an important part of our nature?" (Kastenbaum and Aisenberg, 1972).

The answers to these questions and our responses to these challenges will effect the social and psychological adjustment to acute grief, the special humanness of man, and the meaning of life and death for generations to come. It is imperative that the quest for these answers and these responses be continued and accelerated.

REFERENCES

Binger, C. M., et al.: Childhood leukemia: emotional impact on patient and family. *N Engl J Med, 280*:414-418, 1969.

Bustard, William L.: Funeral service pricing. In Raether, Howard, C., (ed.): *Successful Funeral Service Practice.* New Jersey, Prentice-Hall, 1971, p. 76.

Dønne, John: *Meditation XVII.*

Fulton, Robert: The sacred and the secular: attitudes of the American public toward death, funerals, and funeral directors. In Fulton, Robert, (ed.): *Death and Identity.* New York, Wiley, 1965.

————: A Compilation of Studies Toward Death, Funerals, and Funeral Directors, prepared in 1967.

Fulton, Robert, and Fulton, Julie: A psycho-social aspect of terminal care: anticipatory grief. In Schoenberg, B., Carr, A. C., Peretz, D., and Kutscher, A. H., (eds.): *Psychosocial Aspects of Terminal Care.* New York, Columbia U Pr, 1972.

Gorer, Geoffrey: *Death, Grief, and Mourning.* New York, Doubleday, 1965.

Harmer, Ruth M.: *The High Cost of Dying.* New York, Collier, Macmillan, 1963.

Irion, Paul E.: The Funeral, An Experience of Value, an address given at the 75th Annual Convention of the National Funeral Directors Association, October 24, 1956.

Jackson, Edgar N.: *You and Your Grief.* New York, Channel Press, 1961.

Kalish, Richard: Social distance and the dying. *Community Ment Health J,* 2:152-155, 1966.

Kastenbaum, Robert, and Aisenberg, Ruth: *The Psychology of Death.* New York, Springer Pub, 1972.

Kubler-Ross, Elisabeth: *On Death and Dying.* New York, Macmillan, 1969.

Lamers, William M.: Death, Grief, Mourning, the Funeral and the Child, paper read before the 84th Annual Convention of the National Funeral Directors Association, November 1, 1965, Chicago, Illinois.

Lamers, William M., Jr.: Funerals are good for people—M.D.'s included. *Medical Economics, 46*:4, 1969.

Lindemann, Erich: Symptomatology and management of acute grief. In Fulton, Robert, (ed.): *Death and Identity.* New York, Wiley, 1965.

Mead, Margaret: *Twentieth Century Faith Hope and Survival.* New York, Harper and Row, 1972.

Mitford, Jessica: *The American Way of Death.* New York, Simon and Schuster, 1963.

National Funeral Directors Association: The Code of Professional Practices for Funeral Directors, adopted in 1965.

————: A Statement of Policy, adopted at the annual convention, October 17, 1973.

Nichols, Charles H.: Funeral service pricing. In Raether, Howard C., (ed.): *Successful Funeral Service Practice.* New Jersey, Prentice-Hall, 1971.

Raether, Howard C.: The place of the funeral: the role of the funeral director in contemporary America. *Omega,* Vol. II, 1971.

Shakespeare, William: *Much Ado About Nothing,* III. ii.

Spenser, Edmund: *The Faerie Queene,* I. vii.

Toffler, Alvin: *Future Shock.* New York, Random House, 1970.

Weisman, Avery D.: *On Dying and Denying.* New York, Behavioral Publications, Inc., 1972.

CHAPTER 6

THE SOCIOLOGY OF THE MORTUARY: RELIGION, SEX, AGE, AND KINSHIP VARIABLES

Baheej Khleif

THIS CHAPTER reports results from a study of differences between religion, sex, family position (parent, spouse, etc.), and age groups in attitudes to funerals and ability to cope with death. It is part of a larger survey which investigated attitudes of bereaved to funerals, funeral directors, and behavior of bereaved inside the mortuary in the process of making funeral arrangements. A major portion of that survey was published earlier as a chapter on "Attitudes to the Funeral, Funeral Director, and Funeral Arrangements." That earlier chapter focused on what importance the bereaved give to the funeral in the process of bereavement and on how the bereaved define the role of the funeral director in making funeral arrangements. It also presented findings on how the bereaved feel about several specific items in the funeral arrangements such as casket selection, funeral cost, restoration work, and others. The central findings running throughout the data were that the great majority of bereaved held the funeral and funeral director in very high esteem. Most were satisfied with the cost of the funeral and reacted favorably to the restoration work.[1] There were, however, some interesting differences observed between various groups in the sample. This present chapter offers the additional data on dif-

---

[1] These findings stand very much in opposition to critics of the funeral and funeral director—such as Mitford, Bowman, Harmar, and others. For complete presentation of data supporting these conclusions, please see Baheej Khleif, "Attitudes to the Funeral, Funeral Director, and Funeral Arrangements," in *Grief and the Meaning of the Funeral*, edited by Otto S. Margolis, Howard C. Raether, Austin H. Kutscher, *et al.* (New York: MSS Information, Inc., 1975).

ferences in attitudes according to the religion, sex, and age of the bereaved; and according to the age and family position of the relative
who died. Data are also presented on how the bereaved feel about
expressing their grief and their experience in discussing death in the
family and community.

COLLECTION OF DATA

The data for this study were collected by questionnaire mailed to
bereaved in La Crosse, Wisconsin, in December, 1970. A saturation
sample was taken of all the obituaries which appeared in the La Crosse
Tribune in 1969. The year, 1969, was chosen thinking it was distant
enough to allow for detailed inquiry but recent enough to enable clear
recollection of the funeral process. The questionnaire was mailed to
the next of kin listed in each obituary notice. Addresses were given in
the notices. When a choice had to be made among next of kin (e.g.
when a brother and sister were both the closest relative), the draw
alternated by sex. A follow-up card was sent to each respondent ten
days after the questionnaire was sent. The final sample totaled 189
respondents. The complete questionnaire for the survey, including the
questions for data reported in this chapter, is given in appendix A.

Prior to mailing the questionnaire, a good deal of preliminary work
was done to investigate how willing bereaved would be to talk in detail
about the funeral and funeral arrangements. Moreover, it had to be
determined how this type of data could be collected effectively. These
preliminary steps were taken:

1. Funeral directors in the La Crosse area were interviewed about
   funeral arrangements with the bereaved. At first these interviews were conducted by meeting the funeral director in the
   funeral home. This, however, proved unsatisfactory; it appeared
   that the funeral directors were somewhat confined by their professional role in giving the needed information. After that, steps
   were taken to meet the funeral directors outside their professional
   setting. I joined a local service organization to which several
   funeral directors belonged. This enabled me to meet funeral
   directors informally and socially—and arrange for interviews
   which yielded more information.

2. Interviews were conducted with bereaved in which I received

clear indications that they would be very willing to talk explicitly about the death and the funeral arrangements.

3. Interviews were held with florists who provide flowers for funerals in the area.
4. The owner of a local firm for grave markers was interviewed.
5. A pathologist and several doctors and nurses at the major hospital in La Crosse were interviewed concerning attitudes of the bereaved.
6. A pilot project was conducted which pretested many of the questions and demonstrated that bereaved would be willing to complete a mail questionnaire asking very direct and specific questions on the topic. Also, this pilot project indicated that the funeral director was highly regarded by the bereaved. Since the final questionnaire contained a long section on the professional performance of the funeral director, I decided to inform the funeral directors about these preliminary results. Local funeral directors were mailed a letter telling them about the pilot project and the favorable response of the bereaved to the services they provide. I thought this would minimize the possibility of any interference or negative reaction to the study on the part of the funeral directors.
7. During the week just preceding the mailing of the final questionnaire, news releases were dispatched to the local radio stations and newspaper announcing that a study of attitudes to the funeral was being conducted in the La Crosse area. The study was fortunate to be given very good coverage by the local news media. This was centered on preparing the public for receipt of the questionnaire on this "taboo" topic.

SAMPLE DESCRIPTION

All respondents were next of kin to one who died in 1969. Sixty-three percent of the bereaved in the sample were women; 37 percent were men. Their ages ranged from twenty years old to over eighty years old: 10 percent of the bereaved were twenty to thirty-nine years old, 48 percent were forty to fifty-nine years old, 38 percent were sixty to seventy-nine years old, and 4 percent were eighty and above. The majority of bereaved in the sample were between the ages of forty and seventy-nine.

The education of the bereaved was as follows—highest level completed: 22 percent grade school, 11 percent junior high school, 41 percent high school graduate, 15 percent some college, 7 percent college graduate, and 4 percent graduate degree.

Most of the respondents were living on an approximate annual income of under $10,000: 34 percent on less than $4,000; 16 percent on $4,000 to $5,999; 25 percent on $6,000 to $9,999; 10 percent on $10,000 to $14,999; 6 percent on $15,000 and over; 8 percent just answered "retired" without giving an amount; (and 1% gave no response to this survey question).

Occupations of the bereaved (at the time the questionnaire was completed) were the following: 31 percent housewife; 20 percent retired; 2 percent elementary or high school teacher; 12 percent white collar, clerical, or sales; 6 percent technician, craftsman, or the trades; 5 percent business manager or executive, 10 percent laborer or factory worker; and 10 percent other (including unemployed).

The religious background of the bereaved was 40 percent Catholic, 32 percent Lutheran, and 26 percent Other Protestant—including Methodist (10%), Presbyterian (4%), Congregational (4%), and unspecified Protestant (8%); the remaining 2 percent responded other or none on religious background.

Most of the bereaved were either widowed, 51 percent; or married, 42 percent. Only 4 percent reported they were single; 2 percent were divorced (1% no response).

The age, sex, and family position of the deceased relatives on whose death the bereaved respondents reported were as follows: 67 percent of the deceased were sixty years old or above; 25 percent of the deceased were thirty to fifty-nine years old; and only 8 percent were younger than thirty years old. Fifty-eight percent of the deceased were men; 42 percent were women.

A check on kin-relationships showed that in 38 percent of the cases the deceased was the husband of the respondent; 13 percent, wife; 28 percent, parent (father *or* mother); 6 percent, child of the respondent; 9 percent, sibling (brother *or* sister); and 6 percent, other.

The great majority of respondents, 79 percent, had lost either a spouse or a parent.

FINDINGS

Religion of Bereaved

The religious backgrounds of bereaved in this study fell into three major categories: Catholic, Lutheran, and Other Protestant. In controlling for religion, a distinction was made between Lutheran and other Protestants because of a large Norwegian-Lutheran population in the La Crosse area. (This group had a local reputation for being "liberal" and "individualistic.")

One difference in attitudes between religious groups centered on the question of whether the funeral was more for the living or for the dead. For the sample as a whole, 39 percent of the respondents had answered that the funeral was more "for the living," while 51 percent had felt it was more "for the deceased." Only 8 percent said, "both"; and 2 percent other or no response. Further analysis of these responses indicated a striking difference between Catholic and Protestant bereaved on this question. It was found that Catholics were much more likely to feel that the funeral is for the dead—72 percent of the Catholics expressed the belief that the funeral is more for the dead than for the living. On the other hand, the Protestants put more weight on its value for the living. The Lutherans answered 51 percent "more for the living" and only 49 percent "for the dead." Other Protestants responded 56 percent "for the living" and only 44 percent "for the dead" [2] (Table 6-I)

TABLE 6-I

FUNERAL FOR LIVING OR DECEASED—
BY RELIGION OF BEREAVED

	Living		Deceased		
	n	p	n	p	Total
Catholic	18.	(27.69)	47.	(72.30)	100%
Lutheran	28.	(50.90)	27.	(49.09)	100%
Other Protestant	25.	(55.55)	20.	(44.44)	100%

$X^2 = 10.51$ significant at .01, N = 155[3]

---

[2] Throughout this chapter, quotations such as these indicate the specific wording of questionnaire items.

One explanation for this difference may be rooted in the emphasis of the Catholic Church on masses for the dead and other rituals for the deceased. For example, Hinton points to the fact that "in the Roman Catholic religion masses are celebrated for the dead, and All Souls Day is set apart for the commemoration of the departed awaiting in purgatory" (Hinton, 1967). Sicard also observed that the liturgy of the funeral mass in the Catholic Church emphasizes that the mass is for the dead (Sicard, 1968). Riley contended, "Christianity from a Catholic point of view has no meaning apart from its relation with the life to come. Christ did not come to make the world a better place to live in. His mission was directed towards the happiness of heaven; he thought of the world not as an everlasting abode, but as a place of pilgrimage." He observed that the teachings of the Catholic Church stress the idea that the deceased is judged at the time of death (Fulton, 1961). This also may center attention on the deceased in the funeral ritual. On the other hand, the Protestant clergy seems to place a great deal of stress on the funeral as a ritual for the living. Fulton, for instance, found that the Protestant clergy believe their main role at the funeral is to attend to the living—not the dead (Fulton, 1961).

Another difference between religious groups showed in terms of where funerals were held. When asked about the place of the funeral, the results for the total sample were as shown in Table 6-II.

A sizeable portion, 34 percent, of the funerals were held exclu-

TABLE 6-II

WHERE WAS THE FUNERAL SERVICE HELD?

34% Funeral Home
28% Church
35% Both Funeral Home and Church
0% Home
3% Other

—

100%, N = 189.

[3]Responses of both, other, and no answer were dropped from this comparison. In all tables, if N = less than 189, inappropriate categories have been dropped or some bereaved failed to answer one of the questions in the table.

The format of bivariate tables in this paper is the following: the cell frequencies (n) are followed by percentages in parentheses (p). Percentages are conditioned by the row variable—adding to 100 percent across the rows.

sively in the funeral home—instead of in the church. Sixty-nine percent of the bereaved in the study reported that the funeral service was held in the funeral home or in both the funeral home and the church. Most of those who held services exclusively in the funeral home, however, were from a Protestant background. Catholics indicated a pattern of holding the service in both the funeral home and the church or exclusively in the church. The breakdown of the place of funeral according to religious groups is given in Table 6-III.

TABLE 6-III

PLACE OF FUNERAL—BY RELIGION OF BEREAVED

Religion	*Place of Funeral*					
	Funeral Home		*Church*		*Both Funeral Home and Church*	
	n	p	n	p	n	p
Catholic	9.	(12.00)	24.	(32.00)	42.	(56.00)
Lutheran	26.	(44.06)	18.	(30.50)	13.	(22.03)
Other Protestant	26.	(53.06)	10.	(20.40)	10.	(20.40)
	Home		*Other*		*Total*	
	n	p	n	p		
Catholic	0.	(0.00)	0.	(0.00)	(100%)	
Lutheran	0.	(0.00)	2.	(3.38)	(100%)	
Other Protestant	0.	(0.00)	3.	(6.12)	(100%)	

N = 183

Among Catholics, 88 percent indicated that the church setting was used for the funeral service (either exclusively or along with the funeral home, categories "church" and "both" above). On the other hand, only 53 percent of the Lutherans and 40 percent of the other Protestants held services in the church. Many Protestants favored the funeral home as the setting for the service: 44 percent of the Lutheran group and 53 percent of the other Protestants held the service exclusively in the funeral home. Only 12 percent of the Catholic group held such services. Some Catholics may be concerned about the religious content (or lack of such) in funerals held outside the Church. Articles like "Let's Get Rid of Funeral Homes" in the *U.S. Catholic Jubilee* express this attitude. The author criticized the funeral directors for the secular way in which many handle funerals and contended that "the Christian attitude toward death . . . has been sidetracked into gross misconceptions and faulty thinking" (Reardon, 1971). The theme was that funerals should be held in the Church.

Catholics and Protestants also differed somewhat in their attitude to restoration work. In one question, bereaved were asked, "How did you react to the appearance of the deceased regarding restoration work?" Overall, most bereaved were "pleased" with the restoration work. A breakdown by religious groups suggested, however, that Protestants were a bit more positive in their reactions than Catholics: 86 percent of the Lutherans and 78 percent of the other Protestants were "pleased with appearance" of the deceased regarding restoration work—while only 62 percent of the Catholics gave that response.

Sex of Bereaved

Significant differences were found between responses of men and women in the meaning of the funeral and in how they defined their ability to cope with the death. For instance, in one question respondents were asked, "Do you feel that the funeral was a meaningful way to express love for the deceased?" A significantly greater proportion of women answered, "very much." Results are given in Table 6-IV.

TABLE 6-IV

FUNERAL AS AN EXPRESSION OF LOVE FOR THE DECEASED—
BY SEX OF RESPONDENT

	Expression of Love					
	Not at All		*Somewhat*		*Very Much*	*Total*
	n	*p*	*n*	*p*	*n*	*p*	
Men	9. (13.84)		24. (36.92)		32. (49.23)		100%
Women	8. (6.77)		30. (25.42)		80. (67.79)		100%

$X^2 = 6.49$, significant at .05, N = 183

Sixty-eight percent of the women responded that the funeral is "very much" an expression of love for the deceased, but only 49 percent of the men felt that way. Fourteen percent of the men felt that the funeral was "not at all" an expression of love; only 7 percent of the women gave that response.

In another question, bereaved were asked how upset they were when deciding the details of the funeral. Women, much more often than men, defined themselves as being "very upset" when deciding the details of the funeral (See Table 6-V).

TABLE 6-V

DEGREE TO WHICH THE BEREAVED WAS UPSET WHEN MAKING FUNERAL PLANS—BY SEX OF BEREAVED

	Degree of Being Upset		
	Very Upset	*Somewhat Upset*	*Not Upset At All*
	n p	n p	n p	*Total*
Men	8. (12.50)	20. (31.25)	36. (56.25)	100%
Women	35. (32.11)	39. (35.77)	35. (32.11)	100%

$X^2 = 12.20$, significant at .01, N = 173

The results show that while only 13 percent of the men answered that they were "very upset" in deciding the details of the funeral, 32 percent of the women thought that they were. Fifty-six percent of the men said they were "not upset at all," but only 32 percent of the women said they were "not upset at all" when making funeral arrangements.

A similar theme appeared in response to the question, "How able were you to cope with this death in the family?" Women were significantly more likely than men to feel that it was "very difficult" to cope with the death. The breakdown by sex is given in Table 6-VI.

TABLE 6-VI

ABILITY TO COPE WITH THE DEATH— BY SEX OF THE RESPONDENT

	How Difficult to Cope		
	Very Difficult	*Somewhat Difficult*	*Not Difficult At All*
	n p	n p	n p	*Total*
Men	17. (25.00)	33. (48.52)	18. (26.47)	100%
Women	54. (45.76)	48. (40.67)	16. (13.55)	100%

$X^2 = 9.41$, significant at .01, N = 186

While 46 percent of the women respondents answered that it was "very difficult" to cope with the loss, only 25 percent of the men found it "very difficult." Only 14 percent of the women responded that it was "not at all" difficult for them to cope with this death. Nearly double that amount, 26 percent, of the men answered "not

at all" difficult. These results appear to reflect certain cultural expectations and socialization for sex-role behavior. Also, over half the
women in the study were widows reporting on the death of their
husbands. Many widows—alone and forced by death to assume roles
formerly handled by their husbands—would likely be "very upset"
and find it "very difficult" to cope with the death.

Age of Bereaved

Behavior and attitudes of younger bereaved (39 years old and
younger) differed in several respects from those of older bereaved in
this study. First of all, over half the younger bereaved defined themselves as being "very upset" when making plans for the funeral (See
Table 6-VII).

TABLE 6-VII
DEGREE TO WHICH UPSET WHEN ARRANGING FUNERAL— BY AGE OF BEREAVED

| Age of Bereaved | Degree Upset | | | |
| | Very Upset | Somewhat Upset | Not Upset At All | |
	n p	n p	n p	Total
20-39 yrs.	10. (55.55)	5. (27.77)	3. (16.66)	100%
40-59 yrs.	19. (23.45)	30. (37.03)	32. (39.50)	100%
60-79 yrs.	11. (16.66)	22. (33.33)	33. (50.00)	100%
80 and above	3. (37.50)	2. (25.00)	3. (37.50)	100%
				N = 173

The youngest category of bereaved showed the highest proportion
being "very upset" (56%) when deciding the details of the funeral.
Only 16 percent of those who were thirty-nine or younger claimed
they were "not upset at all." There was, however, a sharp decrease
in reports of being upset as age of bereaved increased. The 40 to 59
year old group had only 23 percent "very upset," but had 40 percent
"not upset at all." In the 60 to 79 year old group, only 16 percent
were "very upset," but 50 percent were "not upset at all." The fact
that there was a small shift back to being "very upset" in the eighty
and above group may be due to their own advanced age. One interpretation for the youngest bereaved (twenty to thirty-nine years old)
being most upset while deciding on the details of the funeral is that

they probably had the least experience in making funeral arrangements. It is reasonable to think that older people have attended and arranged for more funerals than younger people and that this former experience could serve as socialization experience to help minimize the feeling of "being upset."

The bereaved were asked, "When making arrangements within the funeral home, how did the setting (music, furniture, decor, etc.) make you feel?" The relationship between reaction to the setting and age of the bereaved is given in Table 6-VIII.

TABLE 6-VIII

REACTION TO "SETTING" IN THE FUNERAL HOME—
BY AGE OF BEREAVED

Age of Bereaved	How Did Setting Make You Feel			
	Very Strange		Somewhat Strange	
	n	p	n	p
20-39 yrs.	2.	(12.50)	5.	(31.25)
40-59 yrs.	5.	(5.88)	12.	(14.11)
60-79 yrs.	0.	(0.00)	11.	(15.94)
80 and above	0.	(0.00)	1.	(12.50)

Age of Bereaved	Not Strange At All		Did Not Make Arrangements		Total
	n	p	n	p	
20-39 yrs.	7.	(43.75)	2.	(12.50)	100%
40-59 yrs.	61.	(71.76)	7.	(8.23)	100%
60-79 yrs.	50.	(72.46)	8.	(11.59)	100%
80 and above	4.	(50.00)	3.	(37.50)	100%

N = 178

Although most bereaved did not find the funeral home "strange at all," definition of the situation as "very strange" or "somewhat strange" was much more frequent among the youngest age group than among the rest of the bereaved. There was a definite decrease in the definition of the mortuary setting as "very" or "somewhat strange" as age increased. Thirteen percent of bereaved 20 to 39 years old answered, "very strange;" but only 6 percent of those 40 to 59 years old, and not one person over 60 years answered that way. In a similar manner, 31 percent of the youngest group felt it was at least "somewhat" strange, while only 13 to 16 percent of the older bereaved thought so.

Over two thirds of the total sample said they had been influenced by style, color, and cost in their choice of a casket. The relationships between the age of the bereaved and whether or not they were influenced by these items in casket selection are presented in Tables 6-IX, 6-X, and 6-XI.

TABLE 6-IX
INFLUENCED BY STYLE IN SELECTION OF CASKET— BY AGE OF BEREAVED

Age of Bereaved	Influenced by Style of Casket				
	Yes		No		
	n	p	n	p	Total
20-39 yrs.	6.	(46.15)	7.	(53.84)	100%
40-59 yrs.	66.	(86.84)	10.	(13.15)	100%
60-79 yrs.	49.	(81.66)	11.	(18.33)	100%
80 and above	6.	(75.00)	2.	(25.00)	100%

$X^2 = 12.09$, significant at .01, $N = 157$ (Some bereaved said they did not personally select the casket so N less than 189).

TABLE 6-X
INFLUENCED BY COLOR IN SELECTION OF CASKET— BY AGE OF BEREAVED

Age of Bereaved	Influenced by Color of Casket				
	Yes		No		
	n	p	n	p	Total
20-39 yrs.	5.	(45.45)	6.	(54.54)	100%
40-59 yrs.	64.	(83.11)	13.	(16.88)	100%
60-79 yrs.	48.	(81.35)	11.	(18.64)	100%
80 and above	6.	(75.00)	2.	(25.00)	100%

$X^2 = 8.61$, significant at .05, $N = 155$

TABLE 6-XI
INFLUENCED BY COST IN SELECTION OF CASKET— BY AGE OF BEREAVED

Age of Bereaved	Influenced by Cost of Casket				
	Yes		No		
	n	p	n	p	Total
20-39 yrs.	5.	(38.46)	8.	(61.53)	100%
40-59 yrs.	60.	(76.92)	18.	(23.07)	100%
60-79 yrs.	46.	(74.19)	16.	(25.80)	100%
80 and above	5.	(62.50)	3.	(37.50)	100%

$X^2 = 8.70$, significant at .05, $N = 163$

Within the older age groups (forty and above) the great majority of bereaved answered that they were, indeed, influenced (75 to 85% overall) by style, color, and cost of the casket. The majority of bereaved twenty to thirty-nine years old, however, answered that they were not influenced by these considerations. There was at least a 30 percent increase in the proportion who said, "yes," influenced by style, color, and cost between the youngest group and any of the older groups of bereaved. One interpretation for these results may be that bereaved over forty are more interested in the funeral as a traditional ritual and that this is manifest in considerations for the ceremonial items such as style and color of the casket. It is also possible that the older bereaved are more sensitive to the social expectation to present a "proper" funeral.

When the relationship between age of bereaved and whether or not they were pleased with the appearance of the deceased regarding restoration work was studied, the following results were found (Table 6-XII).

TABLE 6-XII
PLEASED WITH APPEARANCE OF DECEASED (RESTORATION WORK) BY AGE OF BEREAVED

Age of Bereaved	Pleased with Appearance	
	Pleased	*Not Pleased*
	n *p*	*n* *p*
20-39 yrs.	5. (29.41)	3. (17.64)
40-59 yrs.	55. (70.51)	7. (8.97)
60-79 yrs.	54. (87.09)	3. (4.83)
80 and over	7. (100)	0. (0.00)

Age of Bereaved	*Undecided*	*Other*	
	n *p*	*n* *p*	*Total*
20-39 yrs.	2. (11.76)	7. (41.17)	100%
40-59 yrs.	9. (11.53)	7. (8.97)	100%
60-79 yrs.	4. (6.45)	1. (1.61)	100%
80 and over	0. (0.00)	0. (0.00)	100%

N = 164

Nearly all the bereaved in age groups forty and above were "pleased with the appearance" of the deceased—ranging in response from 71 percent to 100 percent "pleased with the appearance." On the other hand, only 29 percent of the youngest age group answered that they were pleased with the appearance regarding restoration work. The youngest group had a high percentage of responses in the "other" category. A content analysis of remarks that accompanied the "other" responses revealed hostility to the idea of restoration and open casket visitation among younger bereaved.

The Deceased: Age and Family Position

Kalish maintained that "the dying of the elderly is, by and large, the least disturbing" type of death in American society. He attributes this, in part, to the nuclear family structure. Kalish argued, "the nuclear family has become a part of our culture, and the elderly inevitably stands outside the unit." The function of the elderly as a breadwinner is diminished in importance, and so is his role as advisor to his children—the American culture encourages the independence of children from parents. According to Kalish, "the importance of the elderly person to the world around him has diminished, and simultaneously he may be undergoing the process called disengagement, through which he is withdrawing from some of his involvements in the world. He and his community are moving socially and emotionally away from each other. . . . All these factors conspire to make the death of an elderly person less upsetting to his family and to the community. Added to this the likelihood of his dying at home is relatively slight, so that the family encounter with the dying process of an aged individual has less impact and is less disturbing." Furthermore, Kalish argued that the long term illnesses preceding the deaths of many elderly may constitute a financial hardship on their children. "Resentment over paying the expenses of terminal illness and guilt over this resentment are a common theme in the family of the dying." These pressures may lead the family to anticipate the death with positive feelings. He concluded that the death of the elderly is relatively easy in terms of, "he lived a long, good life," or "how fortunate that he was relieved from his suffering" (Kalish, 1969).

According to Kalish, "the dying of a middle-aged person provokes more emotional reaction" than the dying of an elderly person. Such a death challenges the cultural goal for a "long and healthy life."

The middle-aged person is still productive in his work, and the family is still emotionally and financially dependent on him or her. He observed that the dying of a middle-aged person is very distressing and disruptive to the family and society (Kalish, 1969).

Finally, Kalish maintained that "the younger the dying person (exclusive of infants), the more distress is caused" to the family by the death. People believe that a young person has not had a "chance to live" and that he or she is entitled to this. Thus the family feels that the child has been cheated out of his life, and the death has a "tremendous impact upon the family." Kalish maintained that the parents are likely to feel guilty at the death of a child—feeling that it was due to their carelessness or that it could have been prevented.

Cobb made an additional point concerning the death of a child in his study on the "Psychological Impact of Long Illness and Death of a Child on the Family Circle." He found that a long-term childhood illness serves to prepare the family for the eventual death of the child. The family showed that they were grateful for time they could spend with the child as long as his suffering could be controlled (Cobb, 1956).

Gorer, in his British sample, investigated the impact of death of a spouse, parent, child, brother, or sister on the family. He emphasized that death introduces changes in the social position and status of surviving family members. He found that when both parents died the change of status for other family members seemed slight: "The pattern of holidays, especially Christmas, are liable to change, with fewer or no gatherings of brothers and sisters and their children; but the survivors do not seem to consider their position altered, nor was their grief intense. The death of parents seemed to be 'natural,' in the proper order of things." Gorer, however, recognized that widowhood poses a serious problem for the bereaved in modern society. This is true not only for the bereaved spouse, but when a mother or father is widowed, the children "seem to feel an extra burden of responsibility." He found that the death of a husband or wife was usually characterized by lack of social and emotional preparation. He also found an indication that deaths of brothers and sisters are likely to be deeply mourned. According to Gorer, "the most distressing and longlasting of all griefs is for the loss of a grown child." His respondents felt that it seems "against the order of nature that a child should die before his or her parents" (Gorer, 1956).

Fulton and Fulton have differentiated between "low grief potential" and "high grief potential" deaths. Low grief potential deaths are those cases involving anticipatory grief where the family has rehearsed the death prior to the actual loss and attempted to adjust to it. Characteristic of "low grief" deaths are those of the elderly who had been terminally ill or institutionalized for a long period of time prior to the death. According to Fulton and Fulton, the bereaved have dissipated most of their grief by the time the death occurred and thus show little or no emotion. On the other hand, "high grief potential" deaths are those considered by society as tragic—for example, the death of a child or someone in "the prime of life." Often sudden deaths are "high grief potential" deaths (Fulton and Fulton, 1970).

These studies emphasized the importance of age and family status position on patterns of bereavement. This study attempted to investigate whether age and status position of the deceased within the family affects the attitude of the bereaved to the death and funeral arrangements. In the total sample, the deceased occupied the following age, sex, and status positions:

TABLE 6-XIII

AGE OF DECEASED

7%	1-29
25%	30-59
64%	60 and Above
4%	Other
100%	Total

TABLE 6-XIV

SEX OF DECEASED

58%	Men
42%	Women
100%	Total

TABLE 6-XV

STATUS POSITION OF DECEASED IN THE FAMILY

38%	Husband
13%	Wife
28%	Parent (Father or Mother)
6%	Child
9%	Sibling (Brother, Sister)
6%	Other
100%	Total

Most of those relatives had died in an institutional setting: 61 percent in the hospital, 14 percent in nursing homes—only 17 percent at home, 2 percent at work, 1 percent in traffic accidents, and 5 percent in some other setting.

Sixty-five percent of the bereaved who lost a sibling, 56 percent who lost a husband, and 42 percent who lost a wife answered that it was "very difficult" to cope with the death. On the other hand, none of those who lost a parent and only 19 percent who lost a child said, "very difficult" to cope. The literature on bereavement suggested that the death of a child causes intense grief among the bereaved. These data, however, did not support that expectation. In an effort to explain these results, the relationship between family status position of the deceased and the circumstances of death was investigated. It was found that the majority (51%) who were children of respondents died after an illness of over six months. Moreover, another 23 percent had been sick for up to six months. Thus it is possible that anticipatory grief served to minimize the difficulty of coping with the death of a child. Nearly one third of those who lost either a parent or child said it was "not difficult at all" to cope with the death.

The attitude that the funeral was "very much" a meaningful expression of love for the deceased predominated among those who lost a husband, wife, sibling, or child—but not among those who lost a parent: 76 percent of those who lost a husband, 67 percent of those who lost a wife, 65 percent who lost a sibling, and 50 percent who lost a child thought that the funeral was a meaningful way to express love for the deceased. Only 20 percent who lost a parent, however, felt that way. One third of all those who lost a parent felt the funeral was "not at all a meaningful expression of love for the deceased."

It was found that bereaved who lost a younger family member were much more likely to be "very upset" while deciding details of the funeral than those who lost a relative over 60 years old (See Table 6-XVI).

Fifty percent of those whose relative was 60 or older reported they were "not upset at all" while making funeral plans.

Finally, reactions to restoration work also varied somewhat according to the age of the deceased. The breakdown by age is presented in Table 6-XVII.

The results show that most bereaved who lost a relative 30 years

TABLE 6-XVI

DEGREE TO WHICH BEREAVED WERE UPSET
WHEN MAKING FUNERAL ARRANGEMENTS—
BY AGE OF DECEASED

Age of Deceased	Degree Bereaved Upset When Making Funeral Arrangements						
	Very Upset		Somewhat Upset		Not Upset at All		Total
	n	p	n	p	n	p	
1-29 yrs.	6.	(46.15)	5.	(38.46)	2.	(15.38)	100%
30-59 yrs.	18.	(41.86)	15.	(34.88)	10.	(23.25)	100%
60 and over	19.	(16.23)	39.	(33.33)	59.	(50.42)	100%

X^2 = 18.88, significant at .001, N = 173

TABLE 6-XVII

WHETHER BEREAVED PLEASED WITH RESTORATION WORK—
ACCORDING TO AGE OF DECEASED

Age of Deceased	Reaction to Restoration Work								Total
	Pleased		Not Pleased		Undecided		Other		
	n	p	n	p	n	p	n	p	
1-29	2.	(18.18)	1.	(9.09)	2.	(18.18)	6.	(54.54)	100%
30-59	29.	(72.50)	3.	(7.49)	4.	(10.00)	4.	(10.00)	100%
60 and above	90.	(79.64)	9.	(7.96)	9.	(7.96)	5.	(4.42)	100%

N = 164

old or older were "pleased with the appearance of the deceased regarding restoration work": 73 percent of those whose relative was 30 to 59 years old and 80 percent whose relative was 60 years or older reported they were "pleased with the appearance." However, bereaved who had lost a very young person (below 30 years old) tended to answer "other" or "undecided." Fifty-five percent of that group responded, "other"—with many comments that there is no way they could be pleased about the appearance of one who died so young.

EXPRESSING GRIEF

In his often quoted article, "The Pornography of Death," Gorer emphasized that death was no mystery in the nineteenth century. It was rare to find an individual during that century who had not witnessed at least one actual death. It was discussion of sex—rather than death—that was avoided. Gorer observed that "in the twentieth century, however, there seems to have been an unremarked shift in prudery; whereas copulation has become more and more 'mentionable,' death has become more and more 'unmentionable' as a natural process" (Gorer, 1965).

One factor in understanding the denial of death in modern society is the shift from sacred to secular. Borkenau characterized contemporary society as post-Christian; he contended that, because of the disintegration of belief in immortality, modern society is embracing a philosophy of despair and denial of death. Borkenau saw the trend as a shift toward what he called "modern secularism" (Borkenau, 1965).

Fulton and Geis also observed the shift from sacred to secular in American society. They maintained that death has moved increasingly out of the realm of religious concern and into the realm of scientific investigation. "Theological explanations of the nature and purpose of human life are explicitly and implicitly challenged by medical and social science. So-called wonder drugs, modern hygiene, birth control, and other discoveries . . . have not only extended the span of man's life but have also caused him to question its meaning anew." Furthermore, they maintained that among the secularly oriented, death has become a taboo topic to be dismissed or avoided. In most modern secular societies, including the United States, death is not considered to be an "open or polite topic of conversation, except among the aged" (Fulton and Geis, 1965).

Fulton observed that the bereaved families in our society are expected to quickly come to grips with the reality of another person's death, accept it, and then return to normal life. During bereavement there is an "expectation of stoical acceptance of death. The expression of grief or sympathy for a death is limited to a time and place. The dramaturgy of death moves inexorably to a conclusion—often only three days. Within one week one is expected to be back on the job" (Fulton, 1965).

On the same issue, Peretz maintained, "the dominant social expectation of the bereaved is that he will quickly pick up the pattern of his life; return to work, family responsibilities, and socialization with the community; and be quiet about his grief. With this ethos, the lack of support from family, friends, and neighbors will force the bereaved to abandon his grief prematurely" (Peretz, 1970).

Among the British, Gorer observed the absence of an accepted social ritual to regulate the first contacts between a mourner and his neighbors, acquaintances, and co-workers after a death. He found people wondered if they should speak of the loss or pretend that nothing had happened (Gorer, 1965).

Vernon took a sample of 1,500 students from American colleges and universities; he asked the respondents how they would act if they met someone who had lost a loved one through death since their last encounter. He found that 25 percent of his sample would prefer no mention of the death if they met a mourner; 40 percent said they would wait for the mourner to mention the death; 10 percent responded that they had never considered the situation before; and only 25 percent said they would mention the death to the mourner (Vernon, 1970).

Discussion of death has been routinely and systematically avoided in the hospital setting as well—where elaborate precautions are usually taken to shield patients from death and evade any discussion of the topic (Glazer and Strauss, 1968; 1970. Sudnow, 1967).

It was of interest to this present study to verify what experience bereaved had in discussing death and how they felt they were expected to express their grief. A central theme which appeared in the data was that the bereaved had rarely discussed death within the family or any other social institution. Bereaved were asked if they had been involved in discussions about death in a variety of social situations (See Table 6-XVIII).

Few respondents had discussed death "very much" in any situation.

TABLE 6-XVIII

HAVE YOU BEEN INVOLVED IN DISCUSSIONS ABOUT DEATH
IN ANY OF THE FOLLOWING SITUATIONS?

Degree of Discussion of Death

	Very Much	*Some-what*	*Not At All*	*No Response*	*Totals*
In the Family	16%	64%	14%	6%	100% N = 189
At Church	8%	37%	50%	5%	100% N = 189
At School	2%	11%	60%	27%	100% N = 189
At Work	2%	33%	43%	22%	100% N = 189
With Friends	8%	62%	22%	8%	100% N = 189
With Physicians	6%	29%	56%	9%	100% N = 189

(In this table, each row represents a separate survey question and was answered by the total sample.)

The discussion of death that had taken place seems to have occurred in the family or with friends. It is interesting to note that reports of discussion of death with friends was nearly equal to that within the family. Keeping in mind that the respondents had recently experienced a death of next-of-kin, it is surprising that only 6 percent had discussed death "very much" with physicians—and only 29 percent had discussed it "somewhat" with physicians. Only 2 percent of the total sample said they had discussed death "very much" at school; 60 percent said "not at all." It is quite revealing to observe that the Church, which is traditionally involved in the ritual of death, does not appear as an active setting for discussion of death. Only 8 percent of the sample had discussed death "very much" in the Church—50 percent claimed they had "not discussed death at all" in the Church.

Most bereaved, 85 percent, reported that friends helped them out with routine tasks such as cooking or babysitting during the funeral week. The great majority, 92 percent, found it "very easy" to get off work during the funeral week. Also, bereaved indicated a good deal of pragmatic knowledge and financial preparation for dealing with the death: prior to the death, 65 percent owned a cemetery lot for the deceased; 86 percent knew they needed a burial vault; 93 percent knew a death certificate was required; and nearly half the bereaved in the sample had some special burial funds or insurance to cover the costs. One thing bereaved were not, however, prepared to do was talk about the death. Bereaved were asked two additional questions probing the extent they discussed death with friends or relatives both before and after the death (See Tables 6-XIX and 6-XX).

All bereaved in the study had recently, within the last year or so, experienced the death of a very close relative. This was not, however, reflected in an increased tendency to talk about death. Only 28 percent of the total sample reported discussing death "frequently"—even

TABLE 6-XIX

PRIOR TO THE LOSS IN THE FAMILY, DID YOU DISCUSS
DEATH WITH FRIENDS OR RELATIVES?

28% Frequently
54% Seldom
16% Not At All
2% No Response
100% Total, N = 189

TABLE 6-XX

SINCE THE LOSS IN THE FAMILY DO YOU FIND YOURSELF DISCUSSING DEATH WITH FRIENDS OR RELATIVES?

28% Frequently
56% Seldom
13% Not At All
3% No Response
100% Total, N = 189

after experiencing this loss in the family. Most reported they only "seldom" discussed death. A sizeable minority, 16 percent before the death and 13 percent after the death, claimed they "do not discuss death at all" with friends or relatives.

A further analysis of the results revealed that there was a significant relationship between "discussing death frequently (since the loss)" and ability to cope with the death (Table 6-XXI).

TABLE 6-XXI

FREQUENCY OF DISCUSSION OF DEATH SINCE THE LOSS— BY ABILITY TO COPE WITH DEATH

Ability to Cope	*Frequency of Discussion*						
	Frequently		*Seldom*		*Not at All*		*Total*
	n	p	n	p	n	p	
Very Difficult	33.	(47.82)	29.	(42.02)	7.	(10.14)	100%
Somewhat Difficult	14.	(17.72)	54.	(68.35)	11.	(13.92)	100%
Not Difficult	6.	(17.64)	21.	(61.76)	7.	(20.58)	100%

$X^2 = 19.78$, significant at .001, N = 182

The bereaved who found it "very difficult" to cope with the death tended to discuss death most frequently since the loss. It is possible that, despite the cultural taboo on the topic, talking about the death is one process through which these bereaved could do their grief-work.

It was also found that bereaved who felt the death was "very difficult" to cope with valued the funeral most highly (See Table 6-XXII).

TABLE 6-XXII

FUNERAL IS AN EXPRESSION OF LOVE FOR THE DECEASED— BY ABILITY OF BEREAVED TO COPE WITH THE DEATH

Ability to Cope	*Funeral Is a Meaningful Expression of Love*						
	Not At All		*Somewhat*		*Very Much*		*Total*
	n	p	n	p	n	p	
Very Difficult	3.	(4.34)	13.	(18.84)	53.	(76.81)	100%
Somewhat Difficult	5.	(6.17)	33.	(40.74)	43.	(53.08)	100%
Not Difficult	8.	(25.80)	7.	(22.58)	16.	(51.61)	100%

$X^2 = 23.02$, significant at .001, N = 181

It was within the category "very difficult to cope" that the greatest proportion of bereaved (77%) felt the funeral was "very much" a meaningful expression of love for the deceased.

Finally, bereaved were asked to indicate how they felt they were expected to express their grief—how open they thought they were to be about showing grief; the question was as follows, (Table 6-XXIII):

TABLE 6-XXIII
IN GENERAL, HOW DO YOU FEEL THAT PEOPLE EXPECTED YOU TO EXPRESS YOUR GRIEF?

31% In a Very Open Way
54% In a Somewhat Open Way
10% Not Tolerant of Openly Expressed Grief
5% No Response or Other
100% Total, N = 189

Less than one third of the total sample felt that they should express their grief in a "very open way." The majority thought they should be only "somewhat open" about it: a noticeable minority, 10 percent, felt the community simply was "not tolerant of openly displayed grief." A further analysis of the data pointed out a significant relationship between "ability to cope with the death" and how the bereaved felt they should express their grief (See Table 6-XXIV).

TABLE 6-XXIV
HOW EXPECTED TO EXPRESS GRIEF—
BY ABILITY TO COPE WITH DEATH

Ability to Cope	Express Grief						
	Very Open Way		Somewhat Open		Not Open Way		Total
	n	p	n	p	n	p	
Very Difficult	32.	(47.76)	28.	(41.79)	7.	(10.44)	100%
Somewhat Difficult	18.	(22.50)	57.	(71.25)	5.	(6.25)	100%
Not Difficult	9.	(29.03)	15.	(48.38)	7.	(22.58)	100%

X^2 = 18.83, significant at .01, N = 178

Forty-eight percent of the bereaved who found it "very difficult" to cope with this death indicated that they felt they were "expected to express their grief in a very open way." Only 29 percent of those who found the death "not difficult" to cope with answered that way. It may be that those who were most unable to cope with the death of a close relative perceived the expectation of the group in a way which was supportive for working out their grief.

SUMMARY CONCLUSIONS

The majority of bereaved from Catholic backgrounds defined the funeral as a ritual more for the dead than for the living. The majority of Catholics held the funeral service in the Church; in contrast, a sizeable proportion of the Protestants held the service exclusively in the funeral home. Protestants were somewhat more positive than Catholics to the appearance of the bereaved with regard to restoration work.

Women were more likely than men to consider the funeral to be a meaningful expression of love for the deceased. A significantly greater proportion of women than men felt they were "very upset" when making funeral plans and felt it was "very difficult" to cope with the death.

Younger bereaved (39 years old and younger) were much more likely to have been "very upset" when deciding the details for the funeral and more likely to feel rather "strange" inside the mortuary than were older bereaved. The great majority of bereaved 40 years and older were influenced by color, cost, and style in selecting a casket; the majority of younger bereaved, however, claimed they were not influenced by these considerations in casket selection. Although most of the sample was pleased with the restoration work, a sizeable proportion of younger bereaved (39 years and younger) offered criticism of the practice of restoration on the deceased.

The bereaved indicated that it was most difficult for them to cope with the death of a spouse or sibling. The funeral was considered "very much" an expression of love for the deceased by most who lost a spouse, sibling, or child—but not by most who lost a parent. When the deceased was over sixty years old, the bereaved were much less likely to report they were upset when making funeral arrangments than in the cases of younger deceased. There was a greater satisfaction with the appearance of the deceased over 30 years old (regarding restoration work), than there was with younger deceased.

Most bereaved in the study had very little experience discussing death in any social situation. Bereaved who found it "very difficult" to cope with the death were more likely than other bereaved to talk "frequently" about death since their loss. It was also the case that bereaved who felt it "very difficult" to cope with the death valued the funeral most highly. Most bereaved thought they should be only "somewhat" open about expressing their grief—a noticeable minority were keenly aware that the community was "not tolerant of openly displayed" grief. Those who found the death "very difficult" to cope with were most likely to feel that they were expected to express their grief in a "very open way."

APPENDIX A:

Questionnaire*

This questionnaire is a study about American attitudes toward death which is being conducted by the Sociology Department at Wisconsin State University—La Crosse. Please do not sign your name, so that we may be sure that all replies will be confidential. *In addition, please do not reveal the name of a funeral home, funeral director, clergyman, or other persons.*

Each of these questions or statements is followed by several choices. We would appreciate it if you would please check ONE answer most nearly expressing your way of thinking, your attitude, belief, or opinion.

Your name was selected at random from the obituary columns of the La Crosse Tribune as next of kin to one who died during 1969.

1. Your age: _____ (Exact age was given).
   - _____ 1. 20-39
   - _____ 2. 40-59
   - _____ 3. 60-79
   - _____ 4. 80 and above
     (These categories made for analysis).
2. Your sex:
   - _____ 1. Male
   - _____ 2. Female
3. Your education:
   - _____ 1. Grade school
   - _____ 2. Junior high school
   - _____ 3. High school graduate
   - _____ 4. Some college

*This is the questionnaire for the complete study including questions for the data reported in this chapter.

_____ 5. College graduate

_____ 6. Graduate degree

4. What is your religious background:

_____ 1. Catholic

_____ 2. Lutheran

_____ 3. Methodist, Presbyterian, Congregational, Other Protestant

5. Your marital status:

_____ 1. Single

_____ 2. Married

_____ 3. Separated

_____ 4. Divorced

_____ 5. Widowed

6. Your approximate annual income:

_____ 1. Less than $4,000

_____ 2. $ 4,000 to $ 5,999

_____ 3. $ 6,000 to $ 9,999

_____ 4. $10,000 to $14,999

_____ 5. $15,000 and over

7. Your present occupation:

_____ 1. Elementary or high school teacher

_____ 2. White collar, clerical or sales

_____ 3. Technician, craftsman, or the trades

_____ 4. Business manager or executive

_____ 5. Professional

_____ 6. Laborer, factory worker

_____ 7. Housewife

_____ 8. Retired

_____ 9. Other (including unemployed)

8. Occupation of the deceased relative:

_____ 1. Elementary or high school teacher

_____ 2. White collar, clerical or sales

_____ 3. Technician, craftsman, or the trades

_____ 4. Business manager or executive

_____ 5. Professional

_____ 6. Laborer, factory worker

_____ 7. Housewife

_____ 8. Retired

_____ 9. Other (including unemployed)

9. What relation to you was the deceased?

_____ 1. Husband

_____ 2. Wife

_____ 3. Parent (Father, Mother)

_____ 4. Child

_____ 5. Sibling (Brother, Sister)

10. Age of the deceased? _____ (Exact age was given)

_____ 1. 1-29

_____ 2. 30-59

_____ 3. 60 and above (These categories made for analysis).

11. Sex of the deceased:

_____ 1. Male

_____ 2. Female

12. What were the circumstances surrounding the death?

_____ 1. Sudden death—accident

_____ 2. Illness—not exceeding 6 months

_____ 3. Illness—over 6 months

13. How did you select a funeral home?

_____ 1. The funeral home contacted me

_____ 2. Clergyman's recommendation

_____ 3. Hospital's recommendation

_____ 4. Coroner's recommendation

_____ 5. Physician's recommendation

_____ 6. Religious affiliation of the funeral home

_____ 7. Knew the funeral director

_____ 8. The deceased had specified a preference
for a funeral home

_____ 9. Other

14. Where did the death take place?

_____ 1. At home

_____ 2. In the hospital

_____ 3. In a nursing home

_____ 4. At work

_____ 5. In a traffic accident

_____ 6. Other

15. Did the deceased leave instructions as to the burial details?
    _____ 1. Yes (left written instructions or told someone his wishes)
    _____ 2. No
16. Where was the funeral service held?
    _____ 1. Funeral home
    _____ 2. Church
    _____ 3. Both funeral home and church
    _____ 4. Home
    _____ 5. Other
17. If you are a widow or widower, who made most of the financial decisions during your marriage?
    _____ 1. I did
    _____ 2. My spouse
    _____ 3. My spouse and I jointly
18. Do you feel that the funeral was *more* for the living or for the deceased?
    _____ 1. For the living
    _____ 2. For the deceased
    _____ 3. Both
19. How important do you believe funerals are for the surviving?
    _____ 1. Extremely important
    _____ 2. Somewhat important
    _____ 3. Undecided
    _____ 4. Not very important
    _____ 5. Not important at all
20. How able were you to cope with this death in the family?
    It was:
    _____ 1. Very difficult
    _____ 2. Somewhat difficult
    _____ 3. Not difficult at all
21. Prior to the loss in the family, did you discuss death with friends or relatives?
    _____ 1. Frequently
    _____ 2. Seldom
    _____ 3. Not at all

22. Since the loss in the family, do you find yourself discussing death with friends or relatives?

    _____ 1. Frequently

    _____ 2. Seldom

    _____ 3. Not at all

23. Emotionally, how prepared do you feel you were to cope with this death?

    _____ 1. Very prepared

    _____ 2. Somewhat prepared

    _____ 3. Undecided

    _____ 4. Not very prepared

    _____ 5. Not prepared at all

Have you been involved in discussions about death in any of the following situations?

24. At church?

    _____ 1. Very much

    _____ 2. Somewhat

    _____ 3. Not at all

25. At school?

    _____ 1. Very much

    _____ 2. Somewhat

    _____ 3. Not at all

26. At work?

    _____ 1. Very much

    _____ 2. Somewhat

    _____ 3. Not at all

27. In the family?

    _____ 1. Very much

    _____ 2. Somewhat

    _____ 3. Not at all

28. With friends?

    _____ 1. Very much

    _____ 2. Seldom

    _____ 3. Not at all

29. With physicians?
    _____ 1. Very much
    _____ 2. Seldom
    _____ 3. Not at all

Did you know that you needed:

30. A burial vault?
    _____ 1. Yes
    _____ 2. No

31. A death certificate?
    _____ 1. Yes
    _____ 2. No

32. Prior to the death in the family, did you own a cemetery lot for the deceased?
    _____ 1. Yes
    _____ 2. No

33. Was it easy for you to get off work during the funeral week?
    _____ 1. Very easy
    _____ 2. Somewhat easy
    _____ 3. Not easy at all
    _____ 4. Do not work

34. Did friends help out with routine tasks like cooking and babysitting during the funeral week?
    _____ 1. Yes
    _____ 2. No

35. In general, how do you feel that people expected you to express your grief?
    _____ 1. In a very open way
    _____ 2. In a somewhat open way
    _____ 3. Not tolerant of openly displayed grief

36. Following the week of the funeral, did the funeral director continue to offer his help and sympathy?
    _____ 1. Very much
    _____ 2. Somewhat
    _____ 3. Not at all

37. Did the funeral director help to make you more aware of your new status as a widow, widower, or member of the bereaved family?

    _____ 1. Did not help at all
    _____ 2. Helped somewhat
    _____ 3. He helped me very much

38. Did the funeral director succeed in comforting you during the funeral week?

    _____ 1. Yes
    _____ 2. No

39. Do you feel that the funeral was a meaningful way to express love for the deceased?

    _____ 1. Not at all
    _____ 2. Somewhat
    _____ 3. Very much

40. Did the expectations of your friends affect you in the selection of type of funeral, flowers, and extra services?

    _____ 1. Very much
    _____ 2. Somewhat
    _____ 3. Not at all

41. Did you go to the funeral home to make plans for the funeral?

    _____ 1. Yes
    _____ 2. No

42. Did you go to the funeral home to select a casket?

    _____ 1. Yes
    _____ 2. No

43. Did you make most of the arrangements for the funeral during the meeting with the funeral director in the funeral home?

    _____ 1. Yes
    _____ 2. No

44. Prior to the loss of the deceased, had you visited a funeral home?

    _____ 1. I had never been inside a funeral home
    _____ 2. I had only visited a funeral home during visitation hours

_____ 3. I had visited a funeral home to arrange for other funerals

_____ 4. Other

45. How much did you expect the funeral to cost before the prices were quoted?

_____ 1. Less than $500

_____ 2. $ 500 to $ 799

_____ 3. $ 800 to $ 999

_____ 4. $1,000 to $1,199

_____ 5. $1,200 to $1,499

_____ 6. $1,500 and over

_____ 7. Had no idea of expected cost

46. How much did the funeral actually cost?

_____ 1. Less than expected $ _____

_____ 2. The same as expected

_____ 3. More than expected $ _____

_____ 4. Don't know

47. When you think it over, how much would you have liked to have spent on the funeral?

_____ 1. Less than was spent $ _____

_____ 2. The same amount

_____ 3. More than was spent $ _____

48. By what means were funeral expenses paid?

_____ 1. Savings account

_____ 2. Loan

_____ 3. Special burial funds (burial insurance, public assistance, veteran's benefits, etc.)

_____ 4. Relatives shared cost

_____ 5. Savings and special burial funds

_____ 6. Other

49. Concerning the cost of the casket you selected, was it:

_____ 1. More than you could really afford

_____ 2. Just what you could afford

_____ 3. Less than you could afford

50. When making arrangements, how did the *atmosphere of the funeral home* make you feel?

_____ 1. Very foreign

_____ 2. Somewhat foreign

_____ 3. Not foreign at all

_____ 4. I did not make the arrangements

51. When making arrangements within the funeral home, did the setting (the music, furniture, carpeting, decor, etc.) make you feel:

_____ 1. Very strange

_____ 2. Somewhat strange

_____ 3. Not strange at all

_____ 4. I did not make arrangements

52. How many went to the funeral home to make the funeral arrangements? I went:

_____ 1. By myself

_____ 2. With one other person

_____ 3. With two other persons

_____ 4. With three others

_____ 5. With four others or more

53. Who were the people who accompanied you to the funeral home to make funeral arrangements?

_____ 1. Friend(s)

_____ 2. Relative(s)

_____ 3. Friend(s) and relative(s)

54. Did the people who accompanied you to the funeral home help make the decisions regarding funeral arrangements?

_____ 1. Yes

_____ 2. No

55. If the funeral was for your spouse, whose relatives were more influential in the funeral arrangements and planning the funeral?

_____ 1. My relatives

_____ 2. My spouse's relatives

_____ 3. Deceased was not my spouse

56. When deciding on the details of the funeral, were you:

_____ 1. Very upset

_____ 2. Somewhat upset

_____ 3. Not upset at all

57. How well did you know the funeral director before the death?

_____ 1. Not at all

_____ 2. Casual acquaintance

_____ 3. Friend of mine or of the family

58. Where did you or your family get acquainted with the funeral director?

_____ 1. Church activities

_____ 2. Civic organizations

_____ 3. Friend of the family

_____ 4. Past funerals

59. When you were selecting the casket and vault, did you feel the pressure of limited time in your decision?

_____ 1. Yes

_____ 2. No

_____ 3. I did not select the casket

In the selection of the casket, did you take into consideration or were you influenced by the following:

60. Style of casket?

_____ 1. Yes

_____ 2. No

61. Color of casket?

_____ 1. Yes

_____ 2. No

62. Cost of casket?

_____ 1. Yes

_____ 2. No

63. Relatives or friends?

_____ 1. Yes

_____ 2. No

64. Funeral director?

_____ 1. Yes

_____ 2. No

65. Grief at the time?

_____ 1. Yes

_____ 2. No

66. Did the funeral director seem like a member of the family during the funeral week?

_____ 1. Yes
_____ 2. No

67. How did the funeral director impress you?

_____ 1. He does not seem at all interested in the people he serves

_____ 2. He is somewhat interested in the people he serves

_____ 3. He seems very interested in the people he serves

68. Did it seem that the funeral director went out of his way to help you in your time of grief?

_____ 1. Not at all

_____ 2. Somewhat

_____ 3. Very much

69. How did the funeral director assist you in making funeral arrangements?

_____ 1. I asked him to take over all possible arrangements

_____ 2. I asked him to take over several arrangements

_____ 3. I asked him to take over very few arrangements

Did the funeral director perform any of the following services for you?

70. Order flowers?

_____ 1. Yes
_____ 2. No

71. Contact pallbearers?

_____ 1. Yes
_____ 2. No

72. Notify any relatives?

_____ 1. Yes
_____ 2. No

73. Send thank you cards for you?

_____ 1. Yes
_____ 2. No

74. Select a grave marker?

_____ 1. Yes
_____ 2. No

75. Notify any friends?

　　　　　_____ 1. Yes
　　　　　_____ 2. No

76. How did you find the appearance of the deceased (in regard to the restoration work)?

　　　　　_____ 1. The deceased looked much younger
　　　　　_____ 2. The deceased looked somewhat younger
　　　　　_____ 3. The deceased looked about the same as when alive
　　　　　_____ 4. Other

77. How did you react to the appearance of the deceased?

　　　　　_____ 1. I was pleased with the appearance
　　　　　_____ 2. I was not pleased with the appearance
　　　　　_____ 3. Undecided
　　　　　_____ 4. Other

We wish to thank you for your cooperation in completing this questionnaire. If you would like a copy of the results, please send us a card with your name and address.

If there are comments or additional information you wish to add, please use the space below and the back of the questionnaire.

REFERENCES

Borkenau, Franz: The concept of death. In Fulton, Robert (Ed.): *Death and Identity*. New York, Wiley and Sons, 1965.

Cobb, B.: Psychological impact of long illness and death of a child on the family circle. *J Pediatr, 49*:746, 1956.

Fulton, Robert: The clergyman and the funeral director: a study on role conflict. *Social Forces, 39*:317-323, 1961.

Fulton, Robert: The sacred and the secular: attitudes of the American public toward death, funerals, and funeral directors. In *Death and Identity*. 1965.

Fulton, Robert, and Fulton, Julie: A Psycho-Social Aspect of Terminal Care, a paper presented at the Symposium for Psycho-Social Aspects of Terminal Care, Columbia University, November, 1970.

Fulton, Robert, and Geis, Gilbert: Death and social values. In *Death and Identity*. New York, 1965.

Glazer, Barney, and Strauss, Anselm: *A Time for Dying*. Chicago, 1968.

———: Awareness of dying. In Schoenberg, B., Carr, A.C., Peretz, D., and Kutscher, A.H., (Eds.): *Loss and Grief*. New York, Columbia U Pr. 1970.

Gorer, Goeffrey: *Death, Grief, and Mourning*. New York, Doubleday 1965.

Hinton, John: *Dying*. Baltimore, Pelican Books, 1967.

Kalish, Richard: The effects of death upon the family. In Pearson, Leonard: Cleveland, The Press of Case Western Reserve U, 1969.

Peretz, David: Development and loss. In Schoenberg, B., Carr, A.C., Peretz, D., and Kutscher, A.H., (Eds.): *Loss and Grief: Psychological Management in Medical Practice*. New York, 1970.

Reardon, Patrick P.: Let's get rid of funeral homes. *U.S. Catholic/Jubilee,* January, 1971.

Riley, Thomas J.: Catholic teaching, the child, and a philosophy for life and death. In Grollman, Earl (Ed.): *Explaining Death to Children*. Boston, Beacon Pr, 1967.

Sicard, Damien: The funeral mass. In Wagner, Johannes (Ed.): *Liturgy: Reforming the Rites of Death*. New York, 1968.

Sudnow, David: Passing On: *The Social Organization of Dying*. Englewood Cliffs, Prentice-Hall, 1967.

Vernon, Glenn: *Sociology of Death*. New York, Ronald Pr, 1970.

CHAPTER 7

THE LEGAL ASPECTS OF DEATH

Erwin H. Greenberg

THERE HAVE BEEN considerable writing and much discussion in recent years concerning the legal definition of death—that is, when is a person *legally* dead? Previously, there was never any confusion in the law about the legal definition of death. The common law defines death as the human body deprived of life. The definition itself requires further definition of the phrase "deprived of life." Until now, a body is deprived of life if there is an absence of circulation, of respiration, of body heat and of sensibility to stimuli; or a body is deprived of life if there is present the physical condition of rigor mortis or putrefaction. Therefore, if the heart is still beating, or if the lungs are still respiring, or if there is circulation or body heat, the body is not legally dead—even though the brain has been destroyed or so damaged that it can never reasonably function again.

However, doctors and other scientists no longer are willing to accept this legal definition. Instead, they have adopted the definition of "brain death." If the human brain has been so damaged or destroyed that it can no longer reasonably function and the body in which it is housed can no longer reasonably function; if there is no reasonable hope or expectation that reasonable, normal bodily functions can be resumed in the future, under the "brain death" definition, the body is dead. The impetus for this definition came from the dramatic breakthrough in organ transplantation, when kidney transplantation techniques were perfected, and a few heart transplant recipients survived for a limited period.

Further speculations about the "brain death" definition of death have been initiated by the recent concern with the concept of dying with dignity. Philosophers, theologians, and friends and relatives of those who are dying have raised the question as to whether it is morally, religiously or humanely proper to keep the human body alive by artificial means when it is apparent that the body cannot survive without mechanical assistance. Is one to be kept alive merely because some device can perform necessary functions that the body cannot perform for itself? Is the body to be kept alive by mechanical means even though there is no reasonable hope or expectation for any sort of normal future existence? Is the body to be kept alive by mechanical devices even though with each breath there is added pain, misery and suffering for the body itself and for those to whom that body represents a loved one? And so, the debate rages on. There is no doubt that any redefinition of death will have vast legal, medical, scientific, philosophical and religious consequences. The proposed definition of "brain death" has not yet been adopted by our courts uniformly or written into any statute.

But, regardless of whether the definition of "deprived of life" or the definition of "brain death" is the legal definition of death, the question then arises—what is the legal status of a dead human body?

Our concern is not with the commercial value of a dead human body but with the value and status it carries in regard to the rights which attach to it. Legal rights, generally speaking, attach to that which is tangible property. The question, therefore, naturally arises whether or not the dead body is property in the legal concept of the word "property." In the strict legal sense, a dead body is not property. It cannot be bought, sold or transferred; nor can it be left by will (except where statutes specifically permit it) ; nor does the body descend to the heirs of the deceased. However, for all practical purposes, it makes no difference whether we call the dead body property or not. Our concern is with the legal rights that attach to it and these rights are in the nature of *property rights,* sometimes referred to as quasi-property rights.

A man has full control over his body. He has without question the right to say what is to be done with any portions of it. If he undergoes an operation resulting in the loss of a leg or arm, he, and he alone, has the right to say in what manner the lost member shall be disposed of. Of course, his directions relative to the disposal must be in keeping with rules and regulations concerning public health.

It is also true in some states, though not all, that he may direct the way in which his body shall be buried. If he desires to leave his body by will to some educational or scientific institution, he may do so. However, his right to give his body away is governed by the rules of common decency. He cannot leave it to a member of his family for any purpose other than for disposal. Unless the beneficiary is an accredited institution or scientific research laboratory and the purpose be for the ultimate advancement of science, his desires cannot and should not be carried out. Under normal circumstances, an individual would not will his body for any reason other than for the good of society generally. Anyone making a bizarre or ridiculous disposal of his body could be considered as legally incompetent and, therefore, legally incapable of making a will.

If a man can direct that his body be given away after death for scientific or medical purposes, the question then arises whether or not he has the absolute right to direct the manner in which his body shall be disposed: in other words, if the decedent has requested that his body be buried and the next of kin desire to cremate the body, whose wish would prevail?

The law is clear that upon the death of an individual, one person and one person only in the entire world has the right and duty of disposal. In order to exercise that right and discharge that liability, that person has all of the rights that any owner of property would have, except that the rights may be exercised only for the ultimate purpose of disposal of the body. Because of this a person who has the right and duty of disposal possesses these property rights and the body is considered to have a legal status somewhat akin to tangible property. Thus, upon death, two questions arise: 1. Who has the right and duty of disposal? 2. Whose wishes should prevail: the wishes of the decedent or the wishes of the party who has the right and duty of disposal? The latter question has yet to be answered from a legal point of view.

Let us consider who has the right and duty of disposal.

The husband's right to the custody of his wife's body is superior to all. Her parents, the children and any other relatives have nothing whatsoever to say. It had been his duty to support her and furnish her with all the necessities of life. It is also his duty to give her body a proper disposal upon her death. All of the liabilities as well as all the rights fall upon him.

There is, however, a situation where the husband may not have these rights. If his wife had left him for good and sufficient reasons, and if she had returned to her parents and henceforth lived under their care and support because he had failed to furnish her with any support during this time, it is probably true that the parents' rights would be paramount. But so long as the husband fulfills his duty of support, no one can question his right and duty of disposal.

It would seem that the same is true relative to any children depending upon the father for support. He may be a poor husband and father and may not give a funeral that seems adequate to the relatives, and, in fact, it may or may not be in keeping with the family's social standing, yet it is his right to give what he desires.

As to a surviving wife, her rights to the custody of her husband's body are paramount to all even though, unlike the husband, she does not have to assume all the liabilities. In many cases where the husband and wife have lived apart, she has been given the right to bury him.

The following are two interesting cases in this regard:

Jones was divorced by his wife. In the state where the divorce was granted, the law was that he could not marry again for two years. He went to another state and married; then returned to his home state and died, leaving his new wife surviving. Jones' parents sought to have the custody of his body for purposes of burial. The clash of rights here is between the surviving wife and the parents of the deceased husband. The custody of the body was given to the parents as Jones was not legally married under the laws of his home state and, therefore, the woman with whom he was living was not his legal wife under these laws.

A physician married Mary in 1955, and divorced her in 1964. He then married Joann. The physician had lived with Mary in Tennessee and with Joann in Pennsylvania. In his will (which he had neglected to change), he had specified that he should be buried in Tennessee at the side of Mary if she should die first. Joann, however, wished to have him buried in Pennsylvania. The court designated Joann as the legal wife and, therefore, gave her the right to bury him wherever she saw fit despite the provisions of his Will.

As we have seen, the husband or wife, whichever survives, has the first claim to custody of the body. If there is no husband or wife, the duty of burial as well as the right to the custody of the body falls upon the kin in order of their relationship to the deceased. The order in which these rights and duties vest is in the degree of kinship.

The degree of kinship is as follows:

First Degree—Father, Mother, Son, Daughter

Second Degree—Grandfather, Grandmother, Grandson, Granddaughter, Brothers, Sisters

Third Degree—Great Grandfather, Great Grandmother, Aunts, Uncles, Nephews, Nieces

Fourth Degree—Great Aunts, Great Uncles, First Cousins

Fifth Degree—First Cousins once removed

Sixth Degree—Second Cousins

Some states have passed statutes which place the duty of disposal upon the kin in a certain order. These statutes, however, follow the common law idea that the body belongs to the person charged with the duty of disposal. The following brief summary as to the person on whom the duty of burial falls and to whom the rights belong is practically the same in every state in the Union.

First, the duty and right falls upon the surviving spouse. If the deceased was unmarried, then upon the nearest kin of sufficient age and possessed of enough money to defray the expenses. If no kin, upon the coroner or person having the authority to handle such bodies when an inquest is held. If no inquest, then to the person in charge of the poor. If all these persons above enumerated refuse to act, then the duty falls upon the tenant of the premises where the death occurred, and if no tenant on the premises, then upon the owner. In death at sea, the duty falls upon the master of the vessel or the owner if the vessel has no master.

It is well to note that executors and administrators have not been mentioned. The reason is simply because they have no rights whatsoever in the custody of the dead body of the person whose estate they are handling.

The superintendents of hospitals and public institutions have no rights to the dead body. However, it would seem that if no person can be found upon whom the duty of disposal fell, they would then have the duty of burial as the deceased would fall in the same class as the tenant of premises where the death occurred. This is true, however, only in the absence of laws which permit such bodies to be used for the advancement of medical science.

Most states have statutes which allow such bodies to be given to medical schools—the purpose being to give medical students an opportunity for study so that the public as a whole will benefit. A few states also have statutes which allow such bodies to be given to funeral service education schools.

Although a person has the right to custody of the body, he must exercise this right in keeping with the requirements of society; with respect for the feelings of the members of the family; with respect for the deceased's social position; and with due respect for the deceased's own wishes. But above all, the dead body is entitled to a dignified decent disposal. This is a right which arises out of the belief that the dead body, in life, housed that most magnificent of all man's possessions—the human soul. To dispose of the human body without dignity and without decency was a crime at common law and is a crime today in this country. Perhaps the most vivid illustration of this right of disposal with dignity and decency occurred in one of the New England states. A man burned the body of his sister who had died of natural causes by stuffing it in the basement furnace. He was indicted for indecent and unlawful disposal of the body. In finding him guilty, the court said that although cremation is lawful, the crime is not that the body was burned, but that it was indecently burned in such a manner that the feelings and natural sentiments of the public would be outraged, and, therefore, this was a crime at common law.

In summation, it has been noted that there is now great agitation in our society for a redefinition of death. This controversy has brought out into the open the entire subject of dying, death and dead bodies. For the first time in human history, people are discussing the concepts of death and dying and talking about dead bodies without fear, without superstition, and without hesitation. Death is the final historic event in a man's life. For too long, man has refused to study or discuss death. The fact that he is now studying, exploring and discussing it is a trend of great social, philosophical, religious and historic importance.

CHAPTER 8

THE ROLE OF THE CEMETERY IN GRIEF EXPRESSION

JOHN P. DANGLADE

WITHIN THE HUMAN cycle of birth, maturity and death, the cemetery has traditionally held the final position of the final turn. Its role has been that of the "last resting place," the "silent" grave, the irrevocable "end" to all things. The primary function of the cemetery is to receive the mortal remains of a human being in a lawful and dignified manner and in keeping with such religious or moral principles as may apply.

Yet, there are other functions of the cemetery which transcend this image of finality. These include the charge to memorialize the life and spirit of the human being whose remains it has received; to provide the environment at the time of interment and subsequently so that the impact of death upon the family and friends may become one of peace; and, the administration of endowment care trust funds which provide for maintenance of the property.

Because of this last function, the cemetery as a place of interment becomes a place of beauty and inspiration. And, in this context, the cemetery is indeed a continuing focal point for the expression of grief and the acceptance of death.

As a matter of record, the public view of the cemetery is changing. This modification can be seen in both social and religious applications. It is necessary that those involved with the entire process of death, dying, and loss and grief be aware of these changes to permit them to work in favor of the bereaved.

Memorialization once was the privilege (or the duty) of the few.

Examples of entombment of kings, pharaohs and warriors are evident in every culture and civilization. The individuals who provided the labor for these monuments were nameless, faceless, and generally unrecorded in history.

The ancient Hebrews introduced a new order to life, and consequently to death: each man became worthy of memory. Christianity and other major religions built on this ethic. Burial of the dead with dignity and memorialization became a social and religious duty.

There followed, at what might be described as the beginning of the modern age, a change and an excess, resulting in the "graveyard" image whereby death itself became the prime focus. Gloomy, weed-grown lots, visually broadcasting defeat, despair, and decay were transformed into the exact opposite of the original intention. Headstones, memorials and commemorative works began to be displayed as symbolic art, and society's manifestation of a fascination with death.

With yet another change, in the mid 1800's in the United States, cemeteries were invested with the dual task of returning to the positive memorial ideal on a basis of sound business practices. Nonprofit organizations sprang up in the major population centers, churches and fraternal orders revised their cemetery concepts, and municipalities created cemeteries for the community along these revived guidelines. In this period, we begin to meet the concept of "God's Acre," as a holy ground, deserving of care and attention and with the emphasis upon eternal life. Tree plantings, landscaping, lakes and quiet walks became an integral part of cemetery design. Beauty for the sake of consolation of the bereaved became a leading factor in cemetery planning.

While the older cemeteries were adjusting and conforming to this concept, the new memorial park idea was born. This type of cemetery took an additional step and attempted to eliminate the graveyard image by abolishing upright headstones and substituting markers flush with the turf. The resulting effect was one of a vast lawn, sometimes accented with planting and statuary. During this time, the cemetery also became an important locale for patriotic observances and commemoration of war dead.

Today, the cemetery in the United States retains a measure of the

God's Acre atmosphere, particularly in the cemeteries maintained by the various religious groups. It continues to serve as the focus for continuing grief expression. After the death and the funeral, the cemetery for many remains the touch-point to the memory of the deceased. Obviously, it can serve to bring about the realization and acceptance of death, or to prolong the avoidance of such acceptance.

There are a number of trends currently shaping cemetery design and the cemetery's role within the community of the living. Some of these may prove to be extremely helpful in supporting the desired acceptance of death, while others may not.

The current emphasis on man's use (and misuse) of his environment is a remarkable phenomenon. Although the historian can find references of concern about the environment dating back dozens and perhaps hundreds of years, the mainstream American is today genuinely concerned with the meaning of "ecology" for the first time. The professional cemeterian has realized that over and above considerations of respect for the departed and our traditional protection of sacred ground, the cemetery today provides the green grass, the trees, the open space reservation and even the creature habitat which are the heart of ecological balance. Moreover, the cemetery administrator has come to understand that he was the original ecologist, in the sense that he was setting aside and caring for these dedicated areas before anyone else. Man built cemeteries before he built parks, and he planted grass and trees in cemeteries long before he noticed the black smoke pouring from chimneys and polluting the atmosphere.

Tied closely to these ecological developments is the newer one of multiple use of cemeteries. A subject of current debate among cemeterians is whether these park-like expanses can be opened to increased public use without destroying the dignity and the sacred atmosphere of the cemetery. Cemeterians are discussing the problem in a series of seminars and conferences. As a result, there has been considerable liberalizing of cemetery regulations controlling activities other than interment and memorialization.

While modern cemeteries are looking at their future, we are seeing a related revival of interest in the restoration and preservation of old, sometimes abandoned, pioneer burial grounds. Within the past five years, voluntary associations for such work have been formed in six states. There is also unprecedented activity in such work among civic and fraternal groups, although a certain amount of this interest is without doubt related to the American Revolution Bicentennial. With the assistance of the American Cemetery Association and its individual members, courses on the process of death at both the college and high school level have recently included visits to, and studies of, cemeteries.

The concept and acceptance of the community mausoleum is a major consideration of cemeteries today. These structures offer entombment rather than earth burial and some are being constructed to rise many stories. Cemeterians agree that this development is one which is being fed by public interest and demand. At present, it is estimated that perhaps as much as 30 percent of all professionally-managed cemeteries in the United States have, or are planning, community mausoleums. If it is realized that entombment offered by the mausoleum does not provide the "return to dust" of earth burial, this development in memorialization may be the most uncertain in terms of final acceptance of death.

Still another development in cemetery planning has been brought about by the slow but steady growth in public acceptance of cremation as an alternative to earth burial. More and more cemeteries are installing crematories and providing columbaria for the urns containing cremated remains.

It would appear that the cemetery's role in grief expression may be subject to change as the cemetery itself changes as a factor in the nation's social and religious life. Most states now have laws requiring the establishment of endowment care funds for cemeteries, which should preclude the desolation and abandonment of the past. It is likely that the cemetery's place in the environment, particularly in reference to its positive values as green space and additional usage, will become more and more appreciated by the public.

Continued expansion of the mausoleum plan will provide more efficient land use. Cremations will probably continue to gain public favor. The natural aspect of the cemetery in terms of its beauty will likely increase its value to the individual community. With its role properly interpreted and communicated by those whose task it is to encourage understanding of death and dying, it would seem that the cemetery can be viewed by society as a most valuable asset.

PART TWO

THE FUNERAL AND
THOSE WHO SERVE

CHAPTER 9

GRIEF, BEREAVEMENT, AND MOURNING: THE REALITIES OF LOSS

VANDERLYN R. PINE

IN HIS CLASSIC ARTICLE, Erich Lindemann describes acute grief and its symptomatology (Lindemann, 1944). He points out that acute grief is a definite syndrome with symptoms which are observable and which follow a crisis. The five major characteristics of acute grief are 1. somatic distress (actual physical symptoms), 2. preoccupation with the image of the deceased, 3. guilt, 4. hostile reactions, and 5. loss of patterns of conduct (Lindemann, 1944; Jackson, 1975). Loss of patterns of conduct refers to the situation which occurs when grieving people feel aimless and restless, while at the same time they are unable to begin and complete any meaningful activity. One means of coping with the loss of patterns of conduct following death is the funeral, for it provides an opportunity to carry out some sort of meaningful, structured, social activity.

The funeral has been described as an experience which functions to "make things easier" by providing social support, and mourning and the funeral process may be thought of as "togetherness." If togetherness does not exist, the funeral will not be too effective in fulfilling its purpose. Jackson argues that "to grieve" is connected with the concept of "to love."

Since the publication of Lindemann's article, others have written and talked about it, and grief has developed into a subject of great interest (Parkes, 1972; Weisman, 1972; Clayton, 1975; Fulton, 1965; Schoenberg, 1974; Coelho, 1974). There are several points from these studies that merit attention. The observable or experienced syndrome of acute grief has both psychological and somatic symptoms. For example, when someone has a "disturbed mind," it may be a psychological symptom of acute grief. On the other hand, when someone has an aching stomach, it may reflect a somatic and medically relevant symptom. Most of us experience acute grief at some time or another, and it touches us in a personal fashion.

Too frequently, the words grief, bereavement, and mourning are used with no specification of their differences and on the assumption that their meanings are understood.[1] Since definitions are important in the conceptual development of a general theory, the definitional distinctions among the three terms should be clarified.

Bereavement is an *objective* state of deprivation, and to bereave is to deprive. Thus, bereavement is the loss of some important object or person. Grief is a *psychological* state characterized by anxiety or mental anguish, and it follows or anticipates bereavement. Mourning is a *social* state of grieving the loss of a significant other.

All three states are directly related to loss and loss-threat (Pine, 1974). The sense of loss that occurs following a divorce or a separation, or the separation from relatives or friends because of movement from one place to another, is a form of bereavement, and the grief which results can be just as problematic for people following separation or divorce as it can following a death. At times, in both cases, there is deprivation (bereavement) and mental anguish (grief). Unfortunately, following a divorce, there seldom is a legitimate mourning process such as a funeral. Seen in this context, the funeral may be thought of as a social and emotional support mechanism which provides an opportunity for mourning. It generally involves family, friends and the larger community. My research indicates that without these three components, funerals are far less meaningful to the people who participate in them.

The phenomena that give rise to bereavement, grief and mourning and initiate grief reactions are loss and/or loss-threat.[2] Examination

---

[1] An exception is the perspective set forth by Edgar Jackson, "The Wise Management of Grief," in Otto S. Margolis, et al., *Grief and the Meaning of Funerals* (New York, MSS Information Co., 1975).

[2] Most of the research focuses on the dying person and *loss-threat* rather than on the bereaved survivors. See Elisabeth Kubler-Ross, *On Death and Dying* (New York, The Macmillan Co., 1969); Avery D. Weisman, *On Dying and*

of available resource material and the reactions of people experiencing grief reveals that the theoretical key involves loss and loss-threat as stimuli for these reactions. *Loss* refers specifically to the actual occurrence of death or some other form of permanent irrevocable separation. A potential event is something that is anticipated in the future. For example, the potential that we are going to die is 100 percent. This potential, though, is different from the *threat* of loss Threat is imminent and carries a negative connotation. For example, if a physician tells a patient that he has cancer, the loss-threat that occurs at that time is completely different from the potential that is always present.

When studying death, one's experiential knowledge and personal life history should be taken into account, for the experiences one has had influence the way in which one is able to "face up" to various aspects of death. I believe that it is important for any health professional to be concerned with *his* own life history and *his* own experiential knowledge. For example, how is it that he is what he is? Why does he believe what he believes? What implications do these questions raise?

Let me point out how my experiential knowledge led to the development of my interest in death. My father, grandfather, and great-grandfather all were funeral directors. As a child, I heard every possible joke about death and funeral directors. I was called such epithets as "Digger," and my last name was amenable to "Pine box." Fortunately, in my community these jests were not said in a cruel way. Rather, they were the usual approach of treating death in a humorous fashion when it is not touching people personally; none of my friends ever called me Digger or Pine box when someone close to them died. It should be noted that the less-than-kind allusions

Denying (New York, Behavioral Publications, Inc., 1972); Bernard Schoenberg, et al., *Anticipatory Grief* (New York, Columbia University Press, 1974); and Colin Murray Parkes, *Bereavement Studies of Grief in Adult Life* (New York, International Universities Press, Inc., 1972). Recent attention increasingly is directed toward bereaved people and loss. See Vanderlyn R. Pine, "Grief and Bereavement," a paper presented at a Conference on Death and Dying, Cortland, New York, March 7, 8, 1974; Otto S. Margolis, et al., *Grief and the Meaning of Funerals* (New York, MSS Information Co., 1975); and Robert Fulton, *Death and Identity* (New York, John Wiley and Sons, Inc., 1965).

people often make about funeral directors involve a general aversion to death and not to these professionals as individuals.

When I was a sophomore in college, my father died very suddenly and unexpectedly. Following the common American value, I decided to "carry on the funeral home." I actively practiced funeral service for ten years. In that setting I dealt with over 5,000 bereaved families in some form or another. This background later had a marked influence on my choice of research topics as a student and, still later, on my work as a sociologist.

After ten years as a funeral director, I had the opportunity to return to school to complete my undergraduate work. Then, I went on to graduate school, received my doctorate, and began working and teaching as a sociologist. My background has given me a set of experiences surrounding the idea of death, what it means, and how it affects people. For example, one of my major academic concerns is the funeral as a social-psychological process.

Although I have analyzed various aspects of death-related behavior, neither I nor others have analyzed the relationship between acute grief and the funeral extensively. Funerals have been conducted for countless generations. In 1967, an anthropological investigation reported that in Iraq, a Neanderthal grave was uncovered and in it were found flowers and other artifacts that prove actual funerary treatment of the dead (Sullivan, 1968). This grave, unearthed after sixty thousand years, indicates that Neanderthal people handled death with some sort of affective expression. Egyptian practices are well recorded and rather precisely described by a number of historians, all of whom indicate the Egyptian concern with post-death activities. The ancient Greeks, Romans, and other Europeans also had means of handling death that involved funerals of some kind. In short, people adapted a means for handling death that was relevant to their society and time.

In the United States, funeral customs evolved among diverse sets of people, many of whom came here because they would not have been welcomed in other places. As a result, American funeral practices reflect a wide mixture of backgrounds and beliefs. The funeral that has evolved is adaptive for many people, even though it may be unique for a given area.

Several research projects have found that the funeral director is seen by people as being one of the most helpful professionals with whom the family has contact at the time of a death. This viewpoint may stem partly because of the contrast with medical services when dying may be handled by physicians who do not *seem* to care about anything except technological concerns. When death occurs, the bereaved have to turn to someone else. They leave the hospital and generally go back to their community in which there may well be a clinic physician whom they do not know too well, and a clergyperson whom they may never have met. In these circumstances, the bereaved most often turn to the pragmatic death professional, the funeral director, whose job it is to respond to whatever death needs people have.

Yet history records that the funeral director has been a scapegoat for the technical processes surrounding death. For example, the ancient Egyptians had the Dissector who, during the embalming process, made the incision on the dead body (Habenstein and Lamers, 1955). Following the embalming procedure, the Dissector was stoned, originally in reality and later symbolically, by the family of the deceased because he had defiled the body. Thus, he was made the scapegoat of death.

Today, the funeral director is still one of the scapegoats of death. He is portrayed in the abstract as someone who is less-than-honest and who is motivated by greed. Despite perpetuating this unfair stereotype, people often qualify their negative remarks by saying, "However, I have a friend who is a funeral director, I grew up with his children, and he's really different." Generally, people refer to *their* funeral director as a friend rather than as someone whom they mistrust.

Changes in American society have been responsible for changes in our funeral customs. For instance, the proportion of people in various age categories who died in 1900 as compared to 1970 has changed considerably. In 1900, 53 percent of the deaths were of people under 15, whereas by 1970, over two thirds of those dying were people past 65. In addition, our population has shifted from rural to urban areas. Specifically, in 1900, 60 percent of the population lived in rural areas, while in 1970, 70 percent of the population lived in urban areas. Furthermore, with the development of institutionalized settings and services, it has become increasingly common to place elderly and ill people into hospitals, nursing homes, and other such institutions.

As a result of these changes, the people who do funeral work now differ from those who did the work a number of years ago. In early America, delivering babies was handled by community midwives, all of whom functioned in a medical fashion. Similarly, when a death occurred, there were relatives and friends from the community who knew how to care for the dead. Thus, when our society was largely agrarian, the dead were cared for in an intimate setting.

As time passed, more and more people moved from the country to the cities. In this new, impersonal setting, death tasks began to be carried out by professionals. With further urbanization, there emerged an occupational specialist, the funeral director. At first, the funeral director did most of the work on the body in the home where the death had occurred, and even as recently as the 1920's, it was not uncommon for the family to participate in the embalming of the dead. Remember, these were the same families who also butchered their cows and chickens when they needed food, and they were otherwise involved in the "guts and blood" of life and death. Thus, dealing with the blood of the dead body of a family member was not dreaded, especially since it was the dead body of someone they loved and had nursed in illness.

Because of the tremendous urbanization that we have experienced and the fact that few of us are fortunate enough to see very much of life and death in a natural, meaningful setting, many find these rural community death practices repulsive. Family life was considerably different in the early years of this country, and birth and death were part of daily living.

Contemporary American society tends to elevate science and technology to a high, almost unrealistic, pinnacle. The failure of science and technology to control death, combined with such changes as urban isolation, compounds the severity of the problem for those involved. In an attempt to diminish the destructive features of the impersonal, institutionalized relationships that exist, some hospitals are experimenting with practices in which the family helps care for the dying person —restoring, in a sense, a custom from our past.

Science and technology are unable as yet to solve the problems of acute grief; the funeral is society's response to these. A number of comparable and similar funeral customs are found in our American society and in many differing societies.[3] First, funerals are intended to provide social support through the gathering of relatives and friends. In general, if a funeral is conducted in the absence of other people, it will not be socially functional and will not serve to meet the needs of the bereaved (Pine, 1975).

Second, funerals involve some sort of ritual and ceremony. As used here, the terms "ritual" and "ceremony" may be differentiated. A ritual may be described as an habitual, traditionally practiced behavior which may be carried out by one individual alone. A ceremony incorporates ritualistic behavior in a *social context,* and it always involves more than one person. In most societies, the funeral ceremony is religious, but it need not be.[4]

Third, visual confrontation of the dead body is a common funeral practice in most societies. It may occur at the place of death, e.g. in the hospital bed, or it may occur at the funeral home or in some other setting, e.g. in the private home. The important point is that in almost all societies, funerals involve the visual confrontation, even if it is in a setting unfamiliar to most Americans. There are examples of visual confrontation in unusual settings, even in a contemporary urban setting. For example, some funeral directors have begun to incorporate "old fashioned" family participation in funeral practices. Thus, if the next-of-kin so desire, they may accompany the funeral director to the hospital to pick up the body of their relative, or they may help dress and put the body in a casket.

Fourth, the funeral usually involves a procession. A funeral procession has been described as a family parade (Edgar Jackson, personal communication), and this practice enables people to display their grief publicly. Parades celebrate events which may be happy or sad, and they function as a community expression of emotional reactions.

Fifth, in most societies, some sort of sanitary disposition of the body

---

[3]For a fuller discussion see Vanderlyn R. Pine, Comparative Funeral Practices, *Practical Anthropology, 16*:49-62, 1969.

[4]The value of ritual and ceremony in meeting the needs of the bereaved may be just as effective in a secular society as it is in a sacred society. See Corliss Lamont, "A Humanist Funeral Service," and Paul E. Irion, "The Funeral and the Bereaved" in this book.

is carried out; the dead are interred, cremated, entombed, and so forth in an attempt to dispose of the dead body in a sanitary manner. Often, religious beliefs may influence the means of disposition. For example, in Bali each dead body is disposed of in three ways because of the belief that the three "elements" of life, earth, fire, and water, all should operate to destroy the body. Thus, the dead are buried in the earth until a cremation tower is built. Next, the body is dug up and cremated on a funeral pyre. Then, the cremated ashes and bones are scattered into the sea.

In summary, social support, ritual, ceremony, visual confrontation, a procession, and sanitary disposition are funeral customs present in most societies. These funeral customs involve some kind of expenditure, whether it be in goods, services, or money. The universal practice of expenditure may reflect the guilt component of acute grief.

Rational reactions to death are not always possible (Jackson, 1957). When nonrational behavior is exhibited by a bereaved survivor, the fallibility of the notion of human perfection is demonstrated. We cannot be perfect, and when death occurs, it hurts in nonscientific but human ways. No one close to me has died recently, but the memory of how death had affected me and my family is still very clear. In January, 1957, my father died. In June, my grandfather died. In July, my uncle died. In August, an aunt gave birth to a stillborn baby. Every time the phone rang that summer, we thought that it was going to be the announcement of another death. We did not become accustomed to death, and as each death occurred, our earlier griefs were remembered. The loneliness and the feeling of deprivation still existed and there was nothing we could do about it.

Since that year of so many losses, my family has been fortunate in having been spared the sorrowful experiences of bereavement. However, my grandmother who is now 98 and lives with my mother has begun to become quite senile. When she dies, I do not believe that my present anticipatory grief is going to blunt the pain of losing her. She has lived a full life which means, according to our scheduled society, that it is "o.k. for grandma to go." After all, she is no longer useful to society; her age has placed her in a category with the nearly 70 percent of those who die each year. These people are out of society, and they are at the end of the age spectrum. However, this should not mean that their death will hurt any less because of their societal "uselessness," nor does it mean that their funeral is any less important. Rather, the personal pain will be just as great as was their value to their loved ones.

We all have fears, doubts and questions about death. After a death occurs, these are particularly persistent. I feel that it is important to confront the acute grief pattern at that time by having others around to provide social support. Having others to touch, sharing deep involvement, exhibiting affective behavior, and allowing tears to fall, all come within the context of this social support. The technological and scientific perspectives of American society and Western culture inhibit effective communication when they condition people to believe that they should be able to "take it like a man." This suggests that we should not show emotions, that we should be less than human.

We must be able to show emotions and affective behavior; not to do so is, in a sense, a denial of death. As we strive to express our bereavement, to give vent to our grief, to share our mourning, we can opt for the rituals and ceremonies of the funeral as a means of coping with the reality of loss in a satisfactory fashion. Thus, the funeral serves as an important community and personal event during the period of acute grief because it provides a setting for emotional catharsis with *social support.*

REFERENCES

Clayton, Paula J.: The funeral director and bereavement. In Margolis, O. S., et al.: *Grief and The Meaning of Funerals.* New York, MSS Information Co., 1975.

Coelho, George V., et al.: *Coping and Adaptation.* New York, Basic Books, 1974.

Fulton, Robert: *Death and Identity.* New York, Wiley and Sons, 1965.

Habenstein, Robert W., and Lamers, William M.: *The History of American Funeral Directing.* Milwaukee, Bulfin Printers, 1955, p. 21.

Jackson, Edgar: *Understanding Grief.* New York, Abingdon, 1957.

Jackson, Edgar: The wise management of grief. In Margolis, O. S., et al.: *Grief and the Meaning of Funerals.* New York, MSS Information Co., 1975.

Lindemann, Erich: Symptomatology and management of acute grief. *Am J Psychiatry, 101*:141-148, 1944.

Parkes, Colin Murray: *Bereavement: Studies of Grief in Adult Life.* New York, Intl Univs Pr, 1972.

Pine, Vanderlyn R.: Grief and Bereavement, a paper presented at a Conference on Death and Dying, Cortland, New York, March 7, 8, 1974.

Pine, Vanderlyn R.: *Caretaker of The Dead: The American Funeral Director.* New York, Irvington and Wiley, 1975.

Schoenberg, Bernard, et al.: *Anticipatory Grief.* New York, Columbia U Pr, 1974.

Sullivan, Walter: The Neanderthal man liked flowers. New York Times, June 13, 1968, p. 1 and 43.

Weisman, Avery D.: *On Dying and Denying.* New York, Behavioral Publications, 1972.

CHAPTER 10

SOCIAL MEANINGS OF THE FUNERAL

VANDERLYN R. PINE

C EREMONY IS A powerful force in social control, emphasizing the interconnectedness of the past, the present and the future, and helping to demonstrate the importance not only of society but also of those individuals who form the social group. The value of ceremony is enhanced because its routines are graphic and dramatic presentations which generally appeal to several senses. For example, a ceremony may include singing, dancing, special dress, parading, masks, specific dialogue, and so forth. Furthermore, ceremony represents repetitive discipline for individuals and provides stability to their social group. Of course, in order for ritualized ceremony to have a meaningful utility for people, it must be familiar to them. If it is not, then there generally is a ceremonial tender whose duty and responsibility, i.e. function, is to help people define the nature of that ceremony and the limits to which it may be used. Naturally, this raises an important sociological question which provides the major theoretical focus for this paper. Namely, how, why, and for whom is ceremonial activity familiar, repetitive, and socially valuable?

The ceremonies which surround death provide an opportunity to examine empirically this theoretical question.[1] Moreover, the virtually

This paper was partially facilitated by a National Institutes of Health Fellowship No. 1 FO1 MH3812401A1 from the National Institute of Mental Health. I am particularly indebted to Patricia M. Dalton, Irving Goffman, Patricia P. Pine, Herbert Menzel and Kathy D. Williams for their helpful comments on earlier versions of this paper.
[1]There long have been scholarly works assessing death and reactions to it. These studies have been primarily historical, religious, anthropological and psychological in nature (H. Feifel, ed., *The Meaning of Death* [New York,

universal practice of funerals indicates that such ceremonies have an important societal locus and focus that transcend religious belief or political ideology. However, unlike people in most societies and unlike their associations with many other ceremonies, Americans are generally unfamiliar with funerals. This means that unless they wish to deny the occurrence of death altogether by doing nothing, they must turn to someone familiar with the appropriate ceremonies and their implementation. This person is the American funeral director.

This paper is concerned with the funeral ceremony and with the funeral director who establishes the context in which this ceremony is carried out. Moreover, it is through the perspective of the practicing funeral director as a ceremonial tender that we find one of our central concerns. Specifically, the importance of funeral ceremony is not logically or practically the same for society, for the individually bereaved, or for the funeral director. For society, funeral ceremony exists on a broad level involving individuals, groups, interaction, and the stability or change which occurs over time. For the individually bereaved, funeral ceremony has the unique purpose of providing a context of behavior in which they personally can move through the initial stages of the processes of bereavement and grief. For the funeral director, funeral ceremony is a way of life, in which crisis is treated as routine.

DEATH, FUNERALS, AND FUNERAL DIRECTORS

In nonindustrial societies, proportionately more deaths are concentrated among younger individuals who are the ongoing members of the society. Hertz (1960), Durkheim (1954), and Malinowski (1954) point out that such societies cope with the loss of important societal members by *communally* participating in well-rehearsed and practiced

---

McGraw-Hill, 1959]; R. W. Habenstein, and W.M. Lamers, *The History of American Funeral Directing* [Milwaukee, Bulfin Printing, 1955], *Funeral Customs the World Over* [Milwaukee, Bulfin Printing, 1960]; P. E. Irion, *The Funeral and the Mourners* [New York, Abingdon Press, 1954]; E. N. Jackson, *Understanding Grief* [New York, Abingdon Press, 1957]). However, there are several sociological investigations which recently have been published (W. A. Faunce, and R. Fulton, The sociology of death: a neglected area of research, *Social Forces,* 36:205, 1958; R. Fulton, *Death and Identity* [New York, John Wiley and Sons, 1965]; B. G. Glaser, and A. L. Strauss, *Awareness of Dying* [Chicago, Aldine Publishing Company, 1965]; D. Sudnow, *Passing On* [Englewood Cliffs, Prentice-Hall, 1967]).

funeral ceremonies. Generally, these ceremonies are designed to signify the loss of the individual, demonstrate the cohesion of the group and the solidarity of society, and help to identify publicly the survivor(s) of the dead person.

Today in the United States, proportionately fewer young people die. It is much more common for death to occur among the elderly and the sick who have been more or less separated from active society and whose loss is relatively unimportant to society in general. However, everyone dies, and when a father, mother, spouse, child or other close family member or friend dies, the impact of the specific death emphasizes needs that exist of importance to the community as well as to the survivor. Of course, when death occurs to youthful, important social figures such as John F. Kennedy, Martin Luther King, Robert Kennedy, and so forth, society ceremonializes the loss of these individuals and the nation participates *as a whole* in the ceremonial ending of these important lives. However, when death occurs to individuals less important to the social system, it still has a powerful impact on their relatives and friends.[2]

Since there are funerals for almost everyone, there is a *general* societal awareness of the repetitiveness of funeral ceremony, but this awareness is most salient for funeral directors who function professionally in the performance of funerals.[3] Individual deaths are nonrepetitive events, for each person dies only once. Therefore, ceremonial

---

[2]There have been studies approaching death from the perspective of reactions to the occurrence of death. Among the works from this approach are the writings of W. M. Kephart, Status after death, *American Sociological Review*, 15:635, 1950; G. Gorer, *Death, Grief, and Mourning* (New York, Doubleday, 1965); R. Blauner, Death and social structure, *Psychiatry*, 25:378, 1966; V. R. Pine, Comparative funeral practices, *Practical Anthropology*, March-April, 1969; Social organization and death, *Omega*, 3:149, 1972; Patterns of Information Dissemination in the Dynamics of Death-Related Communications, position paper presented at the Foundation of Thanatology Symposium on Communications and Thanatology, Columbia University, New York, New York, November, 1972; V. R. Pine, and D. Phillips, The cost of dying: a sociological analysis of funeral expenditure, *Social Problems*, Winter, 1970.

[3]Some sociologists have focused their attention on the functionaries of death, such as clergymen, funeral directors, cemetery administrators and monument builders. This approach examines such things as the role conflict between clergymen and funeral directors (R. Fulton, The clergyman and the funeral director: a study in role conflict, *Social Forces*, 39:317, 1961), and the public's orientation toward death and funerals (R. Fulton, *The Sacred and the Secular: Attitudes of the American Public Toward Death* [Milwaukee, Bulfin Printing, 1963]).

funeral behavior may be seen as an attempt by society and funeral directors to impute a repetitiousness to funerals, thereby assisting the bereaved survivors to cope with the death of an individual.

However, it cannot and should not be assumed that such behavior *is* repetitive for the bereaved. It is possible, of course, that prior experiences with death and funerals may have familiarized them with some of the activities and events which generally occur in a funeral. In this sense, there may be a certain familiarity with funeral ceremony, but such ceremonies are not repetitive for the bereaved. It is from this perspective that the funeral director serves as the ceremonial tender of funerals, and it is because of his ongoing activities, practices and experiences that there is repetitive and routine activity. Inasmuch as he is able to impart this sense of ceremony to the bereaved and to society, the funeral takes on value in coping with death and coming to grips with the loss of the dead individual.

The funeral director's position requires him to have a definition of the situation which allows him to treat each death as important and ceremonially worthwhile, even though to society, it may not be so. The bereaved are likely to have an unclear definition of the situation of death and the funeral. Moreover, the bereaved's definition about what is important and unimportant in the funeral ceremony may not resemble what the funeral director believes. Certainly, for society at large, there seems to be little need to define the situation at all, except to note that someone is no longer alive. From the above perspective, the funeral director may be viewed as the institutional tender of American funeral behavior.

As a ceremonial institutional tender, the funeral director is concerned with the everyday practical considerations which constitute funeral behavior. Clearly, the funeral director's behavior will be modified by his definition of each death situation as well as by the particular aspect of the work he is carrying out at the time.

It is important to point out that it is not the definition of death which is problematic for the funeral director.[4] To him, death is only

---

[4]Some investigators have been concerned with the awareness of dying as a social phenomenon. This approach examines the social and psychological problems of terminally ill patients. Studies by D. Sudnow, *Passing On* (Englewood Cliffs, Prentice-Hall, 1967) and B. G. Glaser, and A. L. Strauss, *Awareness of*

the initiating force which gives rise to the need for his specialized skills and knowledge for ceremonializing the dead. Our interests, then, may be contrasted to Sudnow's (1967), whose central theoretical focus is that hospital personnel *define* dying and death according to the relevant tasks and operational activities which they carry out in their day-to-day work procedures.[5] The institutional definitions are far different from the usual definitions of dying and death as held by people not connected with hospitals.

Such *definitional* concerns have little influence on funeral directors for dying as a process is of little consequence to them, except that it is the process leading up to death. Generally, dying is defined by funeral directors much as it is by laypeople, that is, it is used to refer to the state which precedes the ending of an individual's life. Even more important, funeral directors are relatively unconcerned with the medical definition of death and its impact on them. Put somewhat differently, the funeral director treats death as the *start* of a process rather than as a completed event. This means that the funeral director's definition is the initiating force for funeral behavior and explicitly includes (at least) three types of death: 1. *clinical death* is the presence of the physical signs of death; 2. *biological death* is the cessation of cellular activity; and 3. *social death* is the treatment of an individual *as if he were* dead by exclusion from the ongoing processes of the social group.[6]

Instead of being concerned about these aspects of death, the funeral director is interested in the funeral ceremony. It is our contention that through the practical work considerations, the operational activities, and the implementation of his tasks, the funeral director helps provide a definition of the funeral situation on an everyday basis. Thus, although the initiating force is death, it is the activities which arise as its result in which we are most interested. Clearly, the funeral

Dying (Chicago, Aldine Publishing Company, 1965) assess death from the viewpoint of the dying patient, his family, friends, doctors and nurses, and others with whom he must interact.

[5]David Sudnow seeks to provide an ethnography of death in his book *Passing On* (Englewood Cliffs, Prentice-Hall, 1967). It is at the point where his treatment of death stops that the present one begins, namely, at the time death occurs, and thereafter when the dead become the charge of the funeral home.

[6]For development of these types of death see David Sudnow, *Passing On* (Englewood Cliffs, Prentice-Hall, 1967) p. 74.

director's definition of the situation is largely a result of his own experiences, plus the prevailing social norms of the community in which he practices. Therefore, it is certain that funeral directors see certain events as inappropriate for the completion of a successful funeral. Concern about funeral ceremony provides problems for the funeral director in much the same way as dying and death do for physicians and other institutional (hospital) personnel.

Funerals traditionally carry a religious connotation, and for centuries humans have used religious beliefs and practices to fortify walls shaken by death. However, the funeral always has been something far more than a religious ceremony. The funeral is an important social event; an event which helps social groups cope with a specific separation and demonstrates the fact that each member of that group will at sometime die. When a group loses someone for reasons other than death, e.g. moving for a new job, it may be possible to replace that person with a similar one. Of course, most groups are perpetuated either from within by birth or from without by the recruitment of new members. When death occurs, however, it is not easy to find a replacement to fill the vacant spot. There may be substitutes who can "move" from one place to another, but this merely leaves another vacancy which passes down the line until eventually there is no one left to fill the last spot. Put differently, death generally creates an irreplaceable loss.

It is common when people leave a group to have a farewell ceremony which attempts to let the person leaving know of his importance to the group by emphasizing his uniqueness as an individual member of that group. One function of funerals is to pay such a farewell to the dead person. Farewell ceremonies usually are attended not just by those most important to the person leaving but also by a wider circle of those in the group, thereby emphasizing the strength of their networks of friendship and support. This helps to indicate that each individual is important to the group as a whole. Thus, farewell ceremonies are meant to emphasize the value of the person leaving and to emphasize that all members of the group are important and will be affected by the separation.

FUNERARY SOCIAL BEHAVIOR

Most Americans demonstrate some awareness of the customs surrounding death and funerals. Although this knowledge does not appear to be the result of previous funerary experiences, it emerges from a tendency to revert to a socially conditioned human practice. As with so much of human behavior, the lifetime social forces influencing an individual seem to give rise to a facet to cope with death.

For some people, ritual may be utilized as an attempt to purge oneself of guilt. In view of this, funeral rituals attain a special dimension. With death, guilt often consumes the bereaved into a grief-stricken vacuum, from which escape may be difficult. Here, ritual offers a solution, for, as Stein (1965) says: "One of the most important functions of ritual in all societies is to provide a legitimate means of attributing guilt for one's sins and crimes to other persons or outside powers." Religious rituals and death are intimately connected at this level, especially since the ultimate termination of life is so deeply tied to confusion, fear, immortality, superstition, belief and rationalization. It is likely that this combination of factors, plus the contemporary sense of powerlessness, combine to elevate death to a level which can use assistance from any source. This assistance to some extent has been offered by traditional ritual practices; however, the use of such rituals has diminished considerably in American society. The findings of Gorer's (1965) survey on death in England suggest that there is a fairly widespread rejection of traditional funeral rituals and an unwillingness to accept usual death practices and funeral rites. According to his data, Gorer (1965) explains:

> . . . the majority of the British people are today without adequate guidances as to how to treat death and bereavement and without social help in living through and coming to terms with the grief and mourning which are the inevitable responses in human beings to the death of someone they have loved.

Gorer goes on to state that one of the saving factors at the time of death may be deep religious belief. Namely, individuals who are strict adherents of a religious creed seem to display a greater sense of comfort at the time of death. It appears that the traditional forms of sacred funeral rites markedly aid certain people through the crisis of bereavement. Even though "the social ritual which is interwoven with the religious practices" tends to alleviate greatly the grief of the believer, social assistance also might be of measurable help to people with little or no faith (Gorer, 1965).

In the United States the usual funeral service includes a religious portion, which may or may not be a sincere effort to relate death, grief and immortality. Fulton (1965) explains that one of his studies "showed that favorable responses toward funerals . . . varied strongly with religious affiliation." Fulton's findings are similar to Gorer's, that is, both claim that the most traditional churches, as evidenced by their strict adherence to religious dictums, show the most favorable responses to funeral rituals.

According to Mandlebaum (1959), "American culture has . . . for some . . . become deritualized." If this premise is valid, it is likely that at the time of death, undue confusion will often result. Furthermore, broad-scale social changes affect cultural changes to the ceremonies of death. Mandlebaum (1959) goes on to say that although these changes do occur, "the fundamental psychological and social purposes which are accomplished by funeral rites remain quite similar." It seems that Americans might have serious problems in facing death.

FUNERALS AS SOCIAL MECHANISMS IN THE ACCEPTANCE OF DEATH

Mourning practices serve to implement our acceptance of death. Funeral customs traditionally provide a familiar societal support for the bereaved, and the elimination of social mourning practices may result from an unwillingness to accept death and the social separation of individuals. The contemporary emphasis on life and living contributes to the idea held by some that "a modern funeral" should omit the usual practice of viewing the dead body; however, the elimination of this phenomenon may mean that certain aspects of maintaining reality are lost.

Present-day Americans often seem to treat life as if death did not exist. In this way, the denial of death is an effort to rationalize that the dead really are not gone. This unrealistic view fosters the illusion around the death process which implies the hope that death will not be painful and that it will not happen.

Humans have the capability of comprehending death as a force in nature and recognizing the power that death has in the control of human existence. Only if the mechanisms of society help us to accept the role that death plays in life can we truly realize the limits of our own existence. This, of course, contributes to the need to have mechanisms to handle death. Moreover, the implementation of these mechanisms on a social level resides in the funeral traditions of a given culture.

Culture must face the ambiguities of life and death. Since all life must die,[7] to avoid funeral ceremonies may leave the bereaved unattended. If the finiteness of life is not ceremonially connected to the infiniteness of death, we have little more than transitory pains or pleasures. Again, it seems that culture helps provide a means of living through the turmoil of separation. With or without a structured system, humans in a state of distressed emotional balance seldom are factual or rational. It may *appear* that the rituals of death have been designed specifically to support "non-fact" and irrationality. Naturally, this is not the case.

In addition to the religious meaning of the funeral, the *social mechanisms* for death utilize ritual for the resolution of loss. The funeral ceremony provides a time in which people publicly can do things which are not acceptable in most everyday settings. For example, men may cry and women may appear disheveled and both may be in tears much of the time. Statements may be made during this period which would be embarrassing in another setting. For example, when a young child dies, a well-meaning friend might say to her mother, "she was so young," thereby bringing tears. However, to make such a statement in, say, a supermarket, would be upsetting and not socially or emotionally acceptable.

One of the purposes of the ceremony which surrounds death is that it enables people to have an appropriate setting in which to show themselves emotionally. Even though this has been the traditional use of funeral ceremony, some Americans claim it is no longer useful; however, there is nothing in our society which provides stability and gives a chance for the expression of emotional feeling in its place. Put differently, there is not a suitable social climate which substitutes for this way of coping with a highly emotional and up-

---

[7]For development of these types of death see S. Freud, *Beyond the Pleasure Principle* (New York, Bantam Books, 1959), and *Civilization and Its Discontents* (New York, W. W. Norton, 1961).

setting experience. Since this is the case, the ceremony surrounding death is extremely important and worthwhile in providing a humanitarian way for coping with death.

At the funeral ceremonies of John and Robert Kennedy, it was notable that the family members were able to stand almost at attention without overt emotion. However, they had had moments during which they could show their emotions before friends and relatives. In spite of the lack of apparent family emotion, anyone watching these funerals probably was deeply affected with a feeling of compassion. If the bodies had been taken from the places of death with no notice of what was happening, there would have been little chance for Americans in general to express their feeling of loss, guilt and sadness.

CONCLUDING REMARKS

The etiology of funerals seems to be connected to both survivor and survival needs. On the one hand, funerals provide a social vehicle for the expression of sympathy and are an effort to reintegrate the bereaved into society. The bereaved are given an opportunity to express their deep feelings of loss in a socially significant manner. At the same time, the individual who provides a funeral for someone else may be motivated by the thought that someday he will be accorded the final tribute, and this would add a measure of meaning to his life. This act of reaffirmation suggests a nostalgic return to something past and, in this sense, death may be considered a kind of social rebirth.[8]

If death is considered a rebirth in a cyclic manner, funeral rituals make sensible symbolism and imply that there is a beginning and an end to each segment. Furthermore, it is usual that each part of the life cycle is marked by culturally determined and prescribed rites. In this sense, burial has offered a traditional act of return and symbolic rebirth. The implication of the cultural context is that the finality of death and the return to "mother earth" is a logical conclusion to life itself.[9] In this sense, culturally designed rituals add appropriateness

---

[8]For a discussion of the "compulsion to repeat," see S. Freud, *Beyond the Pleasure Principles* (New York, Bantam Books, 1959) pp. 38-47.

[9]For a discussion of "eternal return," see H. Marcuse, *Eros and Civilization: A Philosophical Inquiry Into Freud* (New York, Vintage Books, 1955) pp. 96-114.

to the death of an individual; thus, there are culturally prescribed social obligations of individuals to society at the time of death.

Through funeral ceremony, the bereaved become the center of attention for social support and the extension of sympathy tends to give rise to a sense of comfort and social acceptability. Acceptability is important if we are to live meaningfully after the loss of some key life figure, but to do so is a universal problem. Society has certain established mechanisms which afford us a measure of support through a period of bereavement. These mechanisms are geared to provide help both to individuals and to the society at large. They are arranged to enable us to accept loss, not necessarily through scientific reasoning but through social-psychological empathy. In this sense, one of the values of culture is that it provides socially acceptable channels for the expression of important human needs. Thus, it assists people passing through depressing circumstances by connecting them to others.

REFERENCES

Durkheim, E.: *The Elementary Forms of Religious Life.* (Translated by J. W. Swaine.) London, Allen and Unwin, 1954.

Fulton, R.: *Death and Identity.* New York, John Wiley and Sons, 1965.

Gorer, G.: *Death, Grief, and Mourning.* New York, Doubleday, 1965.

Hertz, R.: *Death and the Right Hand.* (Translated by R. and C. Needham.) Glencoe, Free Pr, 1960.

Malinowski, B.: Death and the reintegration of the grave. In *Magic, Science, and Religion.* New York, Doubleday, 1954.

Stein, M.: *The Eclipse of Community: An Interpretation of American Studies.* New York, Harper and Row, 1960.

Sudnow, D.: *Passing On.* Englewood Cliffs, Prentice-Hall, 1967.

CHAPTER 11

EMPHASIS EMPATHY

KERMIT EDISON

UNLIKE MANY FUNERAL directors who represent a fourth and fifth generation in funeral service, I am a first. However, I do have a son who is a licensed funeral director. When he announced his intention to go into funeral service, as parents we were both pleased and surprised. We were pleased because we were aware of his extraordinary sensitivities to the feelings of his contemporaries when a crisis arose. We were surprised because his background had made him aware of the demands of funeral service, many of which are extremely unpleasant. I am sure he felt the agony of confinement which not only involves the funeral director, but his whole family. He knew what we meant when we talked about availability. He had left the table on a Christmas Eve with me to visit a bereaved family. As a youngster, he had observed me leave the house on Thanksgiving Day, the Fourth of July, and other holidays. He had been told at many breakfasts that I had been up since 2:00 A.M. Knowing all this, he had to be conscious of the fact that in funeral service, one does not count hours; that "others" have the first consideration, and "self" is last.

What has motivated our son and other sons, generation after generation, to take up funeral service as a profession? In essence, it is the personal satisfaction derived from serving people during a very critical period in their lives. One takes a part in the restoration of order where there is chaos; one helps develop understanding where there is hostility, relief where there is despair.

A funeral director can make a tremendous contribution toward the well-being of those who feel the loss of a member of the family through death. In a study done at the Langley Porter Neuropsychiatric Institute and the Department of Pediatrics, University of California, San Francisco Medical Center (reported in the *New England Journal of Medicine*, February 20, 1969), it was noted:

> The pediatric hematology records revealed that 23 children had died of leukemia between January, 1964 and December, 1966. The parents of these children were asked to come to be interviewed by the child psychiatrist regarding the impact of the crisis and its after effects upon their lives. Twenty families agreed to come. . . .

The portion of the findings dealing with references to nurses, clergy, referring physician, social worker, hospital physician and other parents, captioned "Sources of Support to Parents," revealed that:

> Fifteen families expressed positive feelings toward the mortician or funeral director. Their experience with grief reactions makes them skilled in offering solace to grieving families.

Some experiences and comments from families assisted by the author may give some insight into the behind-the-scenes involvements.

Not long ago a young man and woman called for an appointment to discuss funeral arrangements for their father whose death was expected momentarily. They had never made funeral arrangements before, and since their parents were divorced, they knew that any decisions would have to be made by them. They indicated that their primary concerns were price and expediency. Further, their ideas about funerals were expressed in uncomplimentary adjectives. They exhibited no tears, no outward signs of grief. Recognizing that this kind of behavior often indicates deep-seated emotional turbulence, I managed to prolong the conversation, and pointed out values definitely in their best interest. Their father died the next morning, and the whole family participated in viewing, visitation and a religious ceremony. About a week after the funeral, I received the following letter from the young woman:

> We want you to know how very much we appreciate your handling of Dad's funeral. Even when you think you are completely prepared, its effect cannot be fully anticipated. Due to your expert counseling, you made a trying time much less trying! Your ease of taking care of the most incidental of details makes the whole experience one of comfort

rather than confusion. The time you gave to my children stands out in my mind as very meaningful and I know the questions you answered for them will stay with them and help them in the years to come. I feel they are most fortunate to have had that experience; it was a great thing for me as well. Because of your gentle guidance into having a traditional funeral, you gave us the comfort of seeing the outpouring of good will by people who knew Dad years ago, and it made us happy to see that he wasn't as obscure a person as we thought. That was very good to discover! Our basic feeling has been one of a peaceful experience, and we thank you for that. Continued success in helping the living live with greater ease. Most sincerely. . . .

Since receiving the letter, I have had the opportunity to talk with its writer several times, and each time she reiterated remarks she made in her letter. One cannot help but concern himself with the question, "What happened?" Obviously, the funeral for her father became a significant event in her life and her children's lives, an event embodied in richness, compassion and understanding. What only a few days previously had been an unpleasant annoyance became a meaningful occasion.

The funeral has been subjected to many interpretations and definitions. It has been defined as "a group centered response to social reconstruction."

I think my next illustration will give credence to this analogy. A ninety-one-year-old man had died. For more than 40 years, he had been confined to a mental institution. His nephew, a seventy-year-old gentleman, called to say that he and his two sisters were the only relatives, but that he had not talked to his sisters in more than 20 years. Further, he suggested that we should "just bury the old man." We made an appointment to meet at the funeral home at 4:00 o'clock. Shortly afterward, one of the sisters called to say that they had not talked to their brother in 20 years, but that, if I would provide transportation, they would come to the funeral home to make funeral arrangements. At 4:00 o'clock, the brother and sisters met for the first time in 20 years. We did not discuss their problem nor acknowledge that there was a problem but limited our conversation to planning for the funeral for their uncle. When the arrangements were completed, I offered to return the ladies to their home but the brother said, "I'll take them home, we have a lot to talk about." The funeral arrangements for a man whose social contributions were limited in life had played an important part in the social reconciliation and reconstruction of his only relatives.

The need for funeral directors to "recognize their responsibility to counsel families on funeral matters, rather than be consentors" has also been stressed. Counseling on funeral matters has been a role that psychologists, psychiatrists and sociologists have encouraged funeral directors to employ for years. Untimely and tragic deaths cause the greatest need for counseling. Knowing that the funeral director will ultimately help in this critical period, caregivers such as doctors, nurses, and even some clergymen frequently shy away from the uncomfortable task of talking to the bereaved.

The husband and daughter of a young lady we shall call "Mary" were killed in an auto accident. Mary was definitely in shock and had nothing to say to anyone. It was difficult to determine if she even listened when someone spoke to her. Some family members felt that viewing would impose further grief. Mary's mother, a registered nurse, felt that her daughter should participate in the prayers of their church the evening before the funeral. She rationalized that if the caskets were closed, it would be easier for everyone concerned. When she mentioned the idea of closed caskets to me, I said, "But first, Mary should have the opportunity to see her husband and child." Funeral directors do not expect agreement at this time, except from those who understand what happens or who have had similar experiences. The mother said, however, "Because you say so, we will bring Mary in." Mary's sister and brother-in-law brought her to the funeral home, but her mother stayed at home because she was not entirely convinced that visual confrontation with reality would be wise. Two hours later, after Mary had returned home, her mother called to tell me that for the first time in two days, Mary had talked and now was ready to accept the tragic reality.

About two months later, during a seminar on death and dying held for nurses, physicians, clergy and funeral directors, someone questioned the value of viewing a body in the casket. The first person to respond was Mary's mother. Her audience was attentive, and I'm sure convinced by her testimony. No one knows better than this mother what is meant by facing reality and confirming the reality and finality of death through visual confrontation.

The counseling given this family is substantiated by a statement written by Dr. John Bowlby and Dr. C. M. Parkes, British psychiatrists, in the *English Observer*:

> . . . the necessary tasks and rituals, whether religious or not, which surround death serve, however, to bring home gradually to the bereaved persons the reality of the loss they have sustained, and the knowledge that life will never be quite the same again. Drawing the blinds, viewing the body, attending the burial service, lowering the coffin into the grave— all serve to emphasize the finality, the absoluteness of death, and make denial more difficult.

American funeral directors have never been more aware of the impact of emotions on general health, more understanding and perceptive of the need for group support, expression of feelings, and confirmation of the reality and finality of death as they meet the needs of those who mourn.

CHAPTER 12

THE ADAPTIVE FUNERAL

William G. Hardy, Jr.

THE FUNERAL HAS existed through countless generations, in many formats, to serve the needs of diverse cultures and races. The fact of this continuous existence is testimony to man's deep need to formalize his personal bereavement. Customs and ceremonies are the creation not only of the bereaved family members but of the community. "Most community family customs are a public recognition of death, and the value to the life of the community of the person who has died" (Jackson, 1961). The funeral has had to be adaptive or it would have disappeared. Today, we examine the modern funeral in the United States. Is the service adaptive or mechanical? Is it meaningful or sterile? Is the funeral director desirous or even willing to seek out the needs of the individual or does he unconsciously stereotype the funeral service?

A partial examination of these questions requires a review of the funeral director and his professional practices. A generalized description of any group is dangerous and occasionally erroneous. However, if we examine the makeup of the majority of funeral directors, we find two distinctive characteristics: they are usually conservative in their thinking, and traditional in their orientation. Both traits are basic in the exercise of their profession. Conversely, both traits may inhibit a director's ability to adapt a funeral service to individual needs which to him may seem "liberal" or "nontraditional." To be adaptive he must reorient his thinking and his approaches to the families he serves. In the examination of our relatively recent American customs, we realize that today's "traditions" may be relatively new and are yesterday's adaptations to a changing society.

To understand the need for an adaptive approach we must understand the tremendous upheaval in this twentieth century, an "upheaval" some will call a "social revolution." We have changed from a rural culture to a way of life dominated by urban pressures. The breakdown of the family as a cohesive, enduring, multi-generational unit to a nuclear one has created many new problems for bereaved persons and for the care-giving professional who must face these problems.

Each bereaved person is an individual. Each family situation is unique. There are, however, certain groups of persons who, because of their age, social or religious makeup, can be discussed collectively. Professor Paul Irion has commented wisely on the significant need for funeralization for those who reject the formal religions. He emphasizes their need to create rituals and ceremonies to emphasize the value of the life that has been lived. The funeral director must understand this need and help the bereaved family to create a format to adequately express grief—to find meaning in life even though they deny the existence of an afterlife. The funeral director must make available nonsectarian music, writings and material that can be utilized. He will often be asked to officiate in the capacity of surrogate minister and should prepare himself or one of his staff to serve the needs of the bereaved.

The youth of today possess one characteristic that seems predominant. They profess to reject "tradition," preferring "relevance" as a mode of personal expression. One obvious instance is their search for personal expression in their marriage ceremonies. Why then should they be denied some effort to adapt a funeral service to their personal beliefs and life-styles? It is interesting that in many cases the rejection of the traditions of the day results in a reversion to rituals and philosophies of previous cultures or creation of even more elaborate rituals than those discarded.

The actual cases reported in this discussion indicate which needs must be satisfied for those who are in acute grief.

Case History: A sixteen-year-old girl was kidnapped, tortured, raped and murdered. Her decomposed body was found five weeks later in a crude roadside grave. Her parents met the funeral director and arranged for a traditional service involving visitation, a Baptist religious service and earth burial. Several hours after this arrangement conference, four brothers of the deceased came to the funeral home. Their ages were from 13 to 22. The older two are bearded college students. They express their personal grief and anger by attacking the funeral customs. With the guidance of a funeral counselor of their own approximate age and the wisdom of the minister, changes are made in the funeral arrangements. Their choices include a guitar playing vocalist who sings folk songs meaningful to their age group. Philosophical readings from the folklore of American Indian and Oriental cultures are read. In this manner, the brothers begin to work through their deep anger, express personal grief and join their parents in a mutual service of remembrance.

The young are by nature physically active. Their observances of personal bereavement demand physical expression. During the visitation period before the funeral service (either the evning before or the day of the service), it is not uncommon to see the same group of teenage persons return to the visitation room and to the open casket time and again, especially when the deceased is a sibling or a member of their peer group. The bereaved family who chooses a privatized funeral for a deceased young person denies the young friends a meaningful expression of loss. The funeral director should search for ways to involve these young people in some useful physical activity.

Case History: The captain of the football team at a high school in Tennessee is killed in a wreck. The members of the team wish to participate in the funeral beyond the formal service as pallbearers. The funeral director arranges with the cemetery to permit these young men to dig the grave. After serving as pallbearers they go to a nearby shelter, remove their dress clothing, put on work clothing, fill the grave and sod the surface. This physical activity is their gift of service to their friend.

When death occurs to a member of some ethnic minority within the confines of their own group, needful rituals and observances are known. The community and the funeral director anticipate their desires. Due to modern shifts of population death may occur in a strange environment where such rituals are unknown and perhaps viewed with distaste. The parochialism of funeral service should not prohibit the funeral director from listening to their suggestions and within the confines of reasonable action create a climate of accommodation.

Case History: A black Master Sergeant and his family, with roots in the deep South, live in a northern white community near an army post.

A twelve-year-old son dies and a white funeral director is called. In the arrangement conference, the mother exhibits her hostility and makes objections to every suggestion by comparison to observances in her home community. The funeral director calls a local black minister and joins the family in creating some of the home atmosphere. Visiting hours are altered and arrangements are made for special music and written resolutions are prepared. Members of the family and close friends are encouraged to engage in physical involvement with the funeral service. These aids adapted by a northern, white-oriented funeral home in some part meet the requests and desires of an uprooted family in grief.

Most deaths are traumatic to the bereaved. As we view acute grief, we realize that deaths due to accident, murder or suicide pose particular problems in adaptation. A death from suicide often creates a difficult situation for the funeral director. Psychologists have studied the guilt which characterizes grief and bereavement . When death has been caused by suicide, the funeral service must not be routine and stereotyped. An opportunity must be given the bereaved to assume an active role in the planning and execution of the funeral process. It is important that they express and work through their guilt and anger by physical actions. They should never be encouraged to privatize their grief and shield themselves from family and friends. The available social support will mitigate their guilt feelings, confirm the reality of death and give recognition to the value of the life that has been lived. If the death by suicide, murder or other accident resulted in facial disfigurement, cosmetic restoration should be accomplished if it is at all possible. The confrontation with the body can be of value in prohibiting mental escapism and in providing a mental picture less painful and thus more acceptable. The suicidologist seeks to identify the person who may take his or her own life in an attempt to try to keep the suicide from happening. If and when it does, most suicidologists forget the needs of those who survive. Unless their urgent needs are met, there could be another suicide. The funeral with viewing is a way of meeting some of these needs.

As we accept the premise of adaptation in funeral service, what elements may be altered, improved or perhaps eliminated? The basic elements are viewing, visitation, funeral rites or ceremonies, procession and burial/cremation committals. These should be thoroughly discussed with the family so that educated decisions can be made.

In planning the viewing and visitation the funeral director is too often bound by the dictates of local custom, personnel problems and personal predilection. Whenever possible, a flexible approach should be exercised. It has been proven helpful for the funeral director to plan a private viewing before public visitation. Sufficient time should be allowed for the family to express their emotions within the confines of the family circle. Opportunity should then be given for any desired changes in hair-styling, cosmetology and other details before public visitation.

The clothing to be used is extremely important. If the funeral arranger will ask questions and listen to the family, he may find their true desires to be very different from his own concept. This is most true when a young person dies. Too often clothing selected is so different from the life-style of the deceased that an artificial, unreal appearance results. The choice should be the true wish of the bereaved, not a concession to custom or community opinion. Scrupulous care should be taken that hairdressing and cosmetology be individualistic, not routine.

The funeral service, religious or humanist, should be discussed thoroughly. If possible, a joint meeting of the funeral director, minister and bereaved family should be held. The music should provide solace, perhaps expressing the life-style and religious or philosophical beliefs of the deceased. A vivid example is the modern use of the "guitar-mass" in the Catholic Church. Quite often this is accompanied by musical selections not liturgical or secular in character. Occasionally, a friend or relative will serve as musician or vocalist.

Help should be provided the minister or eulogist by preliminary discussions with the family. It may be that the philosophy of the deceased or of the bereaved should be exemplified by readings from literature or philosophy. Care should be exercised that the funeral director does not encroach upon the domain of the church or minister. If understanding exists, the funeral director can be the catalyst that results in a funeral service conforming to the church and meaningful to the family.

The adaptive funeral service will often utilize the active participation of family and/or friends in music and readings as outlined above. There is also a new emphasis on responsive readings which involve

the whole congregation. It is again relevant to point out that this is
not a new creation but rather a return to folk-ways and customs of
previous generations.

The use of the procession and burial/cremation committals varies
in accordance with localities. Weather conditions, traffic congestion,
cemetery rulings are problems which must be met on the local level.
It is imperative that the family discuss and understand what plans are
to be made and what problems must be met. Authorities agree that
a funeral which short cuts or omits the committal at the place of final
disposition is an incomplete funeral.

> *Case History:* A large midwestern cemetery instituted the use of an
> "interment chapel" where committal rites are to be held. A family who
> owned a burial plot there was not informed of the change in committal
> plans. Upon arrival for the final rites for a deceased member of their
> family, they were much disturbed that graveside committal was not the
> practice. They carry a hostility towards the cemetery and the funeral
> home for not properly informing them.

The forms and customs of the actual committal service are probably
as much discussed as any portion of the service. To the logical mind
they may seem extraneous and unimportant. To other persons the
final farewell is extremely meaningful. The excision of this portion
of funeral service may well destroy much of the grief-therapy of the
preceding elements. The accompaniment of the remains to the last
resting place and the visualization of that body in that place may well
serve to eliminate doubts and fears in the minds of persons who because
of their acute grief are temporarily mentally unstable.

A well-planned, cheerful arrangement room assists in establishing
rapport with the bereaved family. Many funeral directors feel that
the room should not be a typical business office. Seating areas are
arranged so that the arranger fits with the family in an informal circle.
The absence of a desk eliminates the psychological block where the
director sitting behind the desk becomes a figure of authority that may
seem overly oppressive or authoritarian.

The first statements made by the funeral arranger to the family
should set the stage for a successful conference. He should express a
desire and a willingness to listen. He should encourage the family to
verbalize their desires, preferences and questions. His statements should

not be to the effect that he knows their wishes and will conform. Rather, he should ask them to inform him of their wishes so that he may make every effort to carry them out.

Whenever possible, the staff of the funeral home should utilize the special talents of the younger persons and/or female persons in discussions with families where their expertise and empathies seem desirable. This brings us to the utmost important adaptive aid—education. The vast majority of funeral directors and arrangers have had little contact with recent studies and experimentation in death, grief and bereavement. The National Funeral Directors Association has done yeoman service in developing resource material and speaking personnel to further funeral service education in this area. Only by the adequate dissemination of this information can conservatively oriented funeral home personnel be directed toward adapting their services to meet the emotional needs of a clientele who are more educated, younger, more affluent and nonreligious.

Members or adherents of the Memorial Society movement pose another delicate challenge for the funeral director. Before death these persons may have decided to eliminate some or all aspects of the funeral. If the funeral director is a dedicated and knowledgeable professional, he has deep convictions concerning the therapeutic value of the funeral. He realizes that the rationale expressed for rejecting funeralization is probably not the true motivating force. He has a responsibility to these expressed and often barely recognized conflicts. Yet by the very nature of his profession, he can be suspect in his protestations. An effective approach is to ask the family to verbalize their reasons for decisions. If they cooperate, he may make valuable suggestions that can adapt a form of funeral to meet their objections and yet preserve the integrity of a funeral service.

This paper has been prepared solely from the standpoint of the funeral director as he assumes his rightful responsibility. The conclusions drawn may seem simplistic, even rudimentary. However, the funeral director labors under a handicap. In a very short period of time he has to counsel grief-stricken persons in planning actions that may influence their mental well-being and emotional security. He has to resolve personality conflicts, either within a family or where his relationships with the bereaved are involved. Often the bereaved family members are complete strangers to him. Perhaps they exhibit hostility toward him as he is for them a symbol of the traumatic death. He must be able to deal with the verbal expressions of their desires. He must be able to sense their unspoken and perhaps unconscious conflicts and confusions. He must act as an occasional arbiter where family ties are strained and latent hostilities become apparent. Each of the methods of adaptation previously discussed may seem insignificant when viewed singly. Professor Robert Slater, Director of the Department of Mortuary Science at the University of Minnesota, said that in the area of funeral service every trifle is tremendous to a bereaved family and the constant challenge for funeral directors is to take each trifle and make it the object of the ultimate service he can provide to those who seek his help. There is no insignificant aspect of funeral service. What may be seemingly unimportant to one family can be essential to another.

In the next decade the success or failure of the funeral director and his profession may depend upon his ability to understand the importance of trifles and his willingness to adapt to the changing personality of his clientele. He can no longer depend on the traditional use of the Judeo-Christian funeral service to insure his future. If he does not adapt to real needs he will be obsolete. The customs and usages of today are the result of past needs. The care-giving professional will exist only so long as he truly cares.

REFERENCES

Jackson, E. N.: *You and Your Grief.* New York, Hawthorn Books, 1961.

CHAPTER 13

THE HUMANIST FUNERAL SERVICE

Corliss Lamont

WHY HAVE A FUNERAL at all? I have found that there are a number of people who do not seem to want to have any such occasion whatsoever when a member of the family dies. Yet I believe that a funeral does honor to the deceased individual. It expresses appreciation for the virtues he had and gives notice to his family and friends that he was a person of some importance and note in the community. A funeral gives friends and family a chance to bid a final farewell which, I think, is an important function. A funeral brings home the fact that the dead individual is really gone. In cases where the death has been sudden, a sense of unreality pervades the atmosphere. We say to each other, "I can't believe that this man (or this beautiful woman) is suddenly dead." And so the funeral provides the realization that a death is real.

On the social level, a funeral enables relatives and friends to get together and share their feelings of grief. It becomes a community occasion with social implications. Of course, a funeral is not the only device that serves these purposes, because a memorial service three or four weeks, or even months, after the death of a person can provide the same sort of function.

In composing my Humanist Funeral Service, my approach was, as the title indicates, from the viewpoint of the humanist philosophy or religion. In other words, it is nonsupernatural and does not even mention personal immortality, survival beyond the grave, or the existence of God. This service stresses social ties, the brotherhood of man and the democracy of death. There can be no doubt that everyone

[139]

becomes equal in the grave—no matter what his position was in life.

This service emphasizes that man is a part of nature and has evolved over millions of years on this earth; he is a natural being without the supernatural characteristics of traditional religion. In this connection the service makes some note of the evolutionary process and the necessary part of death in that process, which has made possible the final appearance of man on this earth. Without death to make real the survival of the fittest, there would have been no man here in the first place. Therefore, in that sense, death is a friend and not an enemy; and it is nature's law that living organisms should finally retire from the scene to make way for newborn generations. Death is the friend of future generations and life affirms itself through death.

An important point in the Humanist Funeral Service is that it makes room for some kind of remarks about the deceased, some kind of personal tribute. When I have attended traditional funeral services of the orthodox religions, I have often been offended by the fact that there is no mention whatsoever of what the person stood for during his or her life. No matter how humble the person may be who has died or how humble his position in life, there is always something of a personal nature that can be said. Therefore, I believe that this personal note should be brought into every funeral service.

Since rituals are a form of art and should appeal to the aesthetic sense, I have included poems and music in this funeral service. These can be selected by the family. My Humanist Funeral Service lists twenty-five different poems, several of which could be read at a funeral service. There are, of course, many possible selections of music.

In concluding this service, I have stressed that the best of all answers to death is the wholehearted and continuing affirmation of life on behalf of the greater glory of humankind. Here, as a humanist, I must state that I have no belief in survival of the personality beyond the grave or the crematory. I believe that when a person dies, his personality is just as nonexistent as it had been before he was born. My suggestion is that in place of the wish for personal immortality, we should seek the immortality of the race of man. This seems to me to be a worthwhile ideal. I believe that man as an animal is the best of all and that it is worthwhile to preserve our race upon this earth.

Astronomists and astrophysicists claim that the sun gives off enough heat to maintain life on this earth for 5 billion years at least. It is possible, too, that when the sun eventually does not have enough heat for the maintenance of life here, scientists will have been able to find a substitute. Some scientists are already talking about ways to change the orbit of the earth around the sun. If the sun does begin to cool off, we can get the earth closer to it, thereby adding another billion years to life here. These speculations deny the prophesy that is sometimes made: that ultimate doom inevitably must come to the human race on this earth. As citizens of the world—as well as of the United States—our program should be that all nations and all men and women upon this planet must work together for the immortality of the human race.

REFERENCE

Lamont, C.: *A Humanist Funeral Service.* Yellow Springs, The American Humanist Association, 1962.

CHAPTER 14

THE ITALIAN FAMILY: HOW IT DEALS WITH ACUTE GRIEF AND THE FUNERAL

FRANK R. GALANTE

THOSE OF ITALIAN DESCENT, like other ethnic groups, are often the subject of jokes and jibes. At times we are stereotyped as possessing certain innate characteristics because of the actions of some individuals. Yet, a most human trait of most of us is the ability to express our emotions freely and unselfconsciously. From 25 years as a funeral director, I believe that I have derived some insight into how Italians face up in part to acute grief through rites and ceremonies of the funeral with the body present.

For most Italians, the funeral is a Roman Catholic religious service. However, there are four components of most Italian funerals which I believe are significant to the study of acute grief and means of helping to resolve it.

THE LA POSTA

Italians often give money to the surviving family at the time of the funeral. This is a custom which dates back to the time when horse-drawn carriages were used. Those who went to the funeral paid for their place in the carriage. For example, in past times, Peter Allioto would come to Anthony Balistere's father's funeral and pay for his place in a carriage. If when Peter's father died, Tony couldn't attend the funeral, he would give the money, $1.00 or $2.00, for the place in the carriage, out of respect and to return the courtesy. This was done at the time of visitation.

As automobiles came into use, this custom was continued. During the depression, La Posta took on a new meaning. It became a means of making a contribution to help out the bereaved family, often more than the one or two dollars.

The custom continues today among Italians at all economic levels. The money is a gift to be used as the family sees fit—for mass offerings, for a charity in memory of the deceased, or to help meet the expenses which come with death.

It has been said that the funeral is a gift received and given by both the deceased and those who survive him. In the same sense, so it is with the La Posta. Most Italians view it as an expression to be accepted and a person seeking emotional support accepts the expression with a feeling that goes beyond the dollar.

FLORAL OFFERINGS OF SIGNIFICANCE

Most Italian families still believe in floral pieces of traditional significance. As examples:

When someone loses his or her spouse, generally a piece depicting a bleeding heart is ordered. The piece—sometimes four to six feet in height —is in the shape of a heart. The heart is usually made of red roses or carnations from which there will be a red streamer ribbon as a symbol of bleeding.

The time of death can also be the design for a floral piece. A simulated clock in a wreath of flowers is made up with the hands showing the time of death.

Religious influences are expressed by a "gates of heaven" piece or the "gates ajar" arrangement, a cross, Holy Bible, vacant chair, broken wheel, broken column.

All these flowers are placed in flower cars in the procession to church and cemetery.

THE FUNERAL PROCESSION

The funeral procession is important to the Italian funeral. Most of the families I serve want the procession to go by the home of the deceased and often by his or her place of business. If the deceased was a civil servant—such as a fireman or policeman—representatives from his fire company or police district play an important role in the funeral.

This was and continues to be a custom of relating or identifying the deceased in death with his or her life. Also it gives those in the area of the home or business a chance to participate, if only to stand in respect as the cortege passes.

THE FAMILY "COLLECTS"

Most Italian families are held together by strong family ties. Even in this day of great mobility, the family "collects" for family occasions. One of the most important of these is the funeral.

I have sat at many funeral director meetings and been told of the fractionalization of the family by age, distance, knowledge and life styles. This is not true of my family. My mother is the head of the household or family. Nor is it true of most other Italian families who call me. Even though there may be a four-generation spread, and the family scattered across the country or the world—all "collect" for the funeral.

I have experienced myself and have observed in others the support the gathered family gives the mourners. I have also heard chiding remarks made about those who did not come or sympathy expressed for them: "How can they grieve by themselves? Why aren't they here where they belong?"

Various cultures pay materially for the benefits of funeralization. This is especially true of the Italian. Some of us do certain things to purge guilt. But most of our people have the funerals they select because they want to express themselves. Sometimes such an expression results in costs which will mean depriving themselves of something for a while. But what is done is done out of love and respect and it is felt that the funeral is not only a declaration that a death occurred, but also testimony that a life has been lived.

As in many other nationalities, there has been intermarrying between Italians with others. Youth is having its impact. But with some meaningful adaptations to the needs of the day, the Italian funeral continues to be a religious rite with the body present. It truly is an experience of value because it does meet the needs of those who mourn.

CHAPTER 15

SOUTHWESTERN PERSPECTIVES ON THE RESOLUTION OF GRIEF

Edward J. Fitzgerald

IT SEEMS TO BE inherent in human nature for every man to think his problems are just a little greater than those of his neighbors. It is true of Americans. It is true of Americans living in the Southwest. It is true of Americans living in the Southwest who are funeral directors. I am one of them, and I am convinced that funeral directors in the Southwest do face problems not found elsewhere. Even when the same problems do occur in other areas, they are not always of the same magnitude.

The so-called Southwestern part of the United States is a rather imprecisely defined geographical area which includes the states of Arizona and New Mexico and some counties in southern Utah, southern Colorado, and western Texas. A clearer description would seem to be one delineating an area with certain characteristics which stem from its climate, culture and geography. Such ingredients as open space and outdoor living, tri-cultural society, variety of topography and scenery, ideal climate, and the openness and honesty of its people all combine to make up what is often called the "land of manana," the Southwestern United States.

Generally speaking, there are no ethnic enclaves in the Southwest as such. That is to say, there are very few places where a neighborhood or a whole town would be comprised of one particular group. There are, however, large numbers of ethnic peoples spread across the length and breadth of the area. Mostly, they are American Indians and Spanish-speaking peoples whose life-style, language and heritage have been preserved in a predominantly Anglo social structure. This is what we call a tri-cultural society.

If the tri-cultural society is an historical, a permanent and an overriding fact of life in the Southwest, we need to look at the effect it has on grief and the funeral. Funeral service practitioners in this area, including those practicing in rural and metropolitan areas as well as in small towns near the bigger cities, generally agree that there are certain unique features in such a society which can and do present challenges to the proper resolution of grief by those who survive a death. It is my purpose in this discussion to set forth from my own subjective experiences the real problems of the area, and to relate these problems to the funeral.

As a fact of history, the American Indian was resident in the area first. The Spanish-speaking people entered in the middle of the sixteenth century. It was another 300 years before any significant number of English-speaking people arrived. However, when they did come, they quickly assumed control of the economy and the government. It is because of this control that the Anglo culture is predominant. In a way, the "gringo" culture has been allowed to exist in an Indian and "chicano" society.

Each culture has maintained its distinctive identity. To become familiar with the customs and needs of three cultures in order to serve families of all three cultures and achieve the right balance from a wide variety of ingredients is quite a challenge to the funeral licensee. The bereaved and those who try to give them solace face nearly the same barriers to effective social action and reaction as exists in certain other situations. It is often very difficult for the "gringo" to act out his part in a "chicano" setting. It is hard for the Indian to understand all the ways of the white man. Yet there are many strong friendships and blood relationships which cross from one group to another.

Linguists will say that some expressions cannot be translated from one language to another. There are also expressions of body and deed that cannot be easily understood by those who do not use them. How does the Indian communicate to the devoutly Roman Catholic "chicano" the meaning of traditions which pre-date the introduction of Christianity during the sixteenth century? How does the "chicano" tell the Anglo the unspoken thoughts symbolized by an "abrazo" (embrace)? What harm is done to the giver of a gift when the receiver is not gracious because he does not understand? I have unwittingly caused feelings to be hurt in some situations. Under other circumstances, I have also been sensitive to what was needed and know that my words and deeds have given comfort.

Not only do differences of custom and language exist among these groups, they are also present within each group. Some mountain "chicano" villages were isolated from the mainstream of life for 200 to 300 years. Customs and language underwent many changes during that time. And yet today there are marriages and births which tie these diverse groups together. The ways of one Indian tribe are significantly different from those of another, and in many instances are off-limits to the white man. These factors often make it impossible for the funeral director to help, no matter how perceptive he might be, to satisfy the needs of those participating in burial rites. The situation was described very well by Oscar Wilde when he wrote: "If he shut the doors of his house of mourning against me . . . if he thought me unworthy, unfit to weep with him, I should feel it as the most poignant humiliation. . . ."

People are now moving into this area from every part of the country. I am convinced that the migration of people to the Southwest is a factor which can influence what is done following a death and the extent to which the funeral does or does not help in the resolution of grief. This migration means the funeral director is generally a stranger to those calling upon him. The family circle is apt to be small, and the family may regard some distant point or former residence as home. It is likely that no local church affiliation exists and that many traditions of family life may have been dissipated.

Between 1960 and 1970 in the United States, the population over age 65 rose .7 percent. In Arizona and New Mexico, the increases were 2.2 percent and 1.6 percent respectively, for the same period. In 1970, the median age for the United States was 28.1 years, while in Arizona it was 26.3 and in New Mexico, 23.9. These figures appear to support the contention of Southwesterners that older people are moving into the area during their retirement years, and that the young are coming also in search of new life-styles and opportunities. Of relevance to the funeral director is the fact that a significant number of senior citizens are dying in this area with little or no family present. Further, there are young people, too, who are making decisions following a death with little to guide them in the way of experience, tradition, or the advice of older family members. Death seems to have less of an impact on some. There are fewer deaths among this younger population and the needs which must be met for these bereaved seem to be less intense.

Some specific questions are often raised in regard to these facts. "Why should we have a ceremony when nobody here cares one way or the other?" "Mom really wanted to be buried back home, but I think it would be better to bury her here." "Do you think we should have a service even though Dad never joined a church here?" "There is no need for anything here, Mr. Funeral Director, because all of the family stayed back home when the folks left there 20 years ago." These and similar remarks are heard by funeral directors daily. Obviously, these are clues to the potential of unsatisfactory arrangements. The funeral director who blindly goes along with such expressions and the wishes apparently expressed by them is a little short on responsibility.

Many studies have revealed that people seek social support following a death. When the circle of family and friends is contracted, how much more important does the presence of the few who are there become? People have to face the fact that many friends at former homes might have moved away or died themselves. If the bulk of friends, no matter how large or small, is to be found at the new home where death has occurred, then I would certainly encourage the survivors to seek their social support at that place. This would be the case whether disposition of the body was to be at the place of death or at some distant point. Circumstances could also require the giving and receiving of social support at both places.

Too often I have seen families decide on a local burial because they thought the cost of transporting the body back home would be more than they could afford. There are also decisions made to cremate the body and send the ashes back home. The funeral director must take the time and trouble to provide facts. If he does not, the survivors will probably not be doing what they really want to do. In my practice, about 25 percent of all arrangements include burial of the body elsewhere. I feel sure that percentage would drop if our staff did not provide factual information about the actual costs of the transportation as well as other costs encountered at the place of burial. The last point is important because uninformed survivors can become very upset when some unexpected expenses arise after they have carefully planned for a burial in a place they have selected as proper.

Many senior citizens live on modest fixed incomes. The anticipated expenses of a traditional ceremony and burial sometimes cause these people to make decisions they would not otherwise have made. Prolonged illness or long life may consume most or all of a person's resources, causing a change in plans previously made. These factors are not unique to my area, but I do feel they are probably present here in a higher percentage of situations than in most other areas of the country.

Older people also have concerns about their general health (really, a lack of it) and their ability to get around and travel. Many elderly people do not or can not drive a car. Too many decisions have been made for local burial or cremation, or for too hurried a disposition with or without ceremony, based on the idea that these kinds of arrangements would help some of those unable to travel or those for whom travel would be difficult, or on the idea that financial resources would be conserved. Here the funeral director has to review what financial benefits might be available and provide what he feels is needed even if he cannot be fully compensated. He should also point out what might be involved in correcting at a later time the arrangements being considered, if such correction would be possible. It is important to understand that the strain of travel could be less than the strain of prolonged emotional adjustment. In my opinion, the location of the ceremony should be the first-choice site of those most intimately involved. Well-meaning friends do no service to mourners when they suggest a location merely for its convenience.

A significant catalyst for funeral activities are traditions, many of which are almost indispensable at the time of a death. Tradition can vary as to geographical areas, religion, family and ethnic group. Even with an increase in our mobility, some traditions will be maintained. Obviously, a person cannot take his geography with him when he moves. Consequently, there is a trend toward discarding traditions which are related to area and ethnic group because of the reasonable fear that the supporting community would not participate in those traditions. For example, the wake or visitation is not widely practiced in the Southwest, and I think it is safe to say that many "newcomers" miss the feeling of personal warmth and the sharing of tears and laughter of this social phenomenon. It is the responsibility of the funeral director to learn, if he can, if a visitation would be successful— even when he is probably dealing with strangers.

The church may not be as strong a social institution in the Southwest as it is elsewhere. There are personal ties which develop across religious lines. However, many people will refrain from participating in religious rites involving a faith with which they are not familiar. It is unfortunate that survivors will be the ones to suffer from this.

While I believe these many factors present a challenge to the resolution of grief and to those who serve as funeral directors in the Southwest, I also believe that there are other factors which have positive effects. In the Southwest, one generally knows his neighbors. The very nature of life helps relieve acute grief. A person is not really bound by customs which might be dysfunctional. If a small social circle and family can create problems, then the importance of a neighbor who volunteers from concern rather than from a sense of duty is very much magnified.

I have attempted to detail part of what I believe to be the facts of funeral service practice in a limited area, the Southwest. It has been my intention to give stress to certain influencing factors. Therefore, it may be a little strange to conclude with two factors which are no doubt universal. There is a reluctance for some people to share their loss with others, and there are those who try to shield the bereaved from the truth of the situation. The informality, openness and friendliness of people in the Southwest should help to overcome such problems, and it is to be hoped that men everywhere can develop social relationships which foster a sharing of all of life's events, including the event of death.

CHAPTER 16

THE FUNERAL DIRECTOR:
SERVING THE LIVING

FRANCIS J. GOMEZ

THE CONTINUING secularization of our society is expanding the role of the funeral director. Formerly, the minister, priest or rabbi was designated as "the person" to tend to the needs of the bereaved. Much of the comfort they offered, and still offer, is based on ritual and religious dogma. However, the recent so-called "liberalization" that has been taking place in many religions has created doubts and uncertainties among many formerly religious people. Increased mobility and urbanization have tended to erode many of the ties people had with their churches. Today it is not uncommon for a clergyman to officiate at services for a person he has never met and to meet the bereaved family for the first and often last time at the funeral home. Additional responsibilities fall to the funeral director as more funeral services are conducted in funeral homes rather than in churches. It is, therefore, only natural that more people will turn to their funeral director for comfort and guidance when a loved one dies.

An essential facet of the enlarging role of the funeral director is to know and be able to explain the role of grief in the mourning process. Grief is essentially an individual response to a social fact (Jackson, 1957). It stands to reason then that the best preparation for effectively dealing with grief can take place outwardly—in the public domain. Thus fortified, an individual can, hopefully, deal more adequately with death when it strikes a loved one.

The funeral director has a unique opportunity to serve the living by preparing them to face, however far in the future, the reality of death. This preparation should include information directly related to the funeral service function, but should also include thoughtful guidance through the normal emotional reactions to death.

THE FUNERAL DIRECTOR AS AN INFORMANT

Every funeral director, to a greater or lesser degree, teaches people about the basic facts of death. Unfortunately, too much of the teaching takes place out of necessity following the death of a loved one. However, all teaching, even under the pressures of time and grief, has a distinct "ripple effect" whereby each person who learns the facts about funeral arrangements is likely to tell several other people and they, in turn, will share their newfound information with others. It is particularly important to make sure that the correct information is given and misunderstandings are avoided. The broad implications of the "ripple effect" are reasons for attempting to educate people *before* they need funeral services, rather than waiting until a grief-stricken individual or family requires assistance.

The typical practices of the ethical funeral director should be a part of community education programs. While it is desirable for people to be counseled prior to their needs, the funeral director must realize that many individuals are still unwilling to discuss death and/or funeral arrangements until they are forced to do so. If permitted, the director can explain alternatives that are available to those who may someday make funeral arrangements, and he can also offer advice about common community practices. A funeral director who willingly provides helpful and financially responsible advice is truly serving the living.

Many publications are available from the National Funeral Directors Association and various state groups on the specifics of funeral arrangements and prices, as well as booklets explaining common funeral customs and even how to explain death to a child. The funeral director should make every effort to have wide distribution of such material in his community. He should also make himself available for speaking engagements before local civic and charitable organizations. When he does so, he is serving the living; but he is also establishing himself as a respected member of the community, one who has made a commitment to serve the community by helping informed clients make rational decisions prior to traumatic events, rather than being stereotyped as someone who is waiting to exploit individuals at a time when grief clouds their judgment.

Some funeral directors have developed their own educational literature for the public. A pamphlet entitled *What Everyone Should Know About Funerals* (Brown, 1965) was originally prepared for J. P. Walsh and Associates in Tuscon, Arizona. It has since been republished and distributed by other funeral directors around the country. One director offers the pamphlet through advertisements in his local newspapers.

THE FUNERAL DIRECTOR AS COUNSELOR

It is in his role as counselor rather than the more clearly defined role as an informant, or provider of specific information, that the funeral director's job is expanding most rapidly. As noted earlier, the growing secularization of our society tends to make the funeral director "the person" that the bereaved is likely to turn to, not just for information, but, more and more, for consolation. The funeral director is expected to offer guidance and counsel in making funeral arrangements. However, he can also provide other assistance and emotional support because he is familiar with and, therefore, can anticipate the typical grief reactions of a person suffering from acute grief.

The funeral director knows and must help the bereaved realize that a funeral is an organized, time-limited, flexible, group-centered response to death (Kutscher, 1969) and that normal grief and its successful resolution are essential to the health of the individual and society. It is a medically known fact that the unwise handling of the grief situation is increasingly causing personality injury and has been linked with the onset of many diseases.

It is important that the funeral director let the bereaved know that normal grief involves symptoms comparable to depression, but that this is a natural part of the mourning process. It is important that he explain that the mourning process is a type of work to which one must apply himself. It is only in this way that the bereaved can disengage himself from the demanding relationship that had existed and reinvest his emotional capital in new and productive directions for the health and welfare of his future life in society (Jackson, 1957).

Death itself often closes lines of communication between and among the surviving individuals as each one seeks to cope with the death in his own way. However, the period immediately following a death is a crucial time for interpersonal relationships. The most helpful communication is with a person who is sympathetic, but who is far enough removed not to be incapacitated by grief. This person has traditionally been a clergyman, but the role is now falling frequently to the funeral director. The funeral director can assist the bereaved by assuring him that ultimate recovery from acute grief will come. The funeral director must also explain that it is not an act of disloyalty for the individual to look for a renewal of pleasures in his life. By explaining that fulfillment in life is truly the greatest tribute to be paid to the memory of a loved one, he helps restore the individual to a life relatively free of the haunting pangs of prolonged grief or guilt.

THE FUNERAL DIRECTOR: SERVING THE LIVING

The funeral director, by virtue of his job, is often said to try to mitigate the reality of death. However, the funeral director is impelled to call attention to death's presence by the very service he renders. Experience has taught the professional funeral director that if the individual does not face death wisely, he is in danger of continuing to live in a state of denial, illusion and unreality (Kutscher, 1969).

It is clear that the role of the funeral director is becoming more demanding and creative all the time. Every new challenge offers those entering and those now in the profession a unique opportunity for service to the public.

REFERENCES

Brown, G. R.: *What Everyone Should Know About Funerals.* Tucson, G. B. R. Publications, 1965.
Hendin, D.: *Death as a Fact of Life.* New York, Norton, 1973.
Jackson, E. N.: *Understanding Grief.* New York, Abingdon Pr, 1957.
Kübler-Ross, E.: *On Death and Dying.* New York, Macmillan, 1969.
Kutscher, A. H. (Ed.): *But Not To Lose.* New York, Frederick Fell, 1969.

CHAPTER 17

GRIEF THERAPY

GENE S. HUTCHENS

SOME INTRODUCTORY THOUGHTS

"THE DEATH BELL of St. Peter's tolls . . . the Pope is dead . . . soon the death bells of all of the churches in Rome will join in . . . and before they cease ringing, his body will be handed up to the embalmers . . . to be prepared for the funeral. Tomorrow, his body will lie in state in the great Basilica of St. Peter's for three days . . . to be viewed and mourned by thousands of the faithful. . . ."[1]

Viewing and mourning are rituals of the ages, whether following the death of a great Pope or of a Missouri farmer. Funeral customs have become the vehicle by which man pauses in his daily routine to acknowledge that a life has been lived—no matter how great or humble—and to express, in some way, respect and sympathy.

A vocal minority in this country insists that the traditional funeral is a paganistic, macabre ritual—perpetuated by the funeral director for financial gain—which serves no useful purpose and is foisted upon the bereaved families contrary to their wishes. But research studies of respected clergymen and psychiatrists have refuted such declarations.

Professor John E. McCaw, Professor of Religion, Drake University, in his essay on culture and death asks: "Why do we need funerals?" and answers: "Every civilization and culture has paid signal attention to funeral procedures and disposal of the dead. . . . The fundamental motives of men in developing such historic practices seem to be universal in both time and place and can be grouped under five main

---

[1]From the news commentator's monologue in the movie "Shoes of the Fisherman."

[155]

categories: 1. religious faith of the deceased and his family; 2. health and sanitation; 3. leadership and responsibility adjustment; 4. emotional adjustment of survivors; and 5. acts honoring the life and memory of the deceased. . . . The *funeral* director as a professional person exists in American culture to support all of the above needs. He functions primarily as agent in some cases, as in health and sanitation, and to facilitate and supplement in others, as in the religious ceremonies. Few situations in modern life can dispense with such services without failing to meet basic needs indicated in the above five categories. . . . Unless there are ways for the grief of separation to be expressed, emotional and physical health of survivors can be affected adversely. . . . To profane the dead, to show indifference and disrespect for the remains of human earthly existence is to give evidence that those who live are indeed already profaning life."

The Reverend James Fulbright, Pastor of St. Mark's Methodist Church in Florissant, Missouri, in a pamphlet ("Guidelines Concerning Funerals") distributed to his congregation stated: "Among the occasions when its [the church's] ministry is needed is when death comes to a family, and a funeral service must be planned and conducted. Few times in a person's life are more charged with emotion, fuller of feeling, and in greater need of tender sympathy and helpful guidance. Our funeral directors have high ethical and moral standards. We accept their dedication to serve the needs of the bereaved with sympathy and dignity. We appreciate their services. A Christian funeral is never a performance staged for morbidly curious or indifferent spectators."

Professor McCaw and Reverend Fulbright represent those clergy who are sensitive to the socio-religious needs of a traditional funeral and recognize the importance of a necessary functionary, the funeral director. Funeral directors have been advised by a group of consultants, each of whom is respected and qualified in a particular discipline, of the value of the funeral, what a funeral director is, what he should be, and about the death-denying proclivities of our society. These subjects have been researched and the findings are well-documented.

A FUNERAL DIRECTOR DOES SOME RESEARCH

Funeral service licensees are not research oriented, but those working with them at the association level have been authorized to retain consultants or others with expertise in attitudinal studies. While certain directors subscribe to services which "follow up" on families they have served, the questions asked do not really probe. One research sociologist said these follow-up services are primarily "ego trips" for the sponsoring funeral home.

With this in mind, I decided to ask families that I have served certain specific questions about the funeral—to find out for myself what the people in my community thought of "the open casket," "the traditional funeral," "the disposal service."

My community, Florissant, Missouri, could be considered a "typical" American city. In 1968, it was selected as one of the 20 All-America cities in the United States. Founded over 200 years ago, it has a rich blending of the old socio-religious heritage and the vibrant modern concepts of youthful America. Springing from a hamlet of 3,700 in 1950, it became the fifth laregst city in Missouri in 1974, with a population of 75,000 with an average mean age of 23.5 years. This city, and the surrounding communities served by my funeral home, have a total population of 250,000. This is the area represented in this survey. Families surveyed include those whose ancestors founded the city and those who have been residents from but a few years to a few months, having come from rural Missouri and other areas such as Kansas, Kentucky, Illinois, Mississippi, Tennessee, Iowa and as far away as Florida, Vermont, North Carolina, Scotland, Germany and Poland.

METHODOLOGY

For this survey, a questionnaire was prepared and sent to 100 families that my firm served between October 1, 1972 and June 30, 1973. This represented approximately 50 percent of the total families served during this period. A total of 63 questionnaires were returned in code reply envelopes and were the basis for this survey. One-half of these questionnaires were returned within ten days after mailing.

The basic criterion for selection of a family to receive a questionnaire was that a funeral "with the body present" had been conducted. Further, consideration was given to selecting respondents in all age categories, so that the survey would reflect the opinions of young adults as well as those of the "golden-age" generation.

Of the 100 families to whom the questionnaire was mailed, 59 were Catholic and 41 were Protestant. Forty-one Catholic families and 22 Protestant families returned the questionnaire. The questionnaires were sent to 50 widows, 13 widowers, 27 children, nine parents and one sister. Twenty-nine widows, nine widowers, 19 children (including one granddaughter), six parents and the one sister replied.

CHANGES REVEALED

The following changes in tradition are developing: of the 41 Catholic funerals, ten were not the traditional funeral Mass conducted in a church. Instead, the Christian Burial Service was held at the funeral home, with a priest officiating. This break from tradition developed in my community, an area steeped in 200 years of conservative Catholicism, in late 1972.

The change to one-night visitation from the two-night visitation has increased considerably during the past three years. This survey shows that 46 percent of the families chose a one-night visitation.

Cremation instead of burial still remains low in this area, with no percentage increase. There was only one cremation reported among the respondent families.

ANECDOTAL REPORTS

The seven queries in the questionnaire and the responses conclude this paper. Before giving the statistical report of the findings, I believe the following anecdotal reports are pertinent to the survey and merit presentation:

Widow about 65 years of age commenting on our services for her husband who died of cancer at 69: "Don't forget to mention that the funeral director's solicitude means so much to the family. And when he doesn't try to talk you into a more expensive funeral than one can afford, it is doubly appreciated. . . ."

Daughter in her sixties, following the death of her mother at 84, had arranged for a brief visitation for all but wanted only family and a few friends at the funeral (a departure from what her family had done previously). She wrote: "I feel that in all fairness to you in answering these questions, I will have to write a little about it. I am writing about my mother. She was more or less an invalid for nine years. She had five operations and seven stays in the hospital. Each time she returned home, she was worse off than before, until she was unable to even move herself in bed and I had to get a hoist. And, finally, we had to put her in a home, and that is a very sad thing. So, in answering the questions, she is the one I have in mind. If she had not been laid up so long or been so bad or if I were writing about a younger person, I don't know if I would have given you the same answers."

Respondent is a widower in his late fifties, Protestant, self-employed. His wife, aged 52, was ill with cancer for several months but death was sudden and unexpected. This family, consisting of the husband, a son and a daughter, presented a most difficult counseling problem. The husband insisted upon cremation; the two children were adamantly opposed and insisted on earth burial. The husband and wife had made a pact long before her death that the one who died first would be cremated and the ashes would be placed in the casket of the survivor at his or her death for earth burial. I privately counseled the children to respect the pact of their parents. They reluctantly agreed. Arrangements: one-night visitation with open casket followed by a funeral service at the Lutheran church and subsequent cremation and in-urnment in a columbarium until the death of the spouse.

The respondents are parents, aged 45 and 50, of the Catholic faith. The deceased was their son, aged 16, who died accidently from an aerosol gas inhalation at an army post. At the time of the visitation, there was some doubt whether the death was accidental or intentional as the young man was being discharged from the army due to his age. The parents were quite emotional, insisted on a four-night visitation, and throughout the visitation period were quite belligerent to my staff. In view of this, it is interesting to review their answers, which were all positive in regard to the funeral with the body present, and negative to an alternate thereto.

Respondent is a father in his middle fifties. The deceased was a son, aged 26, and death was a homicide caused by a gunshot wound in the forehead. A younger son had been killed in an automobile accident about one month before. I had served the family at that time also. Family relations for both services were quite strained because the father and mother were divorced and each had remarried. The first service had been complicated further by a set of foster parents. For both services there was a one-night visitation, open caskets, and the Christian burial service at the funeral home instead of the Catholic Mass. The father wrote: "You and your staff were very kind and comforting to me. I think enough of your service to say, when I take that final step, I do hope that you will take care of me and any of my loved ones as well."

Respondent is a widow in her late fifties or early sixties, owner of a small tailor shop, Protestant (Episcopal). Her husband, aged 67, had suffered from a long, debilitating illness. There was a one-night visitation with open casket, and a funeral service at the local Episcopal church, followed by entombment. Her comment was: "Since I had to experience the death of my husband, I had the feeling that you were sincere in helping me and my family over the difficult hours following my husband's death. I felt as though you had a personal interest in us. Thank you so much for your kindness."

The respondent is a daughter-in-law in her late fifties to early sixties, even though the questionnaire was addressed to her husband, the son of the deceased. The deceased was the respondent's mother-in-law, aged 87, of the Catholic faith. A one-night visitation with open casket was followed by Mass and burial. The reply indicated that no positive value could be found in what was done. However, an honest statement was made: "The above comments represent no reflection on the services rendered recently by Hutchens Mortuary. Everything was handled in good taste. I simply believe, and have believed for many years, that funeral services have become overdone, and provide no real benefit. If one truly believes his religious training, he knows his loved one is safely in the hands of his God, without all of the traditional fanfare. Thank you for the opportunity of expressing my honest opinion."

Respondent is a widower in his middle forties, Catholic, successful salesman, and left with six children ranging in ages from about 19 years to two weeks at the time of his wife's death. He came home from the office and found his wife, aged 44, a victim of a cerebral hemorrhage, unconscious on the bathroom floor. She died within two days, following brain surgery. A one-night visitation with open casket was followed by a Mass and burial. The husband had suffered a tremendous shock and his answers and comments reflect profound grief. The questionnaire was sent to him about three months after his wife's death, and his answers reflected opposition to the traditional funeral. He wrote: "As you get older, you realize that death is inevitable and must be accepted as such, regardless of our feelings. When it involves a younger person, it is especially hard and it is my feeling that the effect on those left behind could be made less burdensome and of shorter duration, without the loss of remembrance. As life continues on, there are constant reminders and memories and they should be beautiful. I don't see how our present [funeral] methods contribute in any way in lessening the sorrow or brightening the future for those left behind."

A granddaughter, about 30, answered the questionnaire instead of her uncle, who was the son of the deceased. The deceased was female, aged 88. She had suffered the infirmities of old age for years. Her body had been grotesquely twisted with arthritis; she had fallen from bed a day or so before death. Lacerations and bruises were on her face. General comment was: "If the casket was not open it would be a horrible memory for life for the whole family as everybody would be wondering what had happened, how death had occurred, if it was as said or something unreal had occurred. I think it would be very hard on the family of a loved one not to at least see her for the last time. You had told me you might have to close the casket and I asked it be open if at all possible. I want to thank you for the job you did. All the relatives and friends said she looked just as they remembered her, not as when she was sick, which made us all feel good."

The respondents are two sets of parents, in their middle to late forties, of the Catholic faith. Each lost a son, aged 19, when the boys' car left the highway and plunged into a flooded drainage ditch, causing death by drowning. I had served both families previously. These two boys had been friends and companions from childhood, so funeral arrangements were made and counseling was done with both sets of parents at the same time. They desired a double funeral and burial.

A departure from family custom was the one-night visitation instead of two nights. Both families were descendants of the earliest settlers of our community and the one-night visitation taxed the funeral home facilities to the utmost. The attendance at the funeral Mass and interment was considered to be the largest in many years. Both young men were popular and well-liked, so we were were able to observe first-hand the grief and reaction to death by literally hundreds of our young people in the community.

Respondent is a daughter in her early fifties. The deceased was her mother, aged 75, Protestant. Visitation was one-night, followed by a service at the funeral home and burial. The deceased had been confined to the state mental hospital for several years before her death. The questionnaire was not answered, but the following letter was written: "From a small child on up, I have never been in favor of open caskets for all the friends and relatives to view, discuss and talk about. I feel it accomplishes nothing. All persons should be remembered as they were before death or when they were in good health and truly themselves. I feel that the body should be viewed by the immediate members of the family to make sure the person is dressed, etc., as they please him or her to be. Then I believe the casket should be closed, and this closed casket lie in state for one or two nights so that friends and relatives may visit and show their respects to the living that are in grief. This gives the loved ones the consolation that the dead person will be remembered by all, as he or she once was and not as that one last look. I think that today as I look ahead to my own death, I would feel content not to be stared at by all others and I know my family and friends would only try to erase what I looked like dead and try and remember me as I was alive. No, I have never agreed with the open casket, but then I'm just one person probably in millions who would think or look at it this way. To answer the questions would be unclear maybe to you, so I wrote you how I felt."

Respondent is a widowed mother, in her late forties, of the Catholic faith, and a registered nurse. Her husband died ten years ago, leaving her with nine children, aged 2 to 15. The husband had had cancer and was ill for many months before death. The deceased now was her son, aged 20, killed instantly in a motorcycle accident. Facial restorative treatment was required. There was a one-night visitation with open casket, followed by a funeral Mass and burial. The respondent had positive feelings about the funeral for her husband, negative for that of her son. She wrote: "Frank [the husband] had been sick for several months and had no chance of recovery. His illness had taken its toll so seeing him looking as he had before his illness did help my grief a great deal. Seeing Freddy [the son] didn't help my grief at all, but it at least did help me to realize that he really was gone. I think most of our traditions are ordeals—graduations, weddings, first communions, etc.—but I would hate to see them done away with; the same goes for the traditional funeral."

Respondent is a widow, about 55, Protestant; the deceased, her husband, had been Catholic. The husband's illness was of several months duration and death was the result of complications of acute alcoholism. This man had been a personal friend of mine for 18 years. The widow privately expressed relief, not sorrow, at his death. There was a two-night visitation and the Christian Burial Service, with a priest officiating, instead of the funeral Mass. This caused strained relations with the husband's family and invoked mild disapproval from the pastor. The priest declined the request to go to the National Cemetery. I gave the committal and said a few words at the grave. The following general comment was made: "I think you did a wonderful job and you were so kind to us. I'm especially indebted to you for the wonderful words you spoke at the graveside. . . ."

The daughter in her early thirties answered the questionnaire instead of her father. Her mother was 57, of the Protestant faith. Visitation was for two nights with open casket followed by a funeral service at the funeral home and burial. As a matter of interest, the funeral and the vault selected were the highest priced for those included in this survey. The daughter wrote: "I was with my mother night and day for one week before she died. And each day her physical appearance got worse and worse. On the morning that she died would have been the picture that would have stayed with me forever, but because of your talent and an open casket I now have a beautiful memory. My mother looked the way she did several years before her illness. And I want to take this opportunity to thank you again for that."

Respondent is a widow, aged 35 to 40, Protestant. Her husband, aged 40, died quite suddenly, apparently of a coronary. They had three young children and there was some doubt in her mind about bringing the youngest, aged 6, to see the father. I talked to her and encouraged her to bring the child. There was a one-night visitation at my funeral home, followed by a one-night visitation and funeral service at the receiving funeral home in a community about 70 miles distant. Her general comment was: "I am thankful I allowed our six-year-old daughter to view her Dad's body. After she saw him in the open casket she realized he would not be coming home any more and would be living in heaven."

The respondents are parents, in their late thirties, of the Catholic faith. The deceased was their fifteen-year-old son who was killed instantly in a motorbike-auto collision. Once more we saw the younger generation of the old community families breaking with the two-night visitation and having one-night. The funeral Mass custom was kept. Facial tissue reduction and some restoration was required and the visitation was with open casket. A general comment was written, I'm sure, by the mother: "When you are standing beside a body of your loved one, my feelings were that of a movie, everyone was talking and moving and you were standing there watching, but not really seeing anyone nor hearing anything. I do not believe you realize how helpful, considerate and kind you are towards a family when they need help the most. We will always remember your kindness and would like you to know it was deeply appreciated."

SOME CONCLUSIONS AND OBSERVATIONS

For the purpose of this research, I queried only those who had a "total" or traditional funeral. My "case" reports give an across-the-board picture of a sample of people who believed in the traditional funeral or at least agreed to have it. Insofar as most of the families that call me want a funeral with the body present, I think the findings of this study show people will continue to want it when death takes someone they love. But there are changes evident. These will force the funeral director to serve each group of survivors according to their needs, not according to what he thinks should be done. But as he serves such families, he must counsel by relying on experiences he has had as he has served others.

QUESTIONS AND TABULATIONS OF ANSWERS AND SOME COMMENTS

Although I lacked knowledge of the mechanics of preparing a questionnaire, I think my sincerity in wanting the families I served to comment on the funeral generically and honestly—not on what I had done specifically as a funeral director—was evident to them. I regret the unfortunate choice of the term "prescription for grief," but could devise no applicable substitute. I do think that those who received the questionnaire knew what I meant.

1. *Do you feel that the open casket and viewing of your loved one helped you realize and accept the fact that he or she was dead?*

   YES: 52 OTHER: 1 marked "yes and no"; 1 with no mark.
   NO: 9
   COMMENTS:
   "Only because no member of family was with him at time of death."
   "Since there was no illness involved, a sudden and accidental death as it was, was difficult and did not seem real."
   "At peace at last."
   "A mature, intelligent individual with any religious belief at all should be able to accept death."
   "It only seemed to be more upsetting to me and my children."
   "The fact is already real, it only hurts more while you stand and look on."

2. *Was the physical appearance of your loved one in the casket such that you have been left with a pleasant memory picture?*

   YES: 55 OTHER: 2 marked "yes and no"; 1 with no mark.
   NO: 5
   COMMENTS:
   "I did not think that you could have done such a good job, the condition she was in . . . also she looked so dead and you made her beautiful."

"Cosmetic treatment was very good."

"I feel that my husband looked at peace, since he had suffered so long."

"My husband had been ill eight years and during past three, suffered greatly. I *feared* a closed casket. I was filled with a sense of unbelievable joy to see my husband look so good."

"I prefer to remember the loved one alive."

3. *Do you feel that recollection of conversations with friends and relatives at the open casket during the visitation or "wake" have helped ease the burden of sorrow?*

YES: 49   OTHER: 2 with no mark

NO: 12

COMMENTS:

"Some . . . so many people remarked what a fine person he was."

"One doesn't realize how many friends one has until a loved one passes on."

"I believe private visits of friends at home would be more appreciated."

"People mean well but only tend to add to the burden at that time."

"It is very difficult to talk to anyone when your heart is so full of sorrow."

4. *In view of your past experience with a funeral would you want the casket of a family member open (if possible) for viewing during the visitation or "wake" period?*

YES: 55   OTHER: 2 marked with a ??; 1 with no mark

NO: 5

COMMENTS:

"No one should be denied last view of deceased."

"I think it helps to realize that he or she is gone forever."

"I would never have felt at ease had I not seen him again. . . ."

"Yes, although the children all said, 'Don't have my casket open, I don't want people staring at me.' "

"Depends upon their views about such things. My husband says YES, but for myself, I am thinking about having mine closed when my time comes. I would rather have people remember me like I was before I got sick. I don't like people looking at the deceased and saying he or she looks good or they look like they suffered a lot or it doesn't look like them at all."

"So many people would not visit the sick or elderly when they should have . . . so why view their remains?"

5. (a) *Do you feel that the "traditional funeral" (which is making funeral arrangements, the one- or two-night visitation or "wake" with open casket for viewing, the funeral service or Mass and the burial) was an experience of value to you at the time of your bereavement?*

YES: 51   OTHER: 1 marked "yes and no"; 2 with no mark
NO: 9
COMMENTS:
"I hope that when I die I will also have the traditional funeral."
"Only to help you assess the truly bereaved and the curious."
"I wanted to have a funeral that would do my husband proud."
"Perhaps yes . . . it was an ordeal, but I felt a necessary one. Life has a lot of ordeals we must endure."
"I believe the 'Traditional Funeral' is an unnecessary strain on the family, both emotionally and financially."
"It took weeks afterward to get over this experience emotionally and physically."

5 (b) *Has its memory helped you in easing your grief?*

YES: 44   OTHER: 1 marked "yes and no"; 3 with no mark
NO: 15
COMMENTS:
"There will always be a sadness involved. We still feel it helped us."
"Yes, some, but you never forget. That is something we will have to get used to."
"The Mass eased our grief to quite an extent."
"My closest relation and children have done the most for me."
"I was glad when it was over so I could be alone with my grief."

6. *In view of your experience with the traditional funeral, would you consider for a member of your family what is known as the "disposal service," which is: No wake or visitation, no viewing*

of the casketed body, no funeral service with the casketed body present . . . just a quick private burial with a memorial service at a later date?

YES: 7   OTHER: 1 was undecided; 3 with no mark
NO: 52
COMMENTS:
"But only for someone who had been laid up for years."
"This is the type of burial I have requested for myself."
"Too much emphasis is put on certain things that are personal and tend to make it a public affair."
"Not as long as the body is viewable and can look nice."
"Never!"
"A person is not just a number and a proper funeral should be a last gesture of love by the family survivors."
"I believe one needs the last viewing to realize the life of the loved one is over."
"Not unless it was the desire of the deceased."

7. *Do you feel that the "open casket" IS a prescription for grief?*
YES: 35   OTHER: 1 marked "yes and no"; 3 with no mark
NO: 24
COMMENTS of those who marked the question "yes":
"One way or another you have grief and I think you owe it to friends and relatives to have an open casket."
"The open casket not only gives the spouse of the deceased comfort, but also the other relatives and friends an opportunity for a last glimpse of their loved one (at least until the resurrection). To me, it spells the difference in the burying of a human being and that of an animal. If we are just whisked away what is to differentiate between God's humans and animals?"
"Whenever I think of my deceased father and mother, I remember them as I last saw them, in the casket, which is better than the way my mother looked after 13 days of being paralyzed."
"Many times it accentuates grief, but should be followed due to comments in question No. 4."
"An open casket is a way of saying good-bye to a loved one. The *final* goodbye is the 'Prescription for Grief.' "

CHAPTER 18

WHO ARE WE – WHAT ARE WE –
WHY WE DO WHAT WE DO

C. Stewart Hausmann

DEFINITION

FUNERAL DIRECTORS most often accept the following definition of a funeral: a funeral is a religious ceremony, in which we serve the living while caring for the dead, with dignity. Further, we accept the premise that a funeral is an experience of value as it meets the needs of those who mourn.

It is helpful to start with a definition even though there are some who may take issue with it and perhaps suggest alternatives. There are those who will say that a funeral need not be religious. Others will object to a ceremony, wanting simpler forms of disposal activities. Most people, however, do accept a funeral as a religious ceremony. In my experience, those who do not, comprise a very small minority.

Funerals, with religious emphasis and ceremony, have been recorded in all of history and in every culture. Yet there are some today who call for a minimum of funeral ceremony. There are also those who demand the most bizarre funeral activities. Most people, however, find their needs filled somewhere in between these extremes.

Funeral directors primarily serve the living. Day by day, we meet and counsel people at a time when we are needed and at a time when almost no one else can help. Our clients are the living, and our clients are in a personal crisis. We bring assistance. In the whole process, no one can or should deny that a death has occurred. A person is dead. A body is present and its needs result. We are prepared to care for these needs, but in the process we always remember that we must give dignity to man in this ultimate and final chapter of human experience.

WHO WE ARE

Historically, in this country, we have been called *undertakers*. This very descriptive term developed in colonial villages where someone simply undertook the care and disposal of the dead and became the village undertaker. This person may have been the colonial barber, dentist or, many times, the furniture maker. It is not unusual still to find a combined funeral home and furniture store in the small towns of middle America. This is a throwback to the day when the furniture manufacturer also made caskets. People would be measured in advance for their caskets, the casket manufacturer crafted and warehoused the casket until needed. Ultimately, at the time of death, the furniture manufacturer who provided the casket, arranged for the funeral as a further service.

Most often today we are called *funeral directors*. Our professional association is called a Funeral Directors' Association. This title has received wide acceptance. It is not always a true description, however, for I believe that in a funeral service at the funeral home or in a church, the clergyman actually directs the service and at that time shares the responsibility for the direction of the funeral with us.

Perhaps a more acceptable modern title might be *mortician*. Our schools are called Mortuary Science Schools. Our regulatory boards are often called Boards of Mortuary Science and my license cites me as a Practitioner of Mortuary Science. Recently, I have even heard us referred to as *crisis intervenors,* which, along with others in the community, we are.

Suffice it to say, whatever people choose to call us, we are actually part of the vital health care service of the community. We are prepared to serve when called upon on a 24-hour basis every day of the year. We must maintain a staff, facilities, vehicles and equipment sufficient to do our job. Unlike the doctor who has a publicly supported hospital in which to work or a lawyer for whom the taxpayers supply a courthouse, we as professionals must provide our own facilities at considerable personal investment.

WHAT WE ARE

Firstly, we are true *professionals.* Licensees in most states are required to invest at least five years beyond high school in academic preparation for examination and licensure. The body of knowledge and demand for more knowledge of the dying, death and bereavement process is expanding day by day.

Our professional counseling is an important help for the bereaved. We bring order out of family chaos. We help families in bereavement to make proper decisions at a time when these decisions are most vital. We assist people in grief and in the process we help mend lives. We give the early aid in the bereavement and grief process and assist people as they take their first steps back into a meaningful life, adjusted to their loss and successful in their grief. These are the goals of our professional practice.

Secondly, we are *technicians.* We bring a deceased person into our preparation facilities. We perform a surgical process called embalming which renders the body clean and free of exterior contamination, preserved so that it may last through the process of the funeral with no further putrefaction, and we present for viewing a body with a natural and acceptable appearance. As technicians, we are part of the community health care services. Embalming is basic to the funeral process.

Lastly, we are *businessmen.* The same economic pressures of the marketplace are upon us as upon any other business enterprise. Capital investment, wages with fringe benefits, taxes and the like are as much a part of our life as they are of any other commercial operation. Obviously, to remain in business we must produce a profit and funerals are priced to provide a reasonable income for the funeral director.

Our modern pricing of funerals is usually broken into five main categories, each descriptive of what it provides. Professional Service Fees head the list, followed by Facility Charges, Merchandise, Transportation and Cash Advances. Obviously, except for the Cash Advances, each category provides its share of the income required to maintain our funeral establishments.

WHY WE DO WHAT WE DO

The funeral is an experience of value. It is a help to those who mourn. We believe this axiom and we use the funeral to provide, among other things, the factors which produce this value.

A funeral helps provide *reality*. It should clearly assert the fact that a death has occurred. Today, in our death-denying, almost death-defying culture, we often try to mask this fundamental fact. People should not die. Doctors, medicines, hospitals, machines—all should be able to save the life. Death is an accident, a doctor's mistake or perhaps the result of someone's ignorance. People blame themselves, their physician, a nurse, the hospital or even God.

People often die today in sterile communities, those of the nursing home or hospital, away from their families who are denied experiencing the reality that death has occurred because they are removed from the presence of death. Older people are often separated from younger generations by being placed in retirement villages for senior citizens, also distant from their loved ones and again making it difficult for those who survive them to accept the fact that the death has actually occurred.

Viewing, as provided at funerals, affirms the reality of death and is often the first step in the successful bereavement process. Persons denied this essential experience often suffer traumatic psychological aftereffects.

Funerals are also important for they give the community *the opportunity to share* a loss. Many want to express their love and this expression of love supports the grieving family members. They want to know that someone cares and shares their loss.

Sometimes families will decide to have a "private" funeral. Private from whom? Office friends or lodge friends are often as close to the dead person as his family. They have shared in his life and should have this opportunity to share in the loss and demonstrate their respect for a life worthily lived.

Sharing a loss through a funeral is a vital tool in the bereavement process. Flowers, memorials, visitations and cards are all part of the social focus which the funeral provides.

Lastly, a funeral must provide *finality*. No one should walk away from a funeral with any lingering doubt that death has occurred. A person has not "passed away," "departed," "gone beyond" or any other phrase which softens the impact. *The person is dead.* A funeral service and the interment or cremation process must make this point crystal clear.

The clergyman's last words might be, "He is dead and buried. Go in peace and may the God of peace go with you." In most cases, a family can leave the experience of a funeral and successfully put together the pieces of life.

The dead are not to be forgotten. They are placed in their proper perspective by the funeral with its attendant ceremonies and supportive experiences. Modern funeral directors are trained to organize the funeral as a necessary step in the process of acute grief.

CHAPTER 19

THE DEATH ANXIETY OF THOSE
WHO WORK IN FUNERAL HOMES

DONALD I. TEMPLER, CAROL F. RUFF AND JOYCE AYERS

THIS PAPER FOCUSES upon the degree of death anxiety of people who work in funeral homes. However, a review of our death anxiety research is necessary to provide adequate background for the findings of this study.

The first step in the death anxiety research program was the construction and validation of the Death Anxiety Scale (DAS) of Templer (1969, 1970). Forty items that seemed to measure the apprehension under consideration were devised on a rational basis. Nine of these items were eliminated by the combined judgment of four psychiatric chaplains and three clinical psychologists. The remaining 31 items were subjected to a statistical analysis to assure that each item would be correlated highly enough with the total scale. The 15 retained items constitute the DAS. The DAS was found to have adequate reliability and to be sufficiently free from response sets. Considerable evidence indicates that the DAS is valid. For example, 16 patients in a state mental hospital who had spontaneously verbalized fear of death to professional personnel were found to have higher DAS scores, to a statistically significant extent, than 16 control patients who were matched for age, sex and psychiatric diagnosis.

In a study that involved over 2,500 subjects (Templer, Ruff and Franks, 1971), the relationships of scores on the DAS to sex, age and parental resemblance were determined. Females were found to have consistently higher DAS scores than males. There was no relationship between DAS score and age with subjects from the teens through the eighties, a finding that contradicts the "common sense" notion that the closer to the end one approaches, the more death anxiety he would be expected to have. The DAS scores of high school students resembled those of their parents, with the correlations with the parent of the same sex being significantly greater than those with the parent of the opposite sex. The highest correlation was between the death anxiety of the two parents. These results strongly imply that death anxiety is not entirely dependent upon genetics or upon early childhood experiences. Rather, intimate interpersonal relationships appear to be crucial in the development of death anxiety.

With college students, there was no relationship between DAS score and a number of religious variables (Templer and Dotson, 1970). This was explained in terms of religion's having relatively little importance in the life of the typical college student. The results were quite different with a group of religiously very involved persons who had participated in interdenominational, predominantly Protestant, retreats (Templer, 1972). These very religiously involved persons had lower DAS scores than were observed in any other research project. Furthermore, within this religiously involved group of individuals, those who were more religious had lower death anxiety.

In a project with elderly individuals, it was found that their mental health was a much more important determinant of death anxiety than their physical health (Templer, 1971). Cigarette smokers, nonsmokers and ex-smokers could not be differentiated on the basis of their DAS scores. However, within the cigarette smoking group, those who smoked less had higher death anxiety (Templer, 1972). Black and white college students demonstrated very similar levels of death anxiety (Pandey and Templer, 1972). Death anxiety is positively associated with various indices of anxiety and depression (Templer, 1969, 1970). In fact, in one project, there was a significant decrease in death anxiety in depressed patients who were symptomatically treated for their depression (Templer, Ruff and Ayers, in preparation).

The research investigation reported in regard to the personnel of funeral homes involved 16 people who worked in seven different funeral homes. Five of these funeral homes are in Hopkinsville, Kentucky, a city of approximately 25,000. Two funeral homes are in small towns near Hopkinsville. Of the 16 persons who completed the DAS, seven were funeral directors, seven were both funeral directors and embalmers, one an assistant funeral director, and one a janitor. Twelve were male and four female. The age range was from 23 to 72 with a median of 51 years.

They obtained a DAS mean of 6.06 and a standard deviation of 2.41. Their DAS mean is strictly within normal limits. In fact, it deviates very little from the median of the means for a number of studies reported by Templer and Ruff (1971). The mean DAS score of 1,271 adults living in Hopkinsville and surrounding communities, as assessed in previously reported research (Templer, Ruff and Franks, 1971), is 6.12. This mean is very similar to and obviously not statistically different from that of the present research. It is acknowledged that because of the rather small funeral home sample, a small difference between the populations of funeral home workers and the general public may not have been detected. However, if any such difference exists, it is probably quite small in view of the present findings. In fact, not one of our present subjects had an exceptionally high or low DAS score. It seems reasonable to conclude that the death anxiety of people who work in funeral homes does not differ greatly from that present in the general population.

One might have speculated that individuals in the funeral industry tend to have high death anxiety because of their continual exposure to the harsh reality of death. It could also have been argued that they tend to have low death anxiety because of their day-to-day routine which could foster a process similar to what behavior therapists call "flooding." Or, it could be argued that only someone with low death anxiety would enter such an occupation. The present research indicates that such speculation would be without basis.

Jessica Mitford (1963) denounced the funeral industry for financial exploitation and other alleged abuses. In her chapter about funeral directors, she stated that "Funeral people are always saying 'funerals are for the living,' yet there is occasional evidence that they have developed an eerie affection, a genuine solicitude, for the dead, in whose company they spend so much time." Although the present investigation did not concern funeral directors' attitudes toward corpses, the fact that their death anxiety tends to be basically average would make the accusation of their other attitudes toward death being pathological seem unwarranted without data to back up such assertions.

It is beyond the scope of competence of the present authors to agree or disagree with Mitford's contention that the fees of professionals in the funeral business are exorbitant. However, it should be pointed out that funeral directors are not the only professionals who demand a lot of money from the bereaved. What we have in mind is that the bereaved sometimes go to professional psychotherapists whose fees can range upward from $50 an hour. We are thinking especially of psychiatrists and clinical psychologists. The findings of most of the well-controlled studies upon the effectiveness of psychotherapy are not especially encouraging. These studies imply that the typical psychotherapy conducted upon the typical patient by the typical therapist produces very limited results. Many contemporary experts believe that the extent to which psychotherapy is effective is primarily a function of the interpersonal relationships between therapist and patient. These experts say that a psychotherapist's understanding, genuineness and warmth are more important than his professional training and university degrees. Such a viewpoint has support from the studies that have found that lay people have handled themselves in psychotherapeutic situations basically on a par with professional therapists. In some situations, a bartender or beautician or neighbor or friend may be just as helpful as the most expensive analyst.

Funeral directors and other persons in the funeral industry probably function at times as psychotherapists. They talk with the bereaved at the time of their greatest sorrow. And, they probably provide much warmth and understanding. Persons of diverse professions such as nurses, clergymen, educators, social workers and dentists are now recognized as providing a psychotherapeutic function. Why not also recognize the workers in the funeral industry?

To summarize this paper which contains two different themes that we fear may be only loosely connected: 1. we found that the death anxiety of people who work in funeral homes is of about the same degree as that of the average person; 2. we suggested that their other death attitudes may be sufficiently similar to those of the norm so that they can empathically and compassionately interact with the bereaved in a psychotherapeutic fashion.

REFERENCES

Mitford, J.: *The American Way of Death.* New York, Simon and Schuster, 1963.

Pandey, R. E., and Templer, D. I.: Use of the death anxiety scale in an interracial setting. *Omega, 3*:127, 1972.

Templer, D. I.: Death anxiety scale. *Proceedings of the 77th Annual Convention of the American Psychological Association,* Washington, A.P.A., 1969.

———: The construction and validation of a death anxiety scale. *J Gen Psychol, 82*:165, 1970.

———: Death anxiety as related to depression and health of retired persons. *J Gerontol, 4*:521, 1971.

———: Death anxiety in religiously very involved persons. *Psychol Rep, 31*: 361, 1972.

———: Death anxiety: extraversion, neuroticism and cigarette smoking. *Omega, 3*:53, 1972.

Templer, D. I., and Dotson, E.: Religious correlates of death anxiety. *Psychol Rep, 26*:895, 1970.

Templer, D. I., and Ruff, C. F.: Death anxiety scale means, standard deviations, and embedding. *Psychol Rep, 29*:173, 1971.

Templer, D. I., Ruff, C. F., and Franks, C. M.: Death anxiety: age, sex, and parental resemblance in diverse populations. *Devel Psychol, 4*:108, 1971.

CHAPTER 20

THE CLERGY ON THE FIRING LINE

Regina Flesch

For a number of years I was the Principal Investigator in a research project supported by the National Institute of Mental Health, (originally through the Center for Studies in Suicide Prevention) designed to study the process of mourning in families bereaved either by vehicular accident or by suicide. Without unnecessary detail about our research plan, it should be noted that family members of hospitalized terminally ill patients suffering from known physiological illnesses are relatively accessible for interviews, and have been the focus of recent research studies. Family members whose bereavements are unexpected are less readily accessible and, therefore, have been studied and written about less. Survivors of major disasters are not alone in their tragedies; they have a feeling of sharing, as have families who lose loved ones in their country's service. Our work has been with interviewees who feel, and in many respects actually are, isolated and alone. Their loved ones often have died alone, in automobile accidents on the highway or through means of their own choosing, leaving survivors who feel abandoned.

My interest in the clergy's work with the bereaved began almost simultaneously with my exploratory interviews with these bereaved respondents. From interviews, it appeared to me that persons with a religious orientation somehow met an unexpected loss with greater resilience than individuals without a religious orientation, however that

The work on which this paper is based was supported by the Commonwealth of Pennsylvania, Department of Public Welfare, and by the United States Public Health Service, National Institute of Mental Health, Research Grants MH15063-01, 15063-02 and 15063-03.

is defined. By "resilience," I mean the ability to continue daily functioning at least in the initial period of loss, the period of acute grief. This observation persuaded me to enlist as co-workers in interviews professional persons who traditionally worked with the bereaved, and who could be expected to have a continuing interest in bereaved individuals. Almost all bereaved families eventually must turn to clergymen to conduct the funeral service. Therefore, I began work with members of the clergy but I soon learned that many clergymen are as poorly equipped as other people to work with the bereaved.

In our research interviews, the first of which we conducted as soon as possible after the funeral, we heard directly about some clerical blunders. One respondent complained that the local rabbi really ought not to have mentioned to members of his congregation that the decedent, our interviewee's wife, had committed suicide. Another respondent, who had had no connection with any church prior to the accidental death of a family member on the highway, related that a local minister had paid him a condolence call to invite him to hold the funeral service in his church. However, during this visit the minister also informed him of the poor financial state of his church, and asked the bereaved family for future financial support as parishioners. His effort was understandably unsuccessful. Another example came from a grieving mother whose only child had committed suicide through the ingestion of drugs. Beyond child-bearing age, and at bitter odds with the boy's step-father, this woman had closeted herself in the house with her boy's belongings and with bottles of gin, but she had opened her door when the clergyman called. He exhorted her to combat her grief, giving her an example from his own life. He said he had lost his beloved wife of many years and was in despair, but he had trust in the Lord. He "kept on," and after a time, he had remarried. He now had a loving wife and a fine new family, so she, too, could remake her life. The woman related this story with a steady look and mirthless laughter.

These examples may be termed clerical "sins of commission." Clerical "sins of omission" can be mentioned more briefly. We have visited many individuals whose clergymen have failed to make even the most superficial condolence call after the funeral service.

In the single funeral that I had to arrange, the rabbi whom I telephoned initially objected to conducting the funeral service in a local church, although there was no synagogue in the village to which he was summoned, and although he on occasion had preached in that church. He suggested instead that the funeral service be held in his synagogue, over 20 miles away, to which the funeral party would have had to drive over the most heavily trafficked stretch of vacation highway in the country, on one of the two most active holiday weekends of the year. His ecumenism may have been stirred by my comment that no funeral party could drive that highway on the third of July, and he finally reluctantly accepted the original plan. Neither the rabbi who had conducted the funeral service nor the rector of the church where the service was held paid a condolence call, although both had promised a call within the week.

A Roman Catholic friend related a similar experience. Her lovely teen-aged daughter had collapsed without warning in school and had died in the mother's arms on the way to the hospital. The distraught parents telephoned their previous parish priest to conduct the funeral service. As he now served in another parish, he referred these heart-broken people to his successor with whom they had had no personal contact. To this day the mother feels bitter because the referral could have been avoided or else handled differently and because their previous priest neither attended the funeral nor paid a condolence call.

A few fortunate interviewees have told us, with pride and pleasure, of condolence calls by their clergymen. Without exception these calls have occurred within the first week after the funeral, and were perfunctory, brief, and final. After the first ten days the bereaved typically are left alone by laity and clergy alike. Clergymen often excuse their failure to keep in touch with parishioners on the grounds of heavy duties, but few clergymen attempt to enlist parishioners in visiting the bereaved. Unable to ask for help and also unable to mobilize themselves to attend a church which could help, bereaved people are neglected by busy clergymen, and thus lose contact with their church and church community. Yet our respondents have been pathetically grateful for any condolence call by a clergyman, and we often have heard how much a single short call by a clergyman has meant to a mourner.

Essentially the above failures in ministry to the bereaved can be subsumed under three headings:

1. Failures in heart—that is, failure in charity and loving kindness.

2. Failures in mind—that is, failure to comprehend the problems of bereavement and grief.

3. Failures in role—that is, failure to fulfill the clerical role as representative of an organized religious faith.

Let us now consider these clerical failures and what may be done about them.

FAILURES IN HEART

Grief as an emotion is poorly understood, partly because there have been few nonretrospective studies (Averill, 1968). I believe it safe to say that most people, even those who have sustained a loss, have little appreciation of the need for patience and understanding with those in grief. Possibly if we consider the psychology of bereavement briefly, the problem will become clear.

Psychologists tell us that man's basic anxiety stems from the first separation anxiety, the separation of the child from its mother. The finality and permanence of separation through the death of a deeply loved person arouses enormous anxiety in the bereaved, so great, in fact, that it has been noted by more than one author that people in grief often fear loss of their sanity. The "work of mourning," (Freud, 1959) must proceed slowly, piecemeal, as the bereaved gradually tries to separate himself from the deceased. While the lost relationship is retained psychologically by the bereaved, he repudiates current reality and clings to the past.

It is easy to become impatient with people in grief, particularly with their reiterated complaints about their loss. Impatience is expressed through comments such as, "You've already told me twice about the day he died," or through nonverbal body language, shifting in the chair and obvious lack of interest, or through actual absence. When the clergyman visits, his impatience may find expression in narration of a personal loss—perhaps not as gross as the example cited earlier, but like the interjection of one young clergyman to an interviewee whose husband recently had committed suicide, "I *know* how you feel because my sister's husband just died." Such responses are correctly perceived by the mourner as signifying lack of understanding. Feeling abandoned and severely anxious, the bereaved person is highly sensitive to the least hint of rejection from others. He reads such signs with accuracy.

It is not necessary to know fully the nature of the lost relationship or the personality pattern of the mourner to understand the need of the grieving individual for support and simple human kindness *over a period of time*. This means not a single, perfunctory condolence call, but a sustained expression of understanding, acceptance and concern, despite the mourner's aversive behavior. Above all, the bereaved need charity, that inestimable gift which traditionally is associated with religious action.

A fine example of clerical charity was provided by a non-Catholic interviewee whose Catholic husband had been killed in a vehicular accident. This decedent's priest came to call after the funeral. When the widow saw him, she let forth a verbal attack against the Lord. I asked what the priest had replied, and she related: "Even when I said I denounced Him, the priest replied: 'He's always the first One that takes it between the eyes.' He said: 'Everybody had a bitter feeling towards God. He's the first One and the only One that takes it all. But He's got broad shoulders; He can take it. And He's forgiving.' " The priest added: "If you can find it in your heart to forgive Him, He'll forgive you." Grief stricken as she was, our interviewee responded to the charity of this reply and spoke of the help she received from that visit.

FAILURES IN MIND

The current literature emphasizes, and the author's clinical experience documents, that one important element in the process of mourning is the disruption of normal patterns of activity. For example, a mother typically will have organized her life around certain routine tasks in relation to a child even after that child is grown and out of the home. She may look forward to weekend visits, to occasional suppers at home, or to contacts with the child's friends who stop in for a meal. Such contacts may be infrequent but are a source of happiness to parents and give *pattern* and meaning to the mother's activity. Even if no longer at home, when the child is removed through death, the mother's entire patern of life is disrupted and may be destroyed permanently.

Typically, the bereaved mother starts to follow her old routines, but fails to carry them through to completion. The routines are no longer purposeful because the person who gave them meaning is no longer among the living. Sociologists term this "role loss" as distinct from "object loss" (Volkert and Stanley, 1966), the loss of the person. After a time, the mother may realize that she should try to do something about her lapses in activity. Recognizing that she should change her routines and develop entirely new areas of activity, she may even be able to accomplish a few changes. However, many bereaved people, by no means in the minority, simply are unable to initiate new activities or to find new roles. As a rule, the initiation of new friendships and new interests, or even the resumption of old patterns, are beyond the capacity of the individual in grief. The duration of this incapacity varies with the individual, with the closeness of the relationship and with other factors, but apathy, lethargy and withdrawal are commonly noted characteristics of grieving individuals. Nevertheless, once someone else starts a bereaved person on something, he may be able to carry through, particularly if the activity involves other people. The clergy can perform very helpful functions during this time, when old patterns of behavior are no longer operable for the individual and when he lacks the capacity to initiate new tasks. Brief condolence calls, even of ten minutes' duration can be enormously reassuring if during these visits there is a simple recognition of the individual's problem. In a brief call, the clergyman can convey understanding of this disruption of daily activities and without exhortation or pressure, he can offer help through the church or through other parishioners for the resumption of former activities and establishment of new roles. What is suggested is first, verbalized recognition of the disrupted life pattern by the clergyman who makes a condolence call, and that this problem be accepted as natural, a matter of course. Second, we suggest that the church community be enlisted in keeping the mourner in contact with the church, and thus, in contact with the community.

There are experimental programs in which lay visitors have been used effectively with the bereaved and, of course, there are church groups which rely on lay contacts to maintain their membership, i.e. the Church of the Lord Jesus Christ of the Latter Day Saints. However, in a large urban community, the enlistment of lay members for this kind of work has been rare. Many of our bereaved interviewees fall away from their church but would continue there if their clergyman had enlisted a church member's aid in their return (I mean not merely transportation, although that may be a factor).

Parishioners who themselves lack meaningful occupation outside their homes could be given basic instruction in how to call on bereaved individuals and how to help them to a religious service. The clergyman who thus coordinates human needs would strengthen the total membership of his church while bringing the bereaved back into the mainstream of life. Thus, this clergyman may build a unified congregation in which all members have a meaningful role.

CLERICAL FAILURE IN ROLE

In addition to loss of a beloved object and loss of a valued role, we have mentioned a third type of loss, the loss of meaning in life that may follow a major bereavement. This may well be the most painful aspect of grief. Meaning in daily life underlies all action and unless one's life has meaning, there is no point in continuing. Our respondents have stated this openly, saying that they take tranquilizers, or drink, or do both, courting oblivion. One of our interviewees, deeply despondent since her husband's death in a vehicular accident, lost all interest in her remaining family, her daughter, her grand-children, and also in her daily existence. She developed some alarming physical symptoms which she described rather casually. When I asked her if she thought much about dying, she gave me a long, slow look and replied, "I have no business here anymore."

Other interviewees have shown that they too need to find meaning in life, but more than this, meaning also in death. From the bereaved one hears again and again the anguished cry of "Why?," and because the need for meaning is so compelling, the listener may be tempted to engage in the search for an answer. In my interviews, I have heard of clergymen who, in an effort to be helpful, have been drawn into the question of, "Why?" and have replied that the loss may "have been for the best," or that it was "God's will," or that the answer would come through prayer. The problem with such answers is that they engender no communication and no rapport with the bereaved. I must confess that I have no simple answer to this question of providing new meaning in the life of the bereaved, but I have the conviction that this is the role *par excellence* of the clergyman. The ultimate meaning in life and death is not a problem which can be referred to the psychologist, psychiatrist or social worker; traditionally it is a problem for religion. In meeting this problem with a bereaved person, it has occurred to me that we may look profitably at some of the principals involved in psychotherapy.

In a typical psychotherapeutic situation, a patient comes in complaining of certain human problems in his life—relationship problems with his wife, his staff, or his children. He usually is absorbed in these complaints which he regards as external, and he is apt to review them without initial willingness to examine his own part in the problem. The good therapist listens quietly and tries to clarify in his own mind how the patient has contributed to the problem. He hopes that the patient eventually can be helped to see this contribution himself—will, in other words, develop "insight" into his difficulties. However, if the therapist tries to inject "insight" into the discussion before the patient himself is ready for it, the patient is apt to terminate treatment prematurely. A bridge must be built for the discussion of the patient's contribution to the situation, and that bridge is the *relationship,* the *rapport,* between the patient and therapist. That rapport also is the *vehicle* for the patient's emotional reorientation. As Alexander and French (1946) put it, "In many cases it is not a matter of insight stimulating or forcing the patient to an emotional reorientation, but rather one in which a very considerable preliminary emotional readjustment is necessary before insight is possible at all." This readjustment may be accomplished only through a foundation of rapport and trust.

Religious faith is similarly the outgrowth of trust directed toward a Supreme Being, as Martin Buber (1959) explains in "I and Thou." Religious faith cannot be engendered by pressure or exhortation, anymore than can insight. The psychotherapist is neither obligated nor able to inject insight where this is lacking nor is the clergyman obligated to inject faith where absent. An active listening to the complaints of the bereaved and an active acceptance are essential to building up that *trust* which must lie at the heart of faith. Like the psychotherapist, the clergyman's obligation is not to answer questions but to supply a nonjudgmental atmosphere in which questions may be raised. This means also a supportive relationship in the context of the example of his own faith, a faith strong enough to withstand the mourner's hostility and doubt. Thus, the clergyman, through his own faith, provides to the bewildered mourner a witness to what that can mean in time of crisis. Father Meissner (1969) says, "Faith provides illumination, direction and meaning to life." "If one cannot be the rose, one can live near it," goes the old saying. Here may lie the clue to why even atheists, despite their own disbelief, acknowledge that they have received solace from the words of a clergyman at the funeral.

Actually, more than providing an example, this means *sharing* the powerful force in life that faith is. Here is the real role of the clergyman, to testify to the bereaved that faith can give meaning to life when object and role are gone.

An example of the kind of meaning that comes through such faith was provided from personal experience. Some weeks before my husband died, when he (but not I) must have realized his time was short, I asked him while I was preoccupied with other matters if he believed in God. Without hesitation the reply came: "Oh, yes." With my attention immediately focused, I questioned again, "Now, how can you, a scientist, believe in God?" He reflected for a moment and, smiling gently, replied: "I will tell you. When I pat a dog on the head and he licks my hand, I think how little he understands of the food I give him, or of the world in which he lives, or of me. As his understanding is of me, so is mine of God. But I believe."

The real role of the clergyman is to share that kind of faith.

REFERENCES

Alexander, F., and French, T.M.: *Psychoanalytic Therapy: Principles and Practice.* New York, Ronald, 1946.

Averill, J.: Grief: its nature and significance. *Psychol Bull,* 70:721, 1968.

Buber, M.: *I and Thou.* New York, Scribner's, 1959.

Freud, S.: Mourning and melancholia. In Riviere, J. (Translator), *Collected Papers.* New York, Basic Books, 1959, vol. IV.

Meissner, W. W.: Notes on the psychology of faith. *Journal of Religion and Health,* 8:47, 1969.

Volkert, E. H., and Stanley, M.: Bereavement and mental health. In Fulton, R. (Ed.): *Death and Identity.* New York, Wiley and Sons, 1966.

CHAPTER 21

THE PASTOR'S PROBLEM WITH HIS OWN DISCOMFORT

Robert B. Reeves, Jr.

IN MINISTERING to the bereaved in the acute period of their grief, one of a pastor's main problems is his own acute discomfort. Grief is grievous to all who behold it, and especially so to those who are expected to assuage it, the pastor perhaps chief of all. He is supposed to bring calm and comfort, but in acute grief the bereaved are often well-nigh inconsolable, and he finds it very painful. What he does, trying to alleviate his own pain, sometimes only makes matters worse.

There seem to be three main ways in which pastors tend to handle their discomfort. One is to cultivate objectivity. Another, is the copious use of ritual. A third is the exercise of doctrine. These all have a place in pastoral practice, when they serve the needs of the bereaved. But when they are employed primarily, although perhaps unwittingly, to serve the pastor's need, they can often do more harm than good.

Objectivity takes many forms, ranging from cold, impassive aloofness to vapid chit-chat, with a business-like, no-nonsense manner somewhere in between. One of the grossest forms is the practice of one minister who invariably arrives at a grief-stricken household smoking a cigar. Less obviously unfeeling is the habit of another who is well-armed with little jokes and pleasantries. Still another form is the somber dead-pan, with speech in stately, measured cadences.

All of these are shields against emotional involvement. The grief of the bereaved is so painful to the pastor that he must wall it out. His demeanor is like a road-sign proclaiming "No Thoroughfare," or a warning notice on a gate, "Keep Out." Sometimes these kinds of objectivity are very effective in imposing momentary self-control upon the bereaved. By sheer refusal to be moved by grief, the pastor is able briefly to stifle it, do his thing, and go on his way. The outburst afterward, of course, finds him at a safe remove. Not many pastors are able to employ this kind of defense and stay very long in any one pastorate. The people soon become resentful at his lack of feeling, and find excuses to get rid of him. Parishioners want a pastor who will "bear their griefs" and "share their sorrows."

More acceptable is the defensive tactic that makes copious use of ritual. Here, at least, is a practice thoroughly in line with religious tradition. Who would criticize a clergyman for praying at a time of bereavement? Indeed, if he did not pray, he would probably be regarded as remiss.

Now, make no mistake—this is not to argue against the use of prayer or other rituals, age-tested in our heritage, when they serve the needs of the bereaved. There is a time and place for prayer. But a pastor must be very clear about whose needs are being served, when, in the face of acute and painful grief, his first impulse is to say, "Let us pray." At that moment, perhaps, the need of a bereaved person may be to curse God, and prayer could be to him like a club beating him into submission.

Ill-timed ritual of any sort, instead of bringing comfort, may only bring reproach. If a pastor, unconsciously defending himself from pain, imposes ritual without regard to the dynamics of the grieving process, he may temporarily produce what externally appears to be calm, but internally, in the bereaved, may be a deeper turmoil, with the hurt of loss compounded by guilt for forbidden anger.

The pastor's defensive use of prayer can be as grossly unfeeling as if he were to blow cigar smoke in the mourners' faces. Precisely because ritual is one of the things expected of a pastor, it can be one of the most insidious ways to protect himself against the pain of grief. He moves serenely in and out of the house of mourning, shielded by the rituals of his faith, and leaves the feelings of the grief-stricken in a shambles.

Also on the side of acceptability is the exercise of doctrine. To the anguished cry of the bereaved, "Why? Why? Why?" it is expected that the pastor will have an answer. Has he not prayed and studied long and hard, precisely to bring answers to people in distress?

Here again, it must at once be stated that doctrine, in some form, is a necessity of faith, and in the working-through of grief there is a time and place for the pastor to try to shed the light of his belief on the mourners' experience of loss. But the timing is of utmost importance, and in the acute stage of grief, it is simply not the time.

The cry, "Why?" uttered in the anguish of immediate loss, is not a plea for theologizing. It is, rather, more likely to be a cry of deep, hurt, angry despair, which must be voiced until it is spent. Often it is expressed as a bitter attack upon God, and the pastor, as God's representative, feels himself to be attacked. If he is not aware of the necessity for this angry attack as a part of grief-work, he may rise in self-defense to justify the ways of the Lord, clamp down upon the bereaved the teachings of the faith, wield doctrine as a bludgeon to silence the anger and the doubt. If he combines this exercise of doctrine with a sanctifying use of prayer, maintaining an emotional aloofness through it all, he may well impose an appearance of quietness upon the scene. But he leaves, not peace, but deep guilty and resentful resignation, which will only break out into anger again in some other, and probably more destructive, way.

What *should* the pastor do at a time of acute grief? Certainly, maintain some degree of objectivity, and be ready, when it is time, to offer prayer or interpret the teachings of the faith. *When it is time*—but until it is time, he must hold his peace, accept the discomfort and pain as his share in his parishioners' experience of loss, be to them one who feels with and understands their feelings, and helps them express even the worst of them, saying, in effect, by his supportive presence, that God, too, feels and understands.

The custom of allowing three days to pass between death and funeral is a sound one, because it gives time for the worst of the acute grief to be spent. If the pastor can give support to the bereaved during this period, then, at the funeral, the time will be much more nearly right for prayer and reaffirmation of the faith.

CHAPTER 22

ACUTE GRIEF, AESCULAPIAN AUTHORITY AND THE CLERGYMAN

Steven A. Moss

As the funeral procession halted a short distance beyond the main office, one of the cemetery's administrators came to our car and asked the bereaved, "Should the procession stay back at a distance while the coffin is removed from the hearse, or do you want to stand by the gravesite while this is done?"

The bereaved, with a confused expression on his face, turned to me and said, "Well, Rabbi, what should we do?"

This was the first funeral that I was attending in a clerical capacity and, unfortunately, I had not anticipated this question but, without more than a second for thought, I said decisively, "We will stay back!"

Two women were standing with me outside a hospital room in which their mother had just died. One of them turned to me and said, "Rabbi, what do I do now? My son is getting married on Sunday. Do we still have the wedding? Can I dance at it? Can we have music playing at all?"

At first, wanting to discover her feelings on the subject, I asked her, "What do you feel most comfortable doing? Are you from a reform or traditional background? Many of these questions pertain to customs and not necessarily laws."

With a distressed and confused expression on her face, she asked, "But Rabbi, what do I do, what do I do?"

I then answered decisively, "This is what you should do. . . ."

In both of these instances, it is obvious that the suddenly bereaved person, that is, one who is experiencing acute grief, would not and could not at this time make any decisions as to his or her proper and moral actions. Unsure of what to do, these people put themselves unequivocally into my hands. As suddenly as their grief had descended upon them, so had they suddenly invested me with the authority to tell them what actions would be proper and moral. They left the decisions up to me.

This type of authority is similar to what has been called the "Aesculapian Authority"[1] which is conferred upon the doctor, just as a king is vested with authority at his coronation. It is necessary for this type of authority to be conferred upon the doctor, especially at an early stage in his career, in order for him to be able to function properly vis à vis the community and the individual patient.

There are three component parts to Aesculapian Authority. They are termed sapiential, moral and charismatic. The doctor's sapiential authority is the "entitlement to be heard by the reason of knowledge or expertness." For example, this knowledge resides in a doctor because of his training and his knowledge of medicine. It is for this reason that the patient regards both a newly-qualified doctor as well as a more experienced man as having sapiential authority. The younger doctor may have more modern techniques, while the older doctor has more experience. But the patient must view and trust both, equally.

The second component, moral authority, is "the entitlement to control and direct by reason of the rightness and goodness according to the methods of the enterprise." The moral authority of the physician is sustained by the assumption that all he does for the patient is for the good of the patient. It is this aspect of the doctor's authority that has sanctioned pain, mutilation and even death—things which without this sanction would have been viewed as forms of torture.

The third component, called charismatic authority, is "the entitlement to control and direct by reason of God-given grace." The doctor is given this type of authority as he is working in a field which encompasses both life and death. These are areas which cannot be ascertained or controlled by knowledge (sapiential authority) alone.

Another professional bestowed with Aesculapian Authority—that is sapiential, moral and charismatic authority—is the clergyman, be he rabbi, minister or priest. The clergyman has been the beholder of

---

[1]See article by Miriam Siegler and Humphrey Osmond in *The Hastings Center Studies,* November 1972.

religious and allied knowledge, therefore he has sapiential authority. It has been assumed that his actions and decisions are for the good of his people, therefore he has moral authority. And since part of the religious realm involves the mysterious and the unknown, he has been invested with charismatic authority.

In an age when all authority—governmental, religious or social—is being questioned, this Aesculapian Authority has diminished in scope. Many people today (except for traditional orthodox followers) view the clergyman's sapiential authority as irrelevant, his moral authority as questionable, and his charismatic authority as deficient. I would suggest, however, that there is still one time when the clergyman is bestowed, unequivocally, with Aesculupian Authority, and that is in moments of acute grief and the accompanying time of funeral and mourning practices.

This confirmation of authority was seen in the instances mentioned above. And it occurred because 1. the bereaved, even if they had the knowledge of what to do, were in a state of shock and confusion which rendered them unable to make any proper and moral decisions; 2. they lacked traditional knowledge and looked to the clergyman for this knowledge, knowing that it was morally necessary, at least out of respect for the deceased, and with trust in the clergyman's ability to do the "right" thing; and 3. they felt vulnerable to outside stress and, therefore, put themselves into the clergyman's hands for protection in life as well as death. The clergyman, thus, became their rock who would do them no harm, who had knowledge of moral standards, and had connections with the mysterious and the unknown.

If these observations are correct and the clergyman is still bestowed with Aesculapian Authority during a person's time of acute grief, I believe that it is moral, ethical and necessary that when this authority is bestowed upon him, he must accept it with speed and diligence. During an age when all authority is questioned, the clergyman wants to step down from any authoritarian role ("priestliness"), but he cannot. I believe that the above noted instances demonstrate that to do so would leave people in a state of confusion during critical times in their lives when they desperately need direction. Therefore, the clergyman must resist the trend toward relinquishing of Aesculapian Authority in order to help people overcome their acute grief and be able to move out once again into the mainstream of life.

CHAPTER 23

SERVING WITH RESPECT AND COMPASSION

Vincent Fish

D URING THE three or four days immediately after death has become an explosive fact, a bereaved person is assaulted by three shock waves of acute grief. The first hits him at the moment when he accepts the fact that death is no longer a future possibility but a present reality. Within a very few hours, the second, long-drawn-out onslaught begins, as the body of the person he loves is first shown to him in its casket, and culminates when that body is shut away from him forever, as the casket is closed. Minutes later, in most cases, the third wave sweeps over him at the moment when all that is left of this one he held dear is put into the ground, and with terrible finality, covered with earth.

At each of these three moments of intense grief, the bereaved person, if he is fortunate, has two professional people with him whose chief purpose is to lessen the impact of his acute grief. The first of these, the clergyman, is, hopefully, well-known to him, a familiar source of help in time of trouble. The second, the funeral director, is usually a stranger, at least in his present capacity, yet his skill and his sense of vocation determine whether the bereaved person will find the events of these days a source of strength rather than a drain on his already overburdened resources. The important point, however, is that if the clergyman and the funeral director are to be of greatest service to a bereaved person, they must work together as chief comforters. If either man is inept in his own area of responsibility, he will cause a disproportionate amount of needless pain and increase the burden of acute grief which the bereaved person must necessarily bear.

The clergyman and the funeral director, then, individually and as a working unity, serve the bereaved person while he is numbed by the shock of the first wave of acute grief, that which follows the actual moment of death. The clergyman, if possible, should be present at the time of death to comfort the dying person and to console those who mourn. Long before death occurs or is even imminent, he will have encouraged the family to choose a funeral director, purchase a burial plot, and inform all those concerned of their specific wishes in connection with the wake and the funeral. If such decisions have not been made, it is the responsibility of the clergyman to help the family to select a funeral director and to remain with them, to assist them, as they make all the necessary arrangements. Furthermore, one of the clergyman's functions is to be sure that the family's wishes and his own requirements are communicated clearly to the funeral director. No matter how much the funeral director may try to comply with these requests, how well he is able to do so depends completely on the accuracy of the information he is given.

On the other hand, the funeral director's chief responsibility at this time, as he concerns himself with the innumerable details connected with the physical preparation of a body for the rites which accompany its burial and for the burial itself, involves the communication of respect and compassion. He will be helpful to those who are suffering the initial acute grief of bereavement in direct proportion to his ability to communicate his compassion, not only for the mourners, but for the person whose body is in his hands.

In their relationship with the mourners, morticians, like all professional people, display a variety of personalities. They possess differing concepts of their role as comforters and aides. In my experience, there have been undertakers, as they used to be called, who wore frock coats and Vandyke beards. There have been those with unshaven faces, who wore rumpled clothing and unpolished shoes. Mannerisms have run the gamut from the obsequious to the forcedly jovial. It is gratifying that these extremes are seldom encountered today. Yet there are always those who lack skill in dealing with the distraught, and this deficiency is glaringly apparent whenever individuals of this sort confer with a bereaved family. The gathering of the proper information and the filling out of necessary forms can be done with gentleness, and need take only a short time. Yet I have witnessed the reactions of mourners to cold, depersonalized references to the person who has just died and to the unmerciful dragging out of the entire procedure by inept and insensitive men.

Even worse than lack of skill, however, is the kind of insensitivity which can reveal a thinly-veiled desire to exploit a tragic situation. Unthinkably callous though certain behavior is, the worst of all the evils which may be perpetrated by a funeral director are those which arise from his failure to treat the body of a beloved person respectfully, tenderly and reverently. There are many people who have a horror of relinquishing the bodies of their loved ones to the care of a funeral director. In one undertaking establishment, for example, I came upon the naked body of a woman to whom I had a short time before given the Last Rites. When I expressed my disapproval of such gross indifference to the dignity of a body which had been the dwelling place of a human soul, I was met with a shrug and a grimace. It was necessary for me to insist that the body be covered.

I can remember stories told by a friend of mine who, many years ago, lived next door to a funeral home. Whenever the body of a young woman was brought in, my friend was invited to view the body, and it became the object of obscene jokes. I have known of a clergyman who was supplied with photographs of accident victims by a funeral director. Unusual though these situations may be, many persons are honestly and justifiably uneasy about what goes on with the bodies of their loved ones. One can conclude only that there are disturbed and cruel people in every profession.

It is understandable that in those professions where life's tragedies are encountered daily, some sort of defense mechanism is necessary. Doctors and nurses also feel this need, as do clergymen. But this fact does not excuse flagrant disrespect for a human body. When professionals are guided by humane principles, the care that they give is sincere and beneficial.

My many experiences with funeral directors have caused me to have great respect and gratitude for their ministrations. I remember the overwhelming love I felt for one man who had come to the hospital toward the end of a long night to get the body of a tiny child. When he arrived, I was with the parents who had only just consented to leave their child's bedside and were standing in the hall. Nothing I could have done would have prevented their watching as their baby was taken away. My fear at this moment of what their reaction to the funeral director might be was almost impossible to contain, but I need not have worried. This compassionate man had come equipped only with a large, soft crib blanket. Without speaking, he went into the room, wrapped the small body in the blanket and, cradling it tenderly in his arms, stepped into the hall. Then, still silent, he stopped in front of the parents. His face, like theirs, was suffused with grief. They moved aside, and with his shoulders hunched protectively over his burden, he walked away from them, down the hall and out of sight. With their faces wet by their first tears, they let him go. So the funeral director and the clergyman, if they are both compassionate men, can serve those who are struggling in the first wave of acute grief.

Initial shock at the fact that death has occurred is quickly replaced by a second wave of grief, of longer duration and greater complexity than the first. At the same time, the bereaved person is attempting to cope with the events which precede the funeral. The exact course of these events depends on the wishes of the family members, who make their decisions according to their own religious, cultural and even community traditions. But often the members of a single family represent a variety of backgrounds. In each tradition represented, there are values that are cherished and not easily relinquished. Prejudices also exist and make for many uncomfortable moments while funeral arrangements are discussed and decisions are made. Stricken with grief, physical and mental weariness, and the inability to deal with so many crucial problems, those already suffering the most severely can also find themselves embroiled in family arguments in which cruel words, the reopening of old wounds, and the revelation of hidden resentments inflict injuries which are very slow to heal. At this juncture, the skill of both the funeral director and the clergyman are vitally necessary and put to the test. Above all, they must support each other if they are to relieve the grief-stricken of some of the pain inherent in these crises.

The clergyman's responsibility during this period is to be with the family as much as he can. One major cause of dissension is lack of knowledge of procedures, combined with heightened sensitivity. The clergyman is the authority here, and all can turn to him with confidence if he is present.

The funeral director's function is to take care of the practical details of this period unobtrusively, to foresee and prevent, if possible, the jarring, disruptive episodes, to provide for the needs of the mourners, and to assist the clergyman at the funeral service and the interment. Unfortunately, too many clergymen consider that their only function is to conduct these services, and the funeral director, in addition to his other duties, must take over the clerical role of chief comforter.

In an ideal situation, such a necessity would not arise. The clergyman and the funeral director would know each other, and each would understand and respect the work of the other. They would be able to communicate by a glance and be responsive to the smallest gesture, with one purpose only, to minister to the bereaved in his moments of acute grief.

During this period, there are two rending crises: the moment when the bereaved person first sees the body in the casket, and the moment when the casket must be closed. No matter how great the mortician's skill, the bereaved person knows with a certainty that this body is not the person he loves but in the truest sense, his "remains." The shock of this realization precipitates an intensity of grief which cannot be comforted by platitudes, but only by reserves of faith. The mortician has done what he can. At this moment, he can do no more. It remains for the clergyman to stand with the suffering soul and to comfort him, not by removing his burden of grief, but by sharing it, carrying it as his own, by suffering with the sufferer. This is what compassion is. This is the work of the clergy.

Eventually the moment must come when the casket is closed, and the second crisis of this period must be faced. The timing of this event poses the most difficult problem for undertaker and clergyman, depending upon the religious convictions of the clergyman and those who mourn. As an Episcopal Priest, it is my duty to insist that the casket be closed before the religious service in the funeral home begins. The theological reason for this is that the body is now in the hands of Christ's Church, and because it was once the tabernacle of the Holy

Spirit, it will have a Christian burial. In the Church Catholic, this concept is understood, and in other Christian sects as well. Yet, the closing of the casket *after* the service is still insisted upon by some persons who cannot see either the religious or the psychological reasons for having it closed.

The third wave of acute grief is that much-dreaded moment when the casket is lowered into the grave. Nothing underscores the finality of death of the body more than the actual burial. It is extremely important that this procedure be accomplished with skill, brevity and smoothness, for this occasion will be etched on the memories of the mourners for a long time. The weather often conspires to make problems, and these must be anticipated and means found to reduce them to a minimum. All of this is the responsibility of the funeral director.

The graveside service, the clergyman's responsibility, should be very brief, and the mourners on their way as quickly as possible to the place where refreshments are usually provided. This social gathering helps to reduce tensions and to ease the bereaved person into the life that must be lived without the deceased.

The three shock waves of acute grief can be met by the mourners, helped by the dedicated teamwork of the clergyman and the mortician. Skill born of experience, plus compassion, dedication, respect and unity of purpose, can be the means by which the bereaved person begins more easily to accept the changed pattern of his life. Thus, the clergyman and the funeral director, each facing his own challenge in ministering to those who mourn, can find by supporting each other's ministry a double strength.

PART THREE

THE FUNERAL AND THOSE WHO SURVIVE

CHAPTER 24

A VIEW OF LIFE AND DEATH

Howard C. Raether and Robert C. Slater

THERE ARE CHILDREN at the age of ten who experience the death of a parent or a sibling, or perhaps even a schoolmate. They feel acute grief and reach out for help.

Many persons get to be 16 without experiencing the death of someone close to them. But when they do, it is a traumatic experience, especially if the death of a parent, a brother or sister or a close friend is sudden.

By age 25, most young women who are going to rear a family have had a child or children. Sometimes a child is born dead or dies shortly thereafter or lives a few months to become a victim of sudden infant death. The grief in these circumstances is most destructive for all members of the bereaved family. Psychiatrists have suggested that the mother should be able to hold the dead child, especially in the case of newborn infants. And a funeral should be held.[1]

At ages 30 and 40, people experience death—sometimes of grandparents, parents, children, other relatives, or other persons with whom they have had a close association.

By the time they get to be 50, almost every individual has been exposed to a death and the acute grief that comes with it. And as long as the grief can be shared with a spouse, that spouse is someone to help with mourning, regardless of what the loss might have been.

[1]An organization for the parents of sudden infant death victims has been formed. Other groups also bring together young mothers who have experienced the death of an infant or a very young child. These women have a bond between them, and they invite others into their fold to help as they share their sorrow and their experiences.

But when the spouse dies, it is as Dr. Thomas H. Holmes, Dr. E. S. Paykel and Alvin Toffler have said—such a death has the greatest impact of any of life's events and usually the grief is most acute.

In November, 1972, Herman B. Brotman, Assistant to the Commissioner for Statistics and Analysis in the Administration on Aging in the Department of Health, Education and Welfare, addressed the annual meeting of the American Public Health Association on "The Fastest Growing Minority: The Aging."

Mr. Brotman made a cogent point—that there seems to be no place in our country for those over 65. But such need not be the case. It is true, as Mr. Brotman reported, that the multigeneration family has been supplanted by the nuclear family. People of different ages live in separate households. In parallel to this, the individually owned business where the head of the family had the "wealth" has frequently been replaced by corporate ownership and a wage economy in crowded urban settings. Young people are prepared to earn a living by formal education rather than by apprenticeships and association with their parents. Mr. Brotman has suggested further that there are three categories of age differences among individuals: those between the young and the old as group averages; those between different individuals within the older group; and those within a single older individual.

All of these sometimes are falsely related to aging. An example thereof is the picture of the decrepit doddering oldster. This is a gross exaggeration and completely misleading. Most older people can manage in the community if society permits. And, the funeral for them can be meaningful.

In the end, it comes down to the younger group's willingness to share on the ordering of our total priorities. In summary, Mr. Brotman indicated that group data can supply only a general or average background. But, someday someone in a specific community will have to apply this knowledge to specific people at specific times to meet specific needs in a specific environment.

Why all this talk of the aging? Simply because the deaths of people over 65 years of age make up almost 70 percent of the deaths which occur annually in our country. And as time goes on, the percentage is going to be even greater.

"Out of sight—out of mind—out of mind and out of heart—out of sentiment" need not be a truism for most of the elderly people who die. Just as there are specific needs which these people have when they are living, there are needs which those have who survive their deaths, be they members of their family, individuals within or outside the family with an attachment to the elderly person, or individuals in a group with which the person associated during the last years or months of his or her life. Sometimes the survivors represent different places and/or periods in the deceased person's life—the family home or town, a nearby extended care facility, or a distant place of retirement. For this reason, an adaptive funeral, or even two services at different places, may be necessary to meet the needs of all the survivors.

The young people of today are also important to those concerned with aging and death because many of the young will be involved in determining what kind of funeral, if any, the older person who has died shall have. Sensitivity to the needs of others, willingness to share and the priority which the young people give the funeral will help determine not only what will be provided for the older generation but also will help determine the post-death activities of those now in their formative years. It is essential that those who believe in the values of the funeral acquaint the young with such values. Funeral directors should show them the facilities they have to offer and the services available. They should impress upon those who have not experienced a death that the services can be adaptive to the death of an octogenarian as well as to the life-style of a young man killed in an automobile accident, a young bride and groom killed on their honeymoon or a young adult dead of a drug overdose.

At this point, it is essential to distinguish between two words— "needs" and "wants." No one really "wants" to arrange a funeral because it implies that someone close to him—often someone very much loved—has died. However, there are needs present in most persons following a death. Personal motivation and grief therapy can be explained by using the mode of motivation structure of A. H. Maslow and G. Allport.

The motivation structure can be applied to the situation which follows death by showing how needs, not wants, are met through the process of funeralization. There is the *physiological* need operative in funeral service decisions as related to tears, dryness of throat, difficulty of expression or an upset or hollow feeling in the stomach. A proper climate for mourning provided by the funeral and the funeral director helps meet such physiological needs.

Following death, those who survive need to feel *secure*. They know they are hurt and hope that their hurt will be one that heals. They hope that what they do through the process of body image for others some day will be done for them and in this way gain a sense of security in the face of the unknown.

Then there are the *social* needs. During the time of the funeral, the sorrows of one do become the sorrows of all. Most times, the funeral is the only ceremony in our culture to which none are invited but all may come. People-to-people needs are always important but perhaps are most essential during times of grief. And through it all, another aspect is at work as the survivors wonder if their actions and arrangements will have community approval and acceptance.

Ego and *love* needs are next. It is well said that the funeral provides one of the few opportunities when love is given and not expected in return.

Finally, in the Maslow-Allport pyramid, there is *self-actualization*. Each person in arranging a funeral wants to become the total person he is capable of becoming. There are no second-chance funerals. That which is done cannot be undone. By the same token, that which is not done shall forever be so.

Self-actualization allows individuals to go beyond "self" to "other." As they do so, they will find a larger meaning of their own life by the actualization of what they have done through the funeral in commemorating a life that has been lived.

As we go from "self" to "other," there are factors which involve status and power within the United States. Shortly after our country had its beginning, the ownership of *land* was a status symbol and a basis for *power* of individuals or institutions. Then there was a shift from the impact of the landowner to that of the individual or the institution that had the *capital*.

To a certain extent this is important, but two things have somewhat changed the picture. In the first place, there is greater affluence among Americans today than ever before. But while the wealthy can do more things more often than people without a large amount of capital, to a degree their overall impact on our society is lessening.

Another factor is the truism that women in this country, having inherited substantial estates from husbands who have predeceased them, control many of the assets of this country. But the money for most of them serves as security, rather than as a means of influence.

The true *power* impact in the United States lies with those who have the *information*—right or wrong—and who disseminate it—properly or improperly. The events of the past few years have shown this to be true—even as to grief and its resolution.

Proper information as to acute grief and the funeral is essential. Interest therein is to be commended, and one should be exhorted to use it at every possible opportunity. There are leaders now who in order to succeed or to have their causes successful must be able to comprehend what people are thinking and must be able to lead on behalf of groups so that in the years which lie ahead, there will be progress toward humanitarian understanding.

In conclusion, the following poem, received from The League of Hospital Friends in England, is cited. Supposedly written by an elderly lady who had been a psychogeriatric patient in a hospital, it was found in her locker after she died.

Cry From a Crabbit Old Woman

What do you see, nurses, what do you see?
Are you thinking when you are looking at me—
A crabbit old woman, not very wise,
Uncertain of habit, with far away eyes,
Who dribbles her food and makes no reply
When you say in a loud voice, "I do wish you'd try,"
Who seems not to notice the things that you do
And forever is losing a stocking or shoe;
Who unresisting or not, lets you do as you will
With bathing and feeding, the long day to fill.
Is that what you are thinking, is that what you see?
Then open your eyes, nurse, you're not looking at me.

I'll tell you who I am as I sit here so still,
As I do as your bidding, as I eat at your will.
I'm a small child of ten with a father and mother,
Brothers and sisters, who love one another;
A young girl of 16 with wings on her feet,
Dreaming that soon now a lover she'll meet;
A bride soon at 20—my heart gives a leap,
Remembering the vows that I promised to keep;
At 25 now I have young of my own
Who need me to build a secure, happy home;
A woman of 30, my young now grow fast,
Bound to each other with ties that should last;
At 40, my young sons have grown and are gone,
But my man's beside me to see I don't mourn.
At 50, once more babies play round my knee,
Again we know children, my loved one and me.
Dark days are upon me, my husband is dead,
I look at the future, I shudder with dread.
For my young are all rearing young of their own,
And I think of the years and the love that I've known.
I'm an old woman now and nature is cruel—
'Tis her jest to make old age look a fool.
The body it crumbles, grace and vigor depart,
There is now a stone where I once had a heart;
But inside this old carcass a young girl still dwells,
And now and again my battered heart swells.
I remember the joys, I remember the pain,
And I'm loving and living life over again.
I think of the years all too few—gone too fast,
And accept the stark fact that nothing can last.
So open your eyes, nurse, open and see
Not a crabbit old woman, look closer—see ME.

CHAPTER 25

IN A HOSPITAL ROOM – AND AFTER

(December 26, 1973)

FLORENCE M. HETZLER

MAY, MRS. DAVID MCCALL, or what was left of this lovely lady, was placed inside the skin of planet earth today. Her last move, a passive one. In dense fog and persistent slate rain, the hearse brought her remains to St. John's Church. Behind the hearse, there followed one lone single slow-moving sleek black car, carrying one friend. Paid bearers bore the light grey coffin to the church aisle. A Magritte, Dali or Tanguy funeral. Either Surrealistic, or perhaps a Marcel Duchamp Dadaist creation, a sociological problem, something alien to the odor of contextual life.

Before the service, I met a lady, Mrs. Peters, who would *substitute* for the regular organist, who had come all the way from Brooklyn "for the *big* services." Her husband, a retired organist, would sing for this service. Lit candles, Christmas decorations and a large crèche formed the backdrop for the last act in the drama of Mrs. McCall's life. The Yule greens reminded me of the flowing pine greens which had been a neighbor's "welcome home" gift to me upon my return from the hospital, and which I had removed and taken with me to the funeral parlor on Christmas Eve when I went to show honor to the past and present of this lady and to her future in my heart, my memory, my being, and the being of those with whom I share my experience.

To my delight, the undertaker (what a feeble word!), instead of placing my ribboned greens behind the coffin in that vast room, put them right on top of it. They became part of that whole work of art,

[209]

that memorial to life—to a former, present and future form of life. Now Mrs. McCall's life, a vicarious one in the lives of those whom her presence had changed, could be memorialized.

There were few of her peers living. She told me on Saturday that she would be 85 on Valentine's Day. Dr. David McCall, her husband, had died the year before. The two had gone together several years ago to a nursing home where they arrived stripped of their belongings, but with one another (and that is all that really mattered). His funeral services had been held in the same church. Perhaps his coffin had covered the same tiles in the church, had made similar shadows. Oh yes, May, in her great pain, about 3 A.M. of the day of her death, had even called her husband's name. She had gotten out of bed twice that morning. Tried to gag herself with her whole hand to get rid of her stomach pain. Rang for the nurse, complained of gas pain, only to be told in icy forcefulness that she was not the only patient on the floor and should relax and go to sleep. When I mentioned that she had truly complained of great pain for a long time, the nurse retorted, "We have to be very hard and cold about these people."

Dying is an act, often a long one, punctuated with many ancillary moves. With thoughts sliced, pierced with harshness, May had not complained of pain from Tuesday, December 19 to Thursday, December 21. But Thursday morning about 5 A.M., she rang for the nurse. She rang again, because she was afraid of wetting the bed. No, not that really, but of the ensuing, "Why did you wet yourself? Why?" And then came the sweet dignity that even the ravages of dying could not diminish, "Pardon me, please pardon me. I did not want to do it." A similar conversation had taken place when I walked in on Monday, December 18, a similar dialogue hit my ears as I doffed my parka and slacks, donned the wrinkly, tieless hospital gown and put myself to bed.

That Thursday morning, the aide who responded to her bell light complained that the ring would wake up others. "Why did you ring twice? Why?" Usually, the "desk" would speak on the intercom to ask what was wanted. When the aide appeared, I explained quietly that no sound had been transmitted into the room. She then started to argue with me. I begged her not to raise her voice in front of the lady. She increased her thrust; I got out of bed and went into the corridor, the blank white cold stillness of 5 A.M., hoping she would continue her explosion out there. When the nurse arrived (the aide had forgotten to turn out the bell light), the aide went on relentlessly. I finally returned to bed. The castigating noise departed.

Then, my dear, defenseless roommate complained of terrible chest pain. Now I trembled as I thought of ringing for help. I rang anyway. A risk worthwhile. Help came. A nurse came; then she sent for an intern. Mrs. McCall said it was pain just like she had at the "home" before she came to the hospital. Yes, there it was. Then came the oxygen, the jabs of demerol, and several hours later, a priest who had never seen her before. He called her name several times. No answer: she was demeroled. Out. He blessed her and left.

There are so many good, caring nurses, but the bad ones can do so much harm. Some plants even may have more sensibility to death and to dying than do some nurses. But there were no plants in our hospital room; she had none, because no one knew where she was, other than those at the "home"; there were no children, no husband. And no one knew where I was; I did not want my students and friends to know what had happened to me or my Christmas plans. If we had had sensitive plants in that room, I think they would have shuddered and died.

The day after Mrs. McCall's attack was Thursday, and with that day came a lovely nurse, a Mrs. Booth. Before I went to the Operating Room for a cystoscopy and retrograde pyelogram, I wondered how my friend would be, if, indeed, she *would* be, when I returned. She was still there, and her pain was worse, her face ashen.

And that noon, a Mrs. Stanton of the OR Housekeeping Department, who also had worked at the nursing home where Mrs. McCall had been, came during a lunch break to arrange May's hair and to encourage her to eat.

I had sent for the Patient Service Representative of the hospital to praise Mrs. Stanton, and to see if the aide who had been so heartless might be spoken to, in order that some other defenseless, dying person might not have to undergo the same knifing. The representative turned out to be someone whose name I had often heard and whose picture I had often seen in an apartment in my own building. And she had heard of me from a friend who had long been night supervisor at the hospital. Small world! We had a delightful talk. We had met and over what seemed something very worthwhile, namely, sensitivity to the defenseless dying.

Friday evening, one of my students, a candy striper, caught sight of me as I walked in the hall. She and her friend came into the room, and we talked with Mrs. McCall who spoke of her husband, of having taught school, the grades, of Cornell Medical where her husband had trained and of the Orangeburg Mental Hospital where he had practiced.

That night May said her prayers. But it was to be a night of excruciating pain, a night of hell, of bellringing for water, for pain soothing—all, I feel, excuses for attention, for a hand to hold, for love, for touch. She got out of bed twice that night. She was trying to get my cardboard water pitcher. Poor soul. She thought it a container for urination. She was afraid to ring for the aide and afraid to wet the bed. Her night was one of living torture, a long night's journey into day; the night nurse was cold, so unwilling to give any compassion, perhaps unable to, perhaps unaware of the beauty of her profession, of its potentialities, of her own capabilities, of the vibrations between human beings. Oh, what she lost in not sharing even one sentence with this dignified lady, dying with so much indignity and so many indignities!

Would negative euthanasia have been better? Or positive euthanasia? Or would that have been murder? And if so, at what point? Or would she have been wiser to have taken her own life? The problems of aging and dying! There are so many unanswered questions here.

Then, the 7 A.M. Saturday shift brought the coldest nurses yet, two icy blondes. "What's the matter, Mrs. McCall?" "Oh, the pain in my stomach, oh, the pain, please." Loudly, the nurse barked, "Do you want an enema?" Those poor bones, that poor intestine. I went for a walk in the hall. There I met an assistant supervisor whose presence I did not think accidental. I told her that I would be leaving that day and wanted to know if I might be informed when Mrs. McCall died since I wanted to attend her funeral. The nurse snarled: "She is not going to die for a long time." And off she went.

After my walk, a fellow patient and I chatted outside my door. He came in for a moment and spoke with my roommate. I explained to him and to her that I was being discharged but would come back and be her visitor on Sunday and that the friend who was coming to pick me up was going to bring a small Christmas tree for Mrs. McCall's Christmas, her last one, I was thinking to myself. I had learned that she had just begun to recover from the depression of her husband's death when she became ill. They had been married for over 60 years and he was over 90 years of age when he died.

Before going for final x-rays that morning, I explained to my fearful, loving roommate that I would be back. She held out her hands and said: "What will I do without you? I shall miss you. They will kill me, you know." I wondered who would ring to have her teeth picked up from the floor. They had fallen during breakfast that morning, and she was so afraid that they had broken. I wondered who would love her, who would be with her when the end came. Her face was so beautiful; her eyes begged for sharing as they faced the annihilation and nothingness of her personal existence. I held her hand and promised to be back, got into my waiting wheelchair and was off.

A volunteer wheeled me from x-rays back to the room. The friend who was to pick me up was not in my room. Neither was Mrs. McCall, whom I wanted my friend to meet and for whom she was bringing the little Christmas tree. Both beds were stripped, mine because I was going home, and hers? Such emptiness. Had they moved her to where they could yell at her more freely, to where she might ring and ring and ring, with no one obliged to answer? Where was she? I looked into the corridor and saw my friend and her Christmas tree and candle. She seemed quiet, but I felt it was because she found the room so full of debris; dirty tissues on the floor, dust balls, a paper cup, and a lone statue of body lotion on Mrs. McCall's nightstand.

A flip blonde nurse came in for something. I explained that I had promised to visit Mrs. McCall on Sunday and wondered where her new room was. "They moved her to a ward and she can't have any visitors," she answered and walked away. I went to the nursing station and asked a second nurse how I might visit Mrs. McCall. In automatic, unfeeling sounds, she pontificated: "You won't be able to visit Mrs. McCall because she is DEAD." Dead—oh, I am so glad for her sake, I thought. So very glad. She is dead. Dead, all gone—bed stripped; but they could not remove all the vestiges of the dignity of that lady and of the cherished addition of her being to my world. So brave—she knew she was all alone, yet, kept saying after the merest gesture of help, "Oh, you are so kind."

I remembered that that morning I had seen her praying. Thinking she had finished, I said, "Did you ask God to take care of you, dear?" After a few minutes she sparkled a bright, "You bet I did. I didn't answer you right away because I didn't want to interrupt my talking to Him. You understand." And now she was *gone*. Even if one does not believe in personal immortality, life is worthwhile. People add to people and this chain is never totally broken. No, never.

At this point, I wondered where the funeral began and where it ended. We often think of a funeral as *the service*. The "viewing," that harsh word, and the burial are often considered apart from the funeral. If that, then what are they? It seems that as soon as people die, their treatment is alien to life, utterly alien. There is a package deal applied to all, like putting mustard on hotdogs, jello, mangoes and artichoke hearts, except, of course, some get bigger blobs of mustard because they can afford more, or because they want people to think they can afford it. People, who have never seen the deceased, lug the box into a church where a "minister," who often has to check the person's name, runs through a form speech—except that he changes the name. A form speech, like a form letter.

Yes, the funeral. What would hers be like? Where would hers be? What would a funeral be like with no relatives, with no one attending, with paid pallbearers, and with paid pallbearers at Christmas time? I called the nursing home, secured the name of the only person, a distant relative, I guess, who could tell me the name of the funeral home. Nursing home. Funeral home. We seem to need the word "home," even though its use can become a habit. I hung up. (That, too, is a strange expression.) I sat on my bed. I thought of cosmic change, of personal change. Truly, the faults and changes of age and deterioration were parts of life's very nature. There is a beauty to be seen in wilting, in color and cell changing in the autumn of life, and in its emergence into winter instead of into spring. There really is beauty in injured being, in wounded ontology. Our feebleness, our fragility is noble, as we live, as we live-die; let us share one another's living-dying, our quality. In doing so, we enhance ourselves, the quality of our being. In going out to others, we come in to ourselves; our destination is man.

Saturday night I called the eighty-five-year-old man whose name I had obtained from the nursing home. He had just been told the time of the funeral by the undertaker. The news was late in coming because the doctor had called him to ask for permission for an autopsy to determine the cause of death. Ye gods, her being piecemealed on the terrestrial skin was not over. The doctor had said that they had no idea of what she died. Part of the etiology may well have been that she was "scared to death," that she was old, that she had been pushed over the brink by poor care, or that she may have decided her time to die, willed death and died. She feared those who should have helped her face her fear of dying, the fear of her own emptiness and of her progression toward the final depletion of her terrestrial personal existence. She had fought so well, so well alone, so well all alone. She may have chosen her death in a final choice of authentic existence, of the validation of her humanity, of her personhood.

That Christmas Eve of 1973 in the funeral "home" will be difficult to forget. There she was, in the biggest room in the establishment, with maybe 250 open, gaping, yawning funeral parlor chairs facing her. Why that big room? Was there estate money to be used up? The coffin was, to my surprise, open. The greens on the coffin, the ones that had been given to welcome me home, were now a goodbye gesture on her pale grey box. But the whole ambiance was an aesthetic incongruity; it was, indeed, unaesthetic, alien to life, like listening to a great symphony performed in a casino where all the one-armed bandits are being "worked." The barren, bulky starkness of that room and the gentility of May's soul were incongruous, almost irrelevant, discordant, mutually insulting.

I took a last look at the total scene that contained this little lady, so obviously alone, yet somehow containing the room with her majesty. In life, I feel, she must have been a fine woman, warm and bright, a good wife to a dedicated psychiatrist. I signed the blank register and left. On Christmas Eve, the street was almost empty and dark. Not a Christmas light. Energy crisis? Apathy? Fear?

I returned to my empty apartment, 46 steps up, and to my door minus its decoration, turned the key, went in, prepared a big mug of coffee, and sat down to think—this time about my own death, my own funeral. I am unmarried—live alone. Will I die alone? Who will help me die? Will I be brave and kind, saying "thank you, you are so kind," to the one who will pick up my false teeth? Will I grin and bear it when someone growls if I ring twice, instead of once, hoping for someone to love me in pain, love both me and my pain, knowing full well that they will not or maybe cannot take the pain away.

And so Christmas Eve passed into Christmas Day—and then the morning after Christmas Day, the day of the funeral of that lovely being who had been treated like a pariah, of the lady who uncosseted faced the almost Augean fact of death, the dear who longed for the hegira from her hospital bed—back to the nursing home, only to be told by the doctors "in a couple of days." It had not all been all bad. There had been fleeting moments of personhood. There were the visits of Mrs. Stanton, the aide who stopped by to give some love; there was the one lovely nurse, Mrs. Booth; there was the candy striper and her friend who came in for a chat. But these moments could be tucked into a few hours.

But the funeral *looked* nice, like a tapestry, perhaps like "Sight," in the "Lady With the Unicorn" series from the Cluny Museum in Paris. Yet, there was the air of Duchamp. There was that one old gentleman in front to the left of the coffin, the priest who had only recently known her, the substitute organist, the substitute singer, the paid pallbearers who never knew her, and me, into whose life May had come for barely four days. Christmas hymns were sung; the coffin drape was white not black; the mass, that of the resurrection; Christmas wreaths symbolized a kind of happiness. There reigned an aesthetics of silence; there were now rest and painlessness. I thought of her raw back, the debris under her bed, the fallen drinking straw, the mattress ticking of her bared bed and of mine, of the final unheard sigh. This is the way the world ends, not with a bang but a gasp!!!

Mrs. McCall's impersonal, strange, almost meaningless funeral, except for the rite and myth reality, will always be a dividend for me, a star twinkling in space, a monument to human ignorance and to the finitude of the funeral "arrangers" but also to the fact of her having transcended all of this.

". . . on ne voit bien qu'avec le coeur. L'essentiel est invisible pour les yeux."[1]

---

[1]"We really see only with the heart. What is essential cannot be seen by the eyes." The message of the fox to the Little Prince. St. Exupery, *Le Petit Prince* (New York, Houghton Mifflin Company, 1946), p. 47.

CHAPTER 26

LOSS AND GRIEF IN THE LATER YEARS OF LIFE

James O. Carpenter

M ODERN SOCIETY EMBODIES a death-denying, age-defying atmosphere. This orientation in the general public is reinforced by the fact that most deaths in the United States today occur within institutional walls where the realities of dying and ultimate extinction are sequestered and hidden from public view. In advanced old age, some older persons are socially devalued by society, find themselves without a meaningful role, suffer recurrent losses and bereavements and, perhaps, ultimately afflicted with chronic and serious illnesses, spend their terminal days in the "vegetable garden" of some long-term facility. The youth-oriented, gerontophobic views of society, in turn, contribute to the shortage of health and related social services required by older people in need, including those older people experiencing the detrimental effects of recurrent bereavements over the loss of loved ones, objects and social status. Those older people who find themselves socially devalued and isolated, in turn, experience the greatest emotional and social deprivation. They may experience depression and view themselves and life in general in negative terms. Indeed, while the younger person presumably looks to the future, the older person is seen as engaging in a life review; a process which, in some instances, may parallel social withdrawal eventuating, in its extreme, in social death.

A first step in overcoming our aversions to death and grief in order to meet the health needs of the dying and bereaved is to peer into the darkness, examining the complex, painful strands of bereavement.

THE PROCESS OF BEREAVEMENT

That bereavement is a complex process has been well documented. The experience of loss accompanying the death of a loved one in which the beloved object, and indeed an integral portion of the survivor's being is ripped away through death, leads to a grief syndrome entailing a series of emotional, physical and social changes in the bereaved. The loss of a loved one is, thus, the loss of an integral portion of the survivor's former being. In the loss of a loved one, we, perhaps, lose something of ourselves. Each must cope with the loss through grief and resolution of such loss, perhaps finding harbor in remembrance of things past. At the same time, the societal impulse toward death denial and the shortage of socially approved means for the expression of grief may enhance difficulties in coping with this loss.

Bereavement appears to entail a number of stages through which the bereaved pass in coping with their great loss. These stages may consist of shock, intense grief and recovery or, in other terms, angry protest, disorganization and reorganization (Blank, 1969; Paul, 1969; Gorer, 1965; Bowlby, 1961). Each stage, in turn, entails complex social, emotional and somatic reactions is the bereaved, some of which have been outlined by Parkes in his study of London widows (1970):

> The most clear-cut transition is likely to be that between the first (numbness) phase and the second. This takes place a few hours to a few days after the bereavement. The second phase has two independent components, "Yearning" and "Protest." "Yearning" is characterized by pangs of intense yearning or pining which are thought to be the principal feature of the urge to unite with the lost object. "Protest" is seen as the restless irritability or bitterness towards others or the self. These components are at their peak during the second to fourth weeks of bereavement and then begin to decline. Tearfulness and the autonomic accompaniments of acute anxiety are the first features to decline; the degree of preoccupation with memories of the lost husband, the sense of his presence, the avoidance of reminders, irritability, and general restlessness and tension decline much more gradually throughout the whole of the first year. . . . As the intensity of yearning and protest diminishes, apathy and aimlessness are the rule and it is this disinclination to look into the future or to see any purpose in life which characterizes the third phase of grief, "Disorganization." . . . About two thirds of the widows described here were still in this phase at the end of their first year of bereavement.

On a more general plane, angry protest, disorganization and reorganization may characterize the stages of bereavement (Bowlby, 1961). Angry protest entails an overwhelming desire to retrieve the loved one from death. In a manner comparable to the stage of shock, the bereaved is bewildered and cannot bring himself to believe that the loved one is irretrievably lost. The stage of shock also appears to act as a sieve in this period, providing some protection from the devastating loss of a loved one by allowing bits and pieces of the tragedy to flow into individual consciousness over time. The bereaved person may act as if the deceased were still alive, trying to substantiate his belief through strenuous efforts to recover the loved one. This response is reflected in weeping, screaming and angry expressions and demands. Hostility toward significant others characterizes the bereaved person during this period and seems a natural outcome of the inevitable failure of family and friends to recover the lost object of love. The expression of anger and other emotions in this period is to be encouraged.

As efforts to recover the deceased are unsuccessful, despair and disorganization loom in the bereaved and are accompanied by disorganized and ineffective behavior. The angry protest or numbness phase in which denial was a crucial element is subsumed by the painful initiation of realization of the actual event and its irreversibility. The painful emptiness accompanying this period seems overwhelming. The bereaved may inquire how can the world go on in the absence of my loved one? The loss of a loved husband or wife, for example, entails the enhanced realization on the part of the survivor of the extent to which each was inextricably intertwined in the existence and being of the other. A period of time to share with loved ones and to meditate alone on the memories of the loved one and past experiences is clearly required during this phase. Moreover, Rees (1971) suggests that hallucinations of the deceased experienced by the bereaved may prove helpful in dealing with this crucial confrontation with reality.

Over a period of time, reorganization or detachment accompanied by active movement toward recovery from loss and resolution of the crisis of bereavement takes place. The bereaved person turns slowly toward life without the loved one. He begins to renew old relationships and establish new ones, starts to review the existing financial and emotional needs of the family and assess family roles. The loved one who is now gone remains in mind and spirit, but the bereaved has reached the point of moving ahead with life within the parameters of an existent reality.

THE EFFECTS OF LOSS AND BEREAVEMENT

Bereavement entails grief work accomplished over a period of time during which the loss of a loved one is confronted, the attachment to the deceased is withdrawn, and the bereaved reaches the point of making adjustments in his life to accommodate his loss and to move beyond it. Failure to move successfully through these stages may be reflected in abnormal grief reactions and have negative consequences for the social, emotional and physical well-being of the bereaved. Lindemann (1944), for example, reports cases of delayed mourning in which a person may engage in frenzied activity to avoid a confrontation with grief and distorted mourning in which a previously unmourned loss may appear within the context of a subsequent loss. Paul (1969) indicates that unresolved grief may, in turn, be reflected in personality and behavior problems. Moreover, mortality rates are higher among bereaved than non-bereaved, and physician consultations for both psychiatric and nonpsychiatric symptoms increase in the presence of grief and loss.

The detrimental effects of grief for older people and other groups have been increasingly documented. In his study (1969) of 4,486 widowers aged 55 years and older, Parkes and his colleagues found that 213 died within six months of the loss of their wives. This figure was 40 percent higher than the expected rate for married men of the same age. After that, the death rate fell to that of married men. The investigators indicate that "If, as seems most likely, the baneful effects of bereavement on physical health are a response to psychological stress, then anything that mitigates the stress can be expected to reduce the risk of its physical effects." Research (Parkes, 1964) also indicates that grief is a syndrome leading to greater physician utilization for both psychiatric and non-psychiatric symptoms. The negative effects of bereavement may be further enhanced in the person of advanced old age who may suffer from various chronic illnesses and impairments and also lack a viable social network of friends and relatives to assist him or her in coping with the loss of a loved one.

Moving older people from their homes to an institution and other forms of forced relocation also entail bereavement in the older person as he finds his mature roots extricated from the rich soil of human interaction. Moving the older patient against his or her wishes may, indeed, provoke a downhill course to death. Thus, controlled studies of the effects of involuntary relocation on the elderly document higher rates of morbidity and mortality in the transferred older populations when compared to matched groups of nonmovers. Gustafson (1972) goes so far as to suggest that the "career" of patients entering a nursing home is that of a dying trajectory. This conceptualization is supported by Weisman and Kastenbaum (1968) who note increased references to the topic of death among older people being transferred to unfamiliar surroundings. Even awaiting a move to a nursing home may have negative effects. The expected loss of family, friends and familiar surroundings clearly involves a period of anticipatory grief in the elderly. Indeed, the features of patients awaiting transfer to an old-age home are clearly reflective of anticipatory grief and bereavement over projected losses. Such persons have been characterized by Prock (1969) as follows:

> . . . general anxiety and tension, high emotional reactivity, a sense of helplessness and powerlessness, a tone of depression accompanied by low self-esteem, interpersonal patterns suggesting an active withdrawal from those about them, and some signs of ego disorganization. A quality of "my life is over" permeated the waiting list group.

Just as bereavement may entail emotional, social and physical ills for the older person, so bereavement and other dislocations including reduced health and social and emotional support may also contribute in complex ways to the problem of suicide in old age. Given the limitations of existing suicide information, there is a clear increase in suicide as age advances, particularly among white males. Whereas white men of all ages experienced 17.2 suicides per 100,000, this figure increases to 65.1 among persons aged 85 and over. Suicide rates also increase with age among white women, peaking at ages 45 to 54 and declining thereafter. The age pattern is less clear for nonwhite persons. Among men, the suicide rate is highest at ages 25 to 34. Nonwhite women reflect the lowest suicide rates in all age categories. These data, limited though they are, suggest the need for health providers to remain aware of the suicide problem in old age.

Bereavement and loss of loved ones and the breaking of the strands of existing relationships may relate in complex ways to suicidal potential in the older population. A role for reduced social support in suicide is suggested in age-specific suicide rates which are lower for married than for single, divorced or widowed persons. Divorced persons experience suicide rates three to five times greater than married persons under 65 years of age and from two to three times greater among persons aged 65 and over. Suicide rates among widowed persons exceed those of the married until about age 65 when the rates become comparable. The extent to which the older person is woven into the social fabric and his conception of this interrelationship may, thus, be related to the risk of suicide. Moreover, Moss and Hamilton (1956) suggest a role for bereavement in suicide attempts. They found that the loss or death of a close relative occurred twice as often for a group of suicide attempters than for a control group. Durkheim's classic thesis (1952) that suicide varies inversely with the degree of integration of the social groups of which the individual forms a part may have considerable applicability to the socially isolated aged in modern society.

Resnik and Cantor (1973) suggest that careful attention be paid to older people experiencing bereavement and loss, psychiatric disorders, serious physical illnesses and those threatening suicide or having a past history of suicidal behavior. They hold that the establishment of trust between provider and patient is the key to treating self-destructive activity. Moreover, the therapist should take authoritative action because "any appropriate realistic step he takes to improve the impasse that overwhelms the victim may lift the feelings of hopelessness and despair." A social psychological diagnostic workup is required to assess the emotional and social attributes and dynamics underlying suicidal motivation or potential. If, in the case of the older patient, family and friends are no longer available to provide support, family surrogates, professionals and volunteers may contribute to the person's social well-being and self-esteem. In the situation of advanced old age, where the patient may be debilitated and isolated through the loss of loved ones, social estrangement culminating in social death may emerge. The answer to this dark visitor is the social environment, including caring health professionals and their commitment to quality care of the older patient.

Bereavement is thus a major health problem requiring intervention and supportive care. Health professionals and community volunteers may help to blunt the traumatic edges of grief in the bereaved person. In a treatment program designed by Gerber (1969) a psychiatric social worker was accepted by 90 percent of bereaved persons who were approached. This degree of program acceptance clearly highlights the need for services to the bereaved who find customary social resources inadequate in dealing with their great loss. In his words, Gerber's program consisted of the following useful approaches:

1. Permitting and guiding the patient to put into words and express the effects involved in (a) the pain, sorrow and finality of bereavement; (b) a review of the relationship to the deceased; and (c) feelings of guilt toward the deceased.
2. Acting as a primer and/or programmer of some of the activities of the patient and organizing among available, suitable friends or relatives a flexible, modest scheme for the same purpose.
3. Assisting the patient in dealing with reality situations, care of children, and legal problems.
4. Mediating referrals to family doctors for prescription of psychic energizers, if necessary, for excessive depression and insomnia.
5. The offer of assistance in making future plans.

Obviously, with the loss of relatives and friends through death or geographic moves, the social resources needed by the elderly to meet new crises and associated bereavements are reduced. The need for a human prosthesis to assist the older person in coping with isolation and loss may, thus, be increased. Unfortunately, few health agencies use death notifications and other approaches to single out older individuals who might need supportive care. Yet, health professionals and community volunteers may be able to aid the bereaved older person. Communities may, for example, organize widow-to-widow programs in which widowed volunteers provide support to newly bereaved women, with some mutual benefit accruing to the volunteers as well.

Similarly, the negative effects of relocation bereavement may be mitigated in some small way by pre-move and follow-up care and support. Allowing patients to participate in the move, familiarizing them with the new facility and staff before moving, supportive counseling during which patients may express their concerns and fears, and finally, adequate follow-up to ensure a successful transition, may prove useful in alleviating this stressful experience.

SOCIETY, THE AGED AND GRIEF

The fact that modern society is death-denying and age-defying harbors clear implications for bereavement in the elderly. The seeming invisibility of death and dying brought about by the institutionalization of the dying patient and the close association between aging and death is conducive to social devaluation of the person in advanced old age. The loss of loved ones with the passage of years further enhances the possibility of multiple bereavements and reduces the pool of social support required by the bereaved older person. The view by society that mourning is obscene and best kept out of sight further reduces outlets for grief work and is enhanced by the limited availability of rituals, roles and predictable situations within which grief work can occur. Failure to deal successfully with the stresses of bereavement are, in turn, reflected in various health problems in the elderly.

While many older people maintain satisfying lives, it remains a truism that with advancing age come substantial losses of various types and each may entail some element of bereavement. The loss of work role and work colleagues through retirement is one such loss. The loss may be heightened for some because of the social devaluation of their persons as a result of no longer being "productive" in the eyes of others. Socially isolated retirees seem to suffer the most from retirement, indicating, in some cases, a low will to live (Ellison, 1966). The loss of loved ones, of spouse, siblings and friends also imposes stress upon the older person and his well-being. Kastenbaum (1969) suggests a cumulative effect for such losses in the older person. Inadequate time and opportunity to complete grieving for one loss prior to the onset of another may leave the older person overwhelmed with loss and grief. Moreover, the older person may require more time for his grief work, especially when he sustains the loss of a loved partner of many years.

The loss of significant others also reduces the social resources available to the older person in coping with his grief. Health workers must be attuned to the need for social support by the bereaved older person. Such support may be provided by volunteers as well as professionals. Other resources and opportunities to express grief may be reduced as well, i.e. establishing new meaningful social contacts, getting satisfaction from a work role. In short, losses may increase while compensatory or coping mechanisms for dealing with loss decrease. For some, depression, isolation and lowered self-esteem may be the ultimate result as avenues for self-fulfillment are closed off by society and recurrent losses take place.

Kastenbaum indicates that older persons may experience a "bereavement overload" because of cumulative losses. This overload may, in turn, be reflected in additional negative outcomes for the aged including a marked preoccupation with bodily functions associated with the physiological accompaniments of grief, a sense of extreme caution in investing emotion into people and objects, a heightened irritability, bitterness or paranoia, and suicide attempts or sub-intentional accidents through neglect of health and nutrition. These correlates of grieving may also lead to withdrawal of others precisely when supportive care is required.

Friends and relatives concerned with an older bereaved person should realize that crying, confusion, talkativeness and somatic complaints are not necessarily precursors of senility, but rather attempts at resolution of grief over loss of a love object. The depression associated with loss in the elderly need not inevitably result in despair, but may be a simple, transient state indicating acceptance of their irretrievable loss, if supportive assistance is provided and additional avenues of self-fulfillment are made available. Hyperactivity, although in some cases connoting adjustment problems, may also be viewed in terms of the need for activity to counteract reduced feelings of self-worth and helplessness in the face of loss. Many of the characteristics of grief such as reminiscences and discussions of the deceased and activities of the past, the expression of pain and anguish through weeping, and activities and decisions required in moving on with life contribute to an awareness of the reality of loss, its acceptance and progression into new relationships and activities.

With increasing illness and reduced social support and function, some older persons head for a new life within institutional walls. The issues of death, dying and bereavement for such an older person may be intertwined with the new environment. The older person being relocated from his own home to a nursing home may experience anticipatory grief over the projected loss of his friends, relatives, community ties, belongings and surroundings. Moreover, while most older people do not express a great fear of death, those persons entering new and unfamiliar surroundings are likely to express concerns about death and dying and, as Weisman and Kastenbaum (1968) note, may protest their loss in the only way they can by inarticulately dying.

The organizational environment of the older patient, including the goal-directed activities of staff members, considerably influences the care and support given. In some long-term institutions, the older dying patient may, for example, be assigned to the "vegetable garden" where the soil is rarely tilled to suggest an atmosphere of dignity and social support. Moreover, as Coombs and others (1973) note, the delicate balance between detachment and concern in medical and related organizations is most often tipped by the patient's age, with the scales weighing decidedly against the elderly. Hinton and others (1967) have noted the covert reluctance of some staff members to care for older patients and particularly for older dying patients. Markson (1971) described one hospital in which "a combination of great age, powerlessness and terminal illness makes one despised by medical and lay people alike and, unless death comes on schedule, suggests transfer to a state mental hospital."

The societal view that death is, in essence, an obscene entity requiring careful camouflaging may also be carried over into the lives of the institutionalized elderly. Townsend (1962) provides an insightful view of this issue and the complex emotions it arouses in the survivors:

> Most of the staff did not care to face up to unpleasant truths about death and took refuge in euphemisms in their relationships with residents. In over half of the institutions it was policy to withhold information. "We try to keep it from them—the old hospital routine, you know. No wreaths, no one goes to funerals. No last respects." "I never tell them if I can help it. I just say they've gone away if I'm asked. We put a screen

round the body and move it as quickly as possible, usually when the others are in the day-room. . . ." A death was hushed up and the body removed swiftly and silently. No doubt the staff were anxious to avoid giving cause for anguish but they failed to realize that by their attitude, they provoked insecurity. Many of the old people were aware that their lives were drawing to a close. Some were fearful, it is true, but most were reconciled to the idea or even welcomed it. The death of others disturbed them less than the concealment of it. And the way death was treated was perhaps a crucial test of the quality of the relationship between staff and residents. Dishonesty over this most serious of matters created distrust over minor affairs. And to avoid the rituals observed in the ordinary community had other consequences. Prompt removal of the body was not only, old people felt, the final indignity which a resident suffered, but it gave no chance to those who were left of paying their last respects to someone who had lived among them, however remotely, and of thereby giving a little more strength, dignity and feeling to the slender relationships between those who continued to share the life of a ward.

CONCLUSIONS

Autumn Leaves on the Wind;
Once Part of the Whole;
Now Scattering; each to
a Separate Destiny.

The increasing concern with the delivery of humane care, the push for open discussion of complex ethical issues, and the fuller recognition that open communication and support for the bereaved has mental and public health value all serve as soft winds on the existing screens of silence, and awaken us to the need to assist bereaved elders and others in resolving the disruptive loss of loved ones.

Some of the negative effects of bereavement seem most devastating to the older person who may suffer recurrent losses and multiple bereavements while social support is waning and avenues for expression of grief may be closing. Some health providers, reflecting the society's negative views of aging, find it difficult to confront the aged or the bereaved. And yet, the deleterious effects of grief comprise a major health problem demanding attention from health workers. Both professionals and volunteers have a vital role to play in providing for the resolution of grief in a supportive social environment. That the bereaved will accept this support and concern has been documented

(Gerber, 1969). Careful attention to the issue of loss and bereavement in the elderly should lead to improvements in the quality of life in old age and pave the way for the comprehensive and humane care which we may hope to experience in the later years of life.

REFERENCES

Blank, H. R.: Mourning. In Kutscher, A. H. (Ed.): *Death and Bereavement.* Springfield, Thomas, 1969, p. 205.

Bowlby, J.: Processes of mourning. *Int J Psychoanal, 42*:317, 1961.

Coombs, R. H., and Goldman, L. J.: Maintenance and discontinuity of coping mechanisms in an intensive care unit. *Social Problems, 20*:342, (Winter), 1973.

Durkheim, E.: (1847), *Suicide.* London, Routledge and Kegan Paul, 1952.

Ellison, D. L.: Alienation and the will to live of retired steelworkers. In Egermann, H.: *Proceedings of the Seventh International Congress of Gerontology,* Vienna, 1966.

Gerber, I.: Bereavement and the acceptance of professional service. *Community Ment Health J, 5*:489, 1969.

Gorer, G.: *Death, Grief and Mourning.* London, The Cresset Press, 1965, pp. 72, 129.

Gustafson, E.: Dying: the care of the nursing home patient. *J Health Soc Behav, 13*:226, 1972.

Hinton, J.: *Dying.* Baltimore, Penguin, 1967.

Kastenbaum, R.: Death and bereavement in later life. In Kutscher, A. H. (Ed.): *Death and Bereavement.* Springfield, Thomas, 1969.

Lindemann, E.: Symptomatology and management of acute grief. *Am J Psychiatry, 101*:141, 1944.

Markson, E.: A hiding place to die. *Trans-action, 9*:48, 1971.

Moss, L. M., and Hamilton, D. M.: Psychotherapy of the suicidal patient. *Am J Psychiatry, 112*:814, 1956.

Parkes, C. M.: Effects of bereavement on physical and mental health—a study of the medical records of widows. *Br Med J, 2*:274, 1964.

————: The First Year of Bereavement. *Psychiatry, 33*:333, 1970.

Parkes, C. M., Benjamin, B., and Fitzgerald, R. G.: Broken heart: a statistical study of increased mortality among widowers. *Br Med J, 1*:740, 1969.

Paul, N.: Psychiatry: its role in the resolution of grief. In Kutscher, A. H. (Ed.): *Death and Bereavement.* Springfield, Thomas, 1969, p. 181.

Prock, V.: Effects of institutionalization: a comparison of community, waiting list, and institutionalized aged persons. *Am J Public Health, 59*:1837, 1969.

Rees, W. D.: The hallucinations of widowhood. *Br Med J, 4*:37, 1971.

Resnik, H., and Cantor, J.: Suicide and aging. In Brantl, V., and Brown, M. (Eds.): *Readings in Gerontology.* Saint Louis, Mosby, 1973.

Townsend, P.: *The Last Refuge: A Survey of Residential Institutions and*

Homes for the Aged in England and Wales. London, Routledge and Kegan Paul, 1962.

Weisman, A. D., and Kastenbaum, R.: *The Psychological Autopsy: A Study of the Terminal Phase of Life.* New York, Behavioral Publications, 1968.

CHAPTER 27

GRIEF, THE FUNERAL AND THE FRIEND

Jeannette R. Folta and Edith S. Deck

THOUGH DEATH is ever present and provides life with an inevitable end, who dies and when make a considerable difference to the living. The death of an individual is one of the most important personal and social events in the lives of humans. Yet as important as it is, until recently death was rarely dealt with in social science literature. Psychiatrists wrote articles about life-death instincts, suicide and pathological grief; theologians about God's role in death, the soul and afterlife; philosophers about the meaning of death; physicians about the prolongation of life; nurses about post-death care of body and goods; morticians about the family and cultural practices of body disposal; statisticians and demographers about rates, causes and places of death; psychologists about grief and sociologists about institutional/organizational structure and the dying. Concern with the phenomena of death and dying as reflected in the geometric proliferation of literature in thanatology, deals primarily with the dying, his caregivers, and the immediate kin (spouse, child, parent, siblings) of the dead. Thus far, the literature in no way demonstrates an awareness much less a concern about the broader population of grieving survivors: the friends. This paper is an attempt to describe the process of grief resolution in the friend-grievor. Perhaps this oversight may be, at least in part, accounted for by first examining two basic fallacious assumptions made about man and his relationships. These include: 1. the notion that the basic structure and the importance of the family are basically unchanged; and 2. the notion that the most important human relationships are to be found in the family.

[231]

FAMILY STRUCTURE

Culture and society are integrated systems that continue to exist only when there is replacement of individuals by others and when there is provision for the means of life. Elemental biological facts of mating and the helplessness of infants become translated into a set of socially defined relationships called "family." The concept of family implies wedlock, which in turn consists of formal prescriptions defining the mutual responsibilities and rights of the couple, their offspring, and society as a whole. One of these responsibilities is the establishment of a household in accordance with custom and law. In the past, custom dictated the establishment of an extended family living together and sharing all responsibilities and rights. Today, in contrast, the newlyweds develop a separate household often geographically separated[1] from their original families and not infrequently within a different social class structure. The separate household structure tends to create a feeling of dual family membership which in turn may create a dispersion of affect and self-involvement and diminish the intimate nature of familial relationships.

While we have the demise of the traditional extended family, we have a longer life of the nuclear family. The presence of death as a frequent occurrence in the family has greatly diminished. In addition, the death rate of the most productive members of the family has decreased. "Today a married couple can expect to spend an average of twenty years together after the last child has left home" (Stub, 1966). The early age of marriage and increased life expectancy means the average child has grandparents for a significant portion of his life and even great-grandparents.

The choice of mate, subsequent family structure, modes of communication and nature of interpersonal relations among family members will vary according to the ethic that predominates the family. Within the Protestant Ethic (Weber, 1930) subculture, males are selected as mates and expected to function as industrious, good providers, be occupationally successful, potential disciplinarians for their children, and be the family's chief spokesman to the outside world. The female is expected to be a good housekeeper, cook and mother with no aspira-

---

[1]Approximately 1 out of 5 Americans changes his residence annually.

tions for a career outside the domain of the home. The Freudian Ethic (LaPierre, 1959) on the other hand, dictates that mates be selected on the basis of a romantic ideal. The marital partners are expected to be good companions who mutually share and enjoy outside activities, be sexually attractive and compatible and potential friends to their children. The Equalitarian Ethic proposes partners who equally share in the instrumental (household and breadwinning chores) and the expressive (emotional feelings) roles. Although these ethics rarely exist in their pure form, the emphasis on one, as opposed to the other, structures the kinds of relationships that exist between husband-wife, parent-child, family member-outside world.

There are, in reality, depending in part on the subcultural group, three types of families:

1. Large extended families who are interdependent and generally mutually supportive. "Because of the multiple relationships in such a family, each member is less vulnerable to the loss of another member, not only because there is more support but also because relationships tend to be a little diluted by their multiplicity" (Ellard, 1968).

2. Small, intimate, nuclear families who share friends, responsibilities, entertainment and have close interpersonal relationships among the members.

3. Small nuclear families that are together by law but are separate in relationships. Here the members have separate circles of friends, separate entertainment and interests and separate relationships and lives with no significant interpersonal relationships among nuclear family members.

HUMAN RELATIONSHIPS

We are a culture which may be characterized as oriented in expressed values toward youth, symbolic of life; the nuclear family symbolic of romantic freedom; and caregivers, symbolic of freedom from unpleasant tasks. We have seen studies that indicate generation gaps and family breakdown, and cry because our youth, especially those of college age, "split" and live in separate dwellings with "strangers" in groups of two to N, independent of family supervision. We decry the seemingly lessening importance of the family and the seeking of gratification from non-immediate kin, yet from cradle to grave we dispense with humans to caregivers, from nursery school and child-care centers to nuclear families to communes to geriatric facilities to morticians. Within this framework there is a shift of primary group relationships from family to friends. In the youth culture, peers often become more significant in importance than do kin. In the early middle-age adult who may be single or married, living near or far from immediate kin, colleagues at work or neighborhood friends often provide the most meaningful and psychologically close relationship. In the increasing geriatric population again friends or nursing-home roommates play the role of intimate primary group kin (Folta and Deck, 1973). Among the elderly, as with youth, the primary group relationship is shifting from (family) kin to (family) friend. More and more elderly as well as youth are living together outside the bonds of matrimony— the law that establishes family kin—and finding primary group relationships among friends. Even outside this type relationship, especially among the elderly who are placed on the periphery of the family group, the fellow inmate or old time friend is the most important person in one's life.

If we consider the above changes in family life and human relationships, what happens to the friend at the time of the death of the significant other non-kin?

GRIEF

While Thomas Eliot (1930) spearheaded the cry for an objective comparative analysis of grief and bereavement in families, it may be said that Lindemann fathered the movement. In his classic study of families of the Coconut Grove Fire victims he pointed out that: 1. acute grief is a definite syndrome; 2. the syndrome may appear immediately, be delayed, be exaggerated or apparently absent; 3. there may appear some distorted picture representing some aspect of the grief syndrome; and 4. by appropriate techniques these distorted pictures can be resolved into a normal grief reaction (1944). Others have confirmed Lindemann's observation of the grief syndrome and the accompanying symptoms.

Patterson (1969) tells us that "grieving is the gradual process of destroying the intense emotional ties to the dead person. The best example of this process is the intense, sad feelings provoked by thinking of the dead person. Each time this happens, it gets the sad person a little closer to being able to think about the dead person without being overwhelmed by the feeling. . . . The other part of grieving is making restitution for the loss. If grief work could be accomplished in more people much chronic unhappiness could be reduced."

Clayton, in her study of bereavement in normal subjects (1968) tells us the symptoms in the bereaved "seem to bear no relationship to age, sex, length of deceased's illness or relation to deceased." (All of her subjects, however, were spouses, parents, children or grandparents of the deceased.) Alistair (1970) also claims, "the closer the relationship to the dead person, the more deeply felt will be the loss." Again Hendin (1973) tells us "whether the loved one is parent, sibling, spouse or child, the closest surviving relatives face perhaps the most trying emotional experience." While all of these studies tell us that grief is a normal phenomenon, the intensity of which corresponds to the closeness of the relationship between the bereaved and the deceased, they fail to take this fact into account. The underlying assumption is that the "closeness of relationship" exists only among spouses and/or immediate kin.

Close friends experience the same grief syndrome and symptoms as described by Lindemann and as pointed out by Clayton and others. The intensity of grief is directly proportional to the "closeness" of the bereaved to the deceased. The difference between kin and friend in grief is to be found not in the definition, syndrome, intensity or process but rather in the modes of resolution available.

FRIEND, GRIEF, FUNERALS

As death happens to us all, so grief is a part of our lives. The study of grief is more than the study of symptoms and possible pathology: it is the study of people and their most intimate relationships. Grief knows no bonds; it is undisciplined by marital law; uncontrolled by kinship boundaries; it floats free among those who love and were loved. It is not grief but its expression in the process of its resolution that varies among human beings. Engel (1964) has identified six stages of normal grief: 1. shock and disbelief, 2. developing awareness, 3. restitution, 4. resolving loss, 5. idealization and 6. outcome. These stages will be utilized to examine differences between kin and friends in grief resolution.

The first stage, shock and disbelief, is characterized by a refusal to accept or understand the fact of death. Many say that prior preparation (i.e. knowing death is coming) helps to decrease grief. "Those closest to the patient deserve some kind of adequate warning," say some physicians. Yet from the moment of hospitalization on, the hospital and physician gear themselves, if at all, toward the statement on the chart that reads "nearest of kin." Rarely are even these kin told of impending death much less are friends notified. At the time of death, health care professionals not only do not notify friends but in several settings such as nursing homes take special precautions to prevent friends from knowing that death has occurred. The growth of the societal values of "death-denying" has often lead to the practices of families hiding the fact of death by refusing to allow public notification through newspapers and the like. It is our experience that it is not infrequent that friends discover the fact of death days, weeks or even months after death has occurred. Given this societal milieu, it is no wonder that friends and distant kin often express feelings of being "stunned" and being "numb."

The reality of death begins to penetrate the consciousness and is followed by feelings of loss, emptiness and anguish. Crying is one mode of release from this period of developing awareness. It is during this time that anger may erupt in feelings of failure; impulsive acting-out behavior and even self-destructive behavior will occur. This is no different for friend or kin; however, when it occurs in the friend it is rarely assumed to be related to the loss. Punishment for such behavior is more severe because our society lacks any acceptable recognizable state of grief for friends.

Engel points out that the third stage in the work of mourning is experienced in the various rituals of the funeral, which helps to initiate the recovery process. One of the ways in which the funeral provides this assistance is described by Jackson (1966), who says:

> Socially and psychologically the funeral with its rites and ceremonies
> can be something we do for ourselves to insure the values of life and to
> protect ourselves against the anxiety of denial. Important but unconscious
> psychological needs are served by the communication and identification

involved in a clear body image of the deceased. Rituals initiate and communicate the process of letting go of someone loved in a way in which the individual, the family, and the group are served and protected.

Covill (1968) enlarges on this process when he says, "the rites of interment and the customs of mourning are a necessary part of normal living. They help the living relate to the dead and lower the tension of grief. The role demanded by modern society wherein grief is suppressed and mourning deemed inappropriate is dysfunctional insofar as it deprives the bereaved of the emotional catharsis needed for the healthy acceptance of bereavement. A minimal ceremony, the discouragement of sending flowers and letters, the suppression of the manifestations of grief, and the destruction of a formalized mourning role are unphysiological and tend toward maladaptation later."

Durkheim (1947) stated a funeral is a ritualistic reconfirmation of society's values and a reintegration of group cohesion. Even the contemporary clergy "believe their major task at a funeral is to attend to the living rather than to the dead" (Fulton, 1961). But by custom the accepted definition of who is bereaved includes only spouse, parents, children and siblings. Consolation is often not given to the person closest to the deceased who is experiencing the greatest grief. For even the one with the greatest grief must give deference to the nearest of kin, as society expects them to experience the greatest grief with decreasing concern and interest as one moves to furthest kin and friends. In fact, it considers interest in the deceased other than by kin as an infringement upon family rights and prerogatives and any say in funeral or burial arrangements is considered an intrusion on the sanctity of the family. Perhaps this is because the law requires that the family or "estate" be liable for all bills incurred, including funeral and burial costs. Thus, even if friends were willing to pay, it is this system of "legal economics" that determines funeral control.

The movement toward abolishment of funerals leads to potential difficulties for families and particularly for friends to achieve "good" grief. Viewing of the body presents the moment of truth and allows for no denying of reality. Our studies have shown that among both families and friends lack of viewing prevents the development of the level of awareness and leads to feelings of disbelief for months and even years after death. For the friend, his only opportunity for mutual sharing of the loss is in his peripheral role at the funeral. When there is no funeral, reality is not confirmed and feelings that are basic to grief response are prohibited. The public funeral provides an opportunity for the entire community to offer support to the family and to themselves. On the other hand, the private funeral disallows the rights of all except the immediate kin to grieve.

The fourth stage, resolving the loss, is a stage in which the mourner attempts to deal with the painful void which may be felt as a defect in the sense of intactness and wholeness in self. In family members this is often manifested in the individual by various bodily sensations or pain which is identical with symptoms experienced by the dead person in the past. In friends this stage is characterized by a projection of self into the dead. Perhaps because friends tend to be so like ourselves in terms of age, interest and values, friends perceive self as the dead and experience fear and anxiety about self and others who are significant to them. Because there is no acceptable ritual which enables him to handle this stage, he often resorts to such activities as extreme concern with his own state of health, frequent visits to physicians, overprotection of loved ones, and frequent phone calls to friends to ascertain their state of aliveness.

The fifth stage, idealization, is a stage in which all negative and hostile feelings toward the deceased are repressed. Here there may be some feelings of remorse, guilt and regrets for past acts or fantasies of unkindness. For the friend not only is there a reliving of the relationship and an intensification of certain aspects of the relationship but also there is often an extreme identification with the dead. Changes in behavior, and exaggeration of values that emulate those of the deceased become important. Since there is no socially acceptable way to validate these feelings, the friend will often either sever other close relationships because he cannot handle another potential loss or he will try to rekindle ex-friendships in which he believes he committed a similar act of unkindness.

In the final stage, outcome, or the ability to remember comfortably and realistically both the pleasures and pains of the relationship, the family has an edge. Because the family can acceptably talk about

and rehash old relationships and receive some comfort and validation from others, his work of grief may be expedited. The friend who
attempts the same tactics may be ostracized from the group or at least
considered "a little weird."

Many authors have talked about pathological grief or unresolved
grief and the relationship of these phenomena to rates of morbidity
and mortality. Programs such as the "widow-to-widow" programs
(Silverman, 1971) have made great strides toward resolving unresolved grief and even in reducing mortality rates. Yet in the highest at risk groups are those friends for whom society has denied
acceptable social means for the resolution of grief. Grief must be
public to be shared and must be shared to be diminished. Friends
are subject to anniversary grief reactions, frequent physical complaints,
frequent visits to physicians, and destructive behavior which may
be other or self-directed. Yet, we do not view these phenomena in
any way as related to unresolved grief. While more study needs to
be done in this area, our preliminary investigation demonstrates that
the rates of morbidity and mortality as a result of unresolved grief
may be in fact higher for friends than for kin.

REFERENCES

Alistair, M.: Bereavement as a psychiatric emergency. *Nursing Times,* July 2,
1970.

Clayton, P., Desmaraus, L., and Winokur, G.: A study of normal bereavement.
Am J Psychiatry, 125:168, 1968.

Covill, F. J.: Bereavement—a public health challenge. *Can J Public Health,
59*:170, 1968.

Durkheim, E.: *The Elementary Forms of Religious Life.* Glencoe, Free Press,
1947.

Eliot, T. D.: The adjusted behavior of bereaved families: a new field of research. *Social Forces, 8*:543, 1930.

Ellard, J.: Emotional reactions associated with death. *Med J Aust,* June 8,
1968.

Engel, G. L.: Grief and grieving. *Am J Nurs, 64*:93, 1964.

Folta, J., and Deck, E. S.: Reconstruccion social despues de la muerte. *Tribuna
Medica,* October 26, 1973.

Fulton, R.: The clergyman and the funeral director: a study in role conflict.
Social Forces, 39:317, 1961.

Hendin, D.: *Death as a Fact of Life.* New York, Norton, 1973.

Jackson, E. N.: *The Christian Funeral.* New York, Channel, 1966.

LaPierre, R.: *The Freudian Ethic*. New York, Duel Slone, 1959.

Lindemann, E.: Symptomatology and the management of acute grief. *Am J Psychiatry, 101*:141, 1944.

Patterson, R. D.: Grief and depression in old people. *Md State Med J, 18*:75, 1969.

Silverman, P.: Widow-to-Widow Program (Paper presented, 1971).

Stub, H. R.: Family structure and the social consequences of death. In Folta, J. R., and Deck, E. S. (Ed.): *A Sociological Framework for Patient Care*. New York, Wiley, 1966, p. 193.

Weber, M.: *The Protestant Ethic and the Spirit of Capitalism*. London, Allan Unwin, 1930.

CHAPTER 28

FUNERAL BEHAVIOR AND UNRESOLVED GRIEF

JOHN J. SCHWAB, PATRICIA B. FARRIS,
SHIRLEY J. CONROY, AND ROBERT E. MARKUSH

A PRELIMINARY REPORT on our Mortality and Grief Studies in Alachua County, Florida, showed that 12 of 24 next of kin were still grieving intensely more than one year after the decedents' deaths. Of the others, three were found to be grieving moderately and nine minimally. We defined the 12 (50%) who were grieving intensely one year after bereavement as having unresolved grief reactions. In this report we are examining the 24 respondents' funeral behaviors to ascertain whether certain behaviors were associated with unresolved grief.

METHOD

The group of 24 interviewed more than one year after bereavement consisted of 9 spouses, 7 adult children, 3 siblings, 1 parent, 2 other relatives, and 2 friends. There were 18 females and 6 males; 13 were white and 11 were black; 16 were under 65 years of age, and 8 were 65 or over.

Each respondent was interviewed in his home by a trained interviewer. The interview schedule contained 209 items about the decedent and 56 about the respondent. In addition, the interviewer recorded 18 of her own observations. The information about the respondent covered four major areas: 1. sociodemographic charac-

*Supported in part by National Institute of Mental Health Contract No. HSM-42-72-206 (ER).

[241]

teristics, 2. physical and mental health, 3. health care, and 4. grief reactions. Six questions related to the funeral: 1. Who was in charge of the arrangements for the funeral? 2. Did you view his/her body? 3. Did you attend the funeral or memorial service? 4. Did you attend the burial? 5. Did you cry at this time? and 6. How much did family and friends help you at this time?

To assess grief reactions, the interviewer prepared a 22-item profile on each respondent (Appendix A). These profiles considered, for example, cause of death, relationship to the deceased, and temporal measures such as the length of illness. Using the profile, each respondent's grief reaction was discussed and impressionistically rated by the interviewers as intense, moderate, or minimal. The group of 12 respondents rated as grieving intensely one year after bereavement (unresolved grief) was compared with the group of 12 rated as grieving moderately or minimally on 6 sociotemporal factors (relationship to decedent, age, race, sex, length of decedent's illness, and length of awareness of impending death) and on the 6 funeral behaviors. We used Fisher's exact test for significance for the statistical analysis since the N in each cell was too small to permit the use of the chi-square.

RESULTS

Sociotemporal Factors

TABLE 28-I

COMPARISON OF SOCIOTEMPORAL FACTORS IN
UNRESOLVED AND RESOLVED GRIEF GROUPS

Relationship	*Unresolved* *N*	*N = 12* *%*	*Resolved* *N*	*N = 12* *%*
Spouse	5	(42)	4	(33)
Nonspouse	7	(58)	8	(67)
Age				
—65	8	(67)	8	(67)
65+	4	(33)	4	(33)
Race				
White	6	(50)	7	(58)
Black	6	(50)	5	(42)
Sex				
Male	3	(25)	3	(25)
Female	9	(75)	9	(75)
Illness				
—1 yr.	4	(33)	9	(75)
1 yr. +	8	(67)	3	(25)
Awareness of *Impending Death*				
—1 wk.	6	(50)	9	(75)
1 wk. +	6	(50)	3	(25)

As shown in Table 28-I, the two groups contained almost equal numbers of spouses and nonspouses. The age, race, and sex distributions in the two groups were similar. But, in the unresolved grief group 67 per cent of the decedents had been ill for more than one year, in contrast to 25 per cent in the resolved grief group. Fifty per cent of the unresolved grief group reported awareness of the decedents' impending deaths for less than one week, in contrast to 75 per cent of the other group. These differences were not statistically significant, but it appears that if the N were larger the two groups would differ significantly on the length of illness factor.

Funeral Behaviors

Table 28-II shows the funeral behaviors of the two groups. A slightly higher percentage of those in the unresolved grief group (64%) than in the resolved grief group (50%) reported that they were personally in charge of the funeral arrangements. Almost all of the respondents in the unresolved grief group (90-100%) viewed the body, attended the funeral service, attended the burial, and cried

TABLE 28-II
COMPARISON OF FUNERAL BEHAVIOR IN
UNRESOLVED AND RESOLVED GRIEF GROUPS

Funeral Behavior	*Unresolved N*	*N = 12 %*	*Resolved N*	*N = 12 %*
Who was in charge of the funeral arrangements?				
Self	7	(64)	6	(50)
Other	4	(36)	6	(50)
Did you view the body?				
Yes	11	(100)	9	(75)
No	0	(0)	3	(25)
Did you attend the funeral ?				
Yes	11	(100)	8	(73)
No	0	(0)	3	(27)
Did you attend the burial?				
Yes	11	(100)	8	(73)
No	0	(0)	3	(27)
Did you cry at this time?				
Yes	10	(91)	7	(78)
No	1	(9)	2	(22)
How much did family and friends help at this time?				
Very much	9	(75)	7	(70)
Less helpful	3	(25)	3	(30)

at the burial, compared to about 75 per cent in the resolved grief group. Almost equal percentages reported that they had received emotional support from family and friends at the time of the funeral. None of the differences between the two groups approached statistical significance.

DISCUSSION

To study unresolved grief we selected two groups of factors, socio-temporal characteristics and funeral behaviors. These particular factors were chosen for a number of reasons, for example: our previous study showed generally that closeness of relationship was directly associated with the intensity of the grief reaction; we hypothesized that lengthy terminal illnesses would allow time for anticipatory grief and reduce the grief reaction; and clinically, we have believed that insufficient participation in funeral ceremonies was related to unresolved grief.

Our major finding, however, was the somewhat surprising lack of differences between the resolved and unresolved grief groups on the factors we selected. The groups differed markedly on only one of the 12 factors—length of illness—and this difference was not in the expected direction. The decedents' lengthier illness tended to be associated with unresolved grief, indicating the possibility that anticipatory grief had not taken place or that anticipatory grief did not diminish the intensity of grief during bereavement. In our previous more general study of grief, we found no associations among length of decedents' illnesses, length of respondents' awareness of the fatal outcome and intensity of grief (Schwab, et al., 1975). Those findings and the contradictory ones in this study concerning length of illness and respondents' awareness suggest that anticipatory grief had not taken place. We can offer several tentative explanations. Perhaps psychic factors such as denial precluded realization of the seriousness of the decedents' illnesses; or, perhaps the next of kin did not receive sufficient detailed information about the prognosis; or possibly, persons with lengthy illnesses of one or more years' duration required so much burdensome daily care that the next of kin had little time or energy to ponder about the outcome. We are inclined to believe that the last possibility may have some validity since many of the decedents were elderly and had been chronically ill, and since the interviewers found that the next of kin had been nursing or caring for the dying persons over a protracted period of time. But the interviewers were also told repeatedly by the next of kin that they had received little information about the nature of the illness.

Another explanation for the association between the factor, extended length of illness, and unresolved grief is that the laws of probability would lead us to expect that one out of any 20 factors would be statistically significant and that one of 12 would be likely to approach significance. Moreover, one of the limitations of our present study is the small N.

From a broad social perspective, participation in funeral rites is believed to serve a variety of functions. For example, in writing about "Conceptions of Death," Kluckholm (1962) states: ". . . it is certain that such doctrines and rituals have promoted the adjustment of individuals and the integration and survival of societies." Habenstein and Lamers (1960-61) conclude that funeral ceremonies allay suffering. Reeves (1970) suggests that psychiatry's concern with grief developed as a result of the passing of the wake, and Lamers (1969) has recently entitled an article "Funerals are Good for People—M.D.'s Included."

The precise function of the funeral is viewed as giving meaning to what is meaningless (Toffler, 1970), as an important source of status (McDonald, 1973), as affirming the importance of the ethnic group (Gorer, 1965), as educating man (Fulton and Geis, 1968), as encouraging man to perform well in everyday living (Gouldner and Gouldner, 1963), or as reorienting the bereaved and assisting the group to adjust to the loss of one of its members (Durkheim, 1926; Mandelbaum, 1959).

For the individual survivor, funeral rites are believed to furnish something to do during a time of crisis (Eliot, 1930; Kane, 1968; Vernon, unpublished), to offer norm role definitions at an uncertain time (Gorer, 1965; Vernon, unpublished), and to provide comfort for the bereaved and grief-sharing by bringing family and friends together (Kane, 1968; Reeves, 1969; Raether, 1971; Parkes, 1972).

Our findings cast doubt on the validity of some assumptions about funeral behaviors, (commonly regarded as important for the grief process) such as viewing the body and crying which were not associated with resolution of grief but were reported more frequently by those with unresolved grief.

There are diverging opinions about the significance of participation in funeral rites and the resolution of grief. For example, in a study of 1,961 subjects, Vernon found that 36 percent reported that grief was most intense when they were first notified of the death; for 17 percent, it was most intense on viewing the deceased, for 16 percent during the funeral, and for 10 percent at the graveside. About one fifth of his subjects felt "constrained to conform to socially expected expressions of grief, sometimes not in accord with true feelings," while about one-fourth noted that expected behavior patterns satisfied their needs. Furthermore, Parkes (1972) thinks of grief as a process of realization and fears that anything which forces reality testing too early in bereavement "is likely to give rise to difficulties." He concludes that the funeral service usually takes place too soon after the death to be of great positive psychological value for the bereaved.

From the results in our study pertaining to funeral behaviors and our interviewers' general observations, we are inclined to believe that the absence of a social support system may be the greatest single factor responsible for unresolved grief. Many of our respondents told plaintively that they had received comfort and aid from family and friends during the funeral ceremonies, but for only a short time thereafter. Within weeks they felt lonely and bereft. We observed that many were living as isolates, often in semideprived situations. In such circumstances, it is possible that the continued grief, in all of its tragedy, is a personal and meaningful emotion which is unlikely to be surrendered when there is nothing to take its place. We intend to pursue these conjectures in our continued research and will be examining unresolved grief in this social psychiatric perspective.

APPENDIX A
GRIEF EVALUATION ITEMS

1. Cause of death
2. Relationship of respondent

3. Interval between awareness and death
4. Interval between death and interview
5. Length of illness
6. Satisfaction with medical care
7. Unresolved grief after one year (assessed by the interviewer)
8. Intensity of grief (assessed by the interviewer)
9. Impact on the interviewer (self-rating by interviewer)
10. Who was in charge of funeral arrangements?
11. Did you cry at this time?
12. How much did family and friends help?
13. Do you have close relatives in the county?
14. Do you have close friends in the county?
15. How often do you cry because of his/her death?
16. How often do you dream of him/her?
17. How often do you have trouble sleeping?
18. How often are you unable to do your usual work?
19. Do you ever have loss of appetite?
20. How often is your mind on him/her?
21. How often do you feel all choked up?
22. What is your total family income?

REFERENCES

Durkheim, E.: *The Elementary Forms of the Religious Life.* New York, Macmillan, 1926.

Eliot, T. D.: The adjustive behavior of bereaved families: a new field for research. *Social Forces,* 7:543, 1930.

Fulton, R. L., and Geis, G.: Social change and social conflict: the rabbi and the funeral director. Western Kentucky University Sociological Symposium, Fall, 1968.

Gorer, G.: *Death, Grief and Mourning.* Garden City, Doubleday, 1965.

Gouldner, A. W., and Gouldner, H. P.: *Modern Sociology.* New York, Harcourt, Brace and World, 1963.

Habenstein, R. W., and Lamers, W. M.: *Funeral Customs the World Over.* Milwaukee, Bulfin, 1960-61.

Kane, J. J.: The Irish wake: a sociological appraisal. Western Kentucky University Sociological Symposium, Fall, 1968.

Kluckhohn, C.: Conceptions of death among the Southwestern Indians. In *Culture and Behavior.* New York, Free Pr, 1962.

Lamers, W. M., Jr.: Funerals are good for people—M.D.'s included. *Medical Economics,* 1969.

Mandelbaum, D. G.: Social uses of funeral rites. In Feifel, H. (Ed.): *The Meaning of Death.* New York, McGraw-Hill, 1959.

McDonald, M. J.: The management of grief: a study of black funeral practices. *Omega, 4*:139, 1973.

Parkes, C. M.: *Bereavement Studies on Grief in Adult Life.* New York, Intl U Pr, 1972.

Raether, H. C.: The place of the funeral: the role of the funeral director in contemporary America. *Omega, 2*:136, 1971.

Reeves, R. B., Jr.: The hospital chaplain looks at grief. In Schoenberg, B., Carr, A. C., Peretz, D., and Kutscher, A. H. (Eds.): *Loss and Grief: Psychological Management in Medical Practice.* New York, Columbia U Pr, 1970.

Schwab, J. J., Chalmers, J. M., Conroy, S. J., Farris, P. B., and Markush, R. E.: Studies in Grief: A Preliminary Report. In Schoenberg, B., Gerber I., Wiener, A., Kutscher, A.H., Peretz, D., and Carr, A.C., (Eds.): *Bereavement: Its Psychosocial Aspects.* New York, Columbia U Pr, 1975.

Toffler, A.: *Future Shock.* New York, Random House, 1970.

Vernon, G. M.: A Study of Attitudes Toward Death, 1968 (Unpublished, analysis in process).

CHAPTER 29

GRIEF, LOVE LOST, AND THE FUNERAL RITE

ALBERT B. HAKIM

CLEARLY, THE FUNERAL is a rite symbolizing, for all, the end of life and, for many, its beginning. The varieties are vast, whether it leads to a pyre whose consuming flames return the body to its primal elements, or the traditional western funeral with wake, prayers and burial, or the latest form of cryonics which, in its own ironic way, seals the departed from the warmth of life. In every case, separation is the burden of the rite, and it transfers its weight to the living; what once was is now no more and has been separated from what is now. The burden on the living is grief.

Though grief may have manifold causes—the guilt of one who feels he might have caused the death, or the uncontrollable aloneness that suddenly overwhelms one—these brief reflections touch upon grief as the felt expression of love lost. As such, it is not tied to the quality of the funeral but to the quality of life led by the dead person; the funeral rite is nothing more than the phenomenological juncture at which the bereaved person begins to express his feeling that somehow more good was given to the world during the lifetime of the deceased and that more love was given to humanity. There is the tender feeling of humanity lived, a sense that, if the meaning of life is ever to be grasped, it is in the direction of the good and that evil, despite its ravages of man throughout life's pilgrimage, is inhuman.

It is the good-as-loved that makes a person happy, and it is precisely the loss of the good-as-loved that makes a person grieve.

Life achieves meaning in the love of the other; it becomes more ample, more sustaining, more joyful, more abiding, more tolerant, more accepting, more giving, more understanding, more outgoing, more in-reaching, more complete. With the death of the other, the meaning of life is momentarily lost until the realization dawns that this very death has within itself the power to support life, not only as a memory of a life gone by but also as a new center of personal strength radiating life for the future. The theme of newness pertains indeed to the person who has died, but just as much to the one who is living.

If sorrow is unaccompanied by hope, a kind of despair closes in; no light seen; no avenue open. As Moltmann writes, "Despair is the premature, arbitrary anticipation of the nonfulfillment of what we hope for from God" (*Theology of Hope,* p. 23). On the contrary, hope, even if seen "through a glass darkly," looks to fulfillment by sharing life anew.

Elie Wiesel lets an incident speak for itself when Juliek the violinist, in a poignant liturgy rising out of a barracks of rotting flesh, celebrates his death in deepest sorrow, yet the legacy left for the young boy was that the mystery of death ineffably enfolds a hope for the future: "I was thinking of this when I heard the sound of a violin. The sound of a violin, in this dark shed, where the dead were heaped on the living. What madman could be playing the violin here, at the brink of his own grave? Or was it really an hallucination? It must have been Juliek. He played a fragment from Beethoven's concerto. I have never heard sounds so pure. In such a silence. How had he managed to free himself? To draw his body from under mine without my being aware of it? It was pitch dark. I could hear only the violin, and it was as though Juliek's soul were the bow. He was playing his life. The whole of his life was gliding on the strings—his lost hopes, his charred past, his extinguished future. He played as he would never play again. I shall never forget Juliek. How could I forget that concert, given to an audience of dying and dead men! To this day, whenever I hear Beethoven played my eyes close and out of the dark rises the sad, pale face of my Polish friend, as he said farewell on his violin to an audience of dying men." (*Night,* chap. 6.)

The shape of the funeral rite, even though it will be appreciated only with the passing of time, should, while being concerned with the liturgy of the dead, bespeak both sorrow and hope for the living. As the preface in the Mass for the dead proclaims, "The sadness of death gives way to the bright promise of immortality." If the Catholic funeral practice laid too much emphasis, in the not too distant past, on the sorrowful side of death, the present practice stresses the belief that life is changed, not ended. The theme of the liturgy is newness of life, the newness heralded by the resurrected Christ, the newness to which all of us are summoned. Indeed, those who mourn are blessed, for they shall be comforted. The good done will never perish; the love given will never be lost. "Only goodness and kindness follow me all the days of my life; and I shall dwell in the house of the Lord for years to come."

CHAPTER 30

"I CAN'T BELIEVE IT YET, HOW CAN SHE?"

ANN S. KLIMAN

WHEN DEATH is sudden and unexpected, it is not possible to do the anticipatory mourning work which facilitates the integration and acceptance of the loss. The very suddenness of such a loss precipitates simultaneous feelings of guilt and helplessness in the bereaved survivors. In adults, the sense of guilt stems from temporary regression to a state of magical thinking in which the adult believes that what he did (or didn't do) in some way caused the death. "If only I had been home, I could have . . .," or, "If only I hadn't been so angry when . . ." is often the way the unrealistic guilt is verbalized. The helplessness results, in part, from the impotent passivity that accompanies the inability to thwart death. The rituals of mourning inherent in the activities before, after and during a funeral are helpful in structuring adaptive, active work which, in turn, decreases the sense of helplessness.

Active participation by adults in the rites and rituals of mourning has long been acknowledged and has been built into the fabric of our society, religion and ethics. However, only recently has attention been paid to the vulnerable position of children who must cope with death. If, indeed, magical thinking and helplessness are temporary regressive phases of suddenly bereaved adults, they are constant, age-appropriate stages of development of all children under age eight. The evolution from magical thinking, the belief that what one thinks, dreams or wishes makes things happen, to rational thinking occurs in the process of maturation. Thus, a child of three, or five, or seven, believes that when someone dies, it is his fault because he, the child, was "bad" or "mad" or "mean," or because he had angry thoughts or wishes. It is these young children, so developmentally vulnerable, who are often excluded from the network of support available to bereaved adults.

Case Report

Five-year-old Stanley's father was killed in an auto accident early one evening. Stanley did not cry when told his father was dead, but several hours later he accidentally slammed his finger in a door. That night, and for several nights thereafter, Stanley had screaming nightmares. During the day, he teased and provoked his older brother and mother into getting angry and telling him how bad he was. In kindergarten, Stanley crashed toy cars into block barriers saying, "He's dead. I killed him." Then he would contrive to hurt himself with the blocks.

Stanley's mother remembered that he used to jump around in the car when he went driving with his father, and his father used to shout, "Sit down, you'll cause an accident!" or, "Be quiet before you kill us all!" As it became observably obvious that Stanley believed that his jumping, his "badness," had caused his father's accident, his mother was able to share with him how the accident had really happened. And, equally important, she shared with him that she too felt sad and sorry about the times she had been angry with Daddy. With this support, there was a reduction in Stanley's provocativeness and accidents since he felt less of a need to be punished.

Young children are excluded from the family coping rituals of mourning not out of cruelty or even insensitivity, but rather because of the adults' desire to protect the young from the grimness, sadness and fear of death. But not talking to children about death, not helping them to understand or deal with what they observe and overhear, not encouraging active, sharing ways of coping with loss do not protect. Rather, the child is isolated, removed from the security available from caring adults, and forced to deal with observable changes and confusions all alone. As experience has taught us, the fantasies a young child experiences when faced with a grieving but uncommunicative family are usually more terrifying than the saddest reality. Ironically, the death of a loved one produces the temporary loss of many of the child's most important and caring family members. The adults are mourning the loss of one person with the support of family and friends; the young child grieves for the loss of all his family without support.

Case Report

Four-year-old Alicia's mother died suddenly, following a cerebral vascular accident. Alicia was picked up at nursery school by a neighbor who told her that she would stay at her house because her mother "went on a trip." For the next four days, Alicia stayed with the neighbor because her father felt that she was "too young to understand" and would be "upset and frightened by all the people and all the crying . . . and besides, *I* can't believe it yet, how can she!" The neighbor lived on her block and Alicia saw the stream of people who moved in and out of the home to which she was not allowed to return. She also realized that no one would tell her where Mommy was, or Daddy, or her grandparents (who usually cared for her when her parents went away), and at nursery school, the teacher looked at her sadly and started hugging her a lot.

Alicia became increasingly frightened as her questions about when Mommy and Daddy were coming home went unanswered. Remembering how angry she had been with Mommy lately, she became convinced that her anger drove Mommy and Daddy away, and that they did not love her and would never come back to a girl who was so angry and mean.

In an apparent effort to spare her, Alicia's father forced her to live in a strange house, with unfamiliar people who had different patterns: people who didn't understand why she demanded so many cookies, cried when they were given to her, and said they were "no good"; people who kept telling her that "everything was all right" when for Alicia everything was very strange and very wrong.

The family's and friends' "protection" of Alicia arose out of their need to isolate themselves from, and to deny Alicia's, painful feelings. By not telling her of her mother's death, by assuming that she could not understand, they projected onto her their own avoidance and denial. She became their island of innocence.

At The Center for Preventive Psychiatry, (White Plains, New York) where work is done extensively with young children, it has been observed that children play and talk freely about death when adults do not avoid listening. After three-year-old Andy found a dead goldfish, he talked and played out his questions, concerns and worries. With support from adults, he coped with his questions and worries by becoming active. He wanted to "bury the fish," to make a clay model of "lots of fishes," and to draw a picture of little goldfish. He made up a song and put on a puppet show which dramatized in tolerable ways his sad, "scary" feelings. And he began to learn to accept and cope with loss, bit by bit, very slowly, even inconsistently, but always with the support of adults who acknowledged his feelings and were willing to share them.

The involvement of a young child in the work of mourning for such a relatively unimportant object as a goldfish serves as a model for involving a child in the crucial mourning work for a parent, sibling or other relative. Keeping the young child within the supportive, sharing, acknowledging framework of the family, and encouraging him to know and feel, allows him to grow and cope, even as it allows bereaved adults an active task at the time when helplessness is most overwhelming. When we cannot change a reality we can, at least, facilitate healthy, growth-promoting adaptation to the reality.

CHAPTER 31

HELPING THE CHILD TO MOURN

ROBERT A. FURMAN

INTRODUCTION

FROM WORK as an analyst, both of adults and children, and from consulting experiences with preschool teachers, I have developed certain convictions regarding the way a child should be handled at the time of acute grief and in relation to participation in funeral rites. To delineate my point of view, let me cite an example derived from a young man in analysis. He described to me the death of his pet parakeet which occurred when he was six years old. This was a loss in which his sadness was shared by his parents, as demonstrated by their respectfully helping him bury his pet in their back yard. He reported the experience as a completed one, painful but wholesome. In striking contrast, his parents gave away a beloved dog without preparing or warning him when, seven years later, they moved to an apartment where pets were not allowed. In his hurt, fury, confusion and feelings of betrayal, he had been unable to express sadness or grief. To this day, he feels haunted "by the tears inside I have never cried, the tears I want so much to cry. But I cannot. It is so painful, so uncomfortable."

Less innocuous examples have involved the loss of siblings at almost the same ages. An earlier one was mastered because parental support had been given, but a later one, with tacit prohibition of response, as above, had not been resolved. Likewise, examples could be given where the outcome was not just a sense of being haunted but either a permanent state of inhibition of feeling and relationship or a paralyzing lifetime state of depression. It is my conviction, derived from my own work and that of others, that from about four years of age on a child can mourn and master a loss if he is supported and sustained in this work by the adults responsible for him (Furman, 1974). If one is convinced of the dreadful potential of an incompleted mourning and of a child's capacity to mourn successfully if he is sustained and supported in that work, then one tries to do something about it.

ACUTE GRIEF

We must ask that parents make themselves available to assist their children through a period of painful feelings when they themselves, as parents, are suffering from grief. However, those able to accept this extra burden have found gratification in being able to help others at a time when their own feelings have rendered them almost overwhelmingly helpless.

Grieving over the loss of a parent, a spouse or a child, adults can easily overlook the needs of their children; sometimes it even seems desperately necessary to overlook those needs. It is often so hard for us, as professionals, to have the opportunity to reach such parents, to have immediate contact with them. Some are referred because our interest and willingness to help is somewhat known at a local level; we try to reach others through nursery school and elementary school teachers. But how much greater are the doctors', nurses', ministers', priests', rabbis' and funeral directors' opportunities to make such referrals when the need is evident.

If, at the time of a death, the survivors were to be asked about children involved and whether their needs have been considered in the immediate planning, it is possible that the initial period of mourning could then be better managed. The needs of the children might be brought to the position of prominence they merit. So much can be done at the time of acute grief and the funeral that is simple and effective in bringing a child's needs into proper perspective and, further, actively demonstrating the possibilities of successful mastery.

This point cannot be made too strongly. What is done at the time of acute grief and the funeral is crucial in what it initiates about the awareness adults should have of the child's needs and their management in regard to the painful but healing process we know as mourning. Guidance and support by professionals for the surviving adults or parents could even be considered judiciously at this point.

To start, the simple principle of honesty, a principle often easier to support than to implement, should be employed. A child should be told honestly what death is—*the absence of life*—in terms that he can understand. He should be told the feelings his parents have about the death that has just occurred. Religious convictions, helpful to adults at such times, are confusing and disturbing to the more concrete thinking child. Crucial here is the distinction between a body that remains after life has ceased and a living person. A funeral can make no sense, can only be terrifying to a child, unless it is clear that a lifeless body and not a living being is involved.

At this time of acute grief, the father of one of my young patients explained the reality of their mother's death to my patient and his two older brothers. He then told them that there were no feelings or thoughts that they could not discuss and share together and that although there would be many sad times ahead, they would manage them together. When asked who would take the mother's place, he replied that no one would ever take her place in their feelings, but that he would see to it that all her jobs would always be done.

In our frame of reference, he was stating that their needs would always be met, an enormous task which he achieved successfully. He gave them the fundamental security necessary for them to be able to approach their feeling responses to the loss. His sons responded in ways appropriate to their respective ages because he had also been honest with them through the long days of their mother's chronic illness. In more acute situations, children often react with an apparently insensitive indifference, returning to play or television, in a manner shocking and disturbing to the unprepared adult. If this apparent indifference can be anticipated and compared to the adult's initial shock reaction of disbelief at the time of a sudden loss, it is more easily tolerated and dealt with.

THE FUNERAL

The loss that involves a child will usually be a death within a family, thereby making it a family loss and experience. As a member of the family, a child should have the right to participate in that experience as he wishes and is able. At a time of loss, with its accompanying loneliness, to be with family and not arbitrarily left out of what is happening seems only humane and just.

I know of no way anyone, except the child, can decide what is bearable and best for him at a time of acute grief. If consulted, I usually suggest that the funeral and interment be explained honestly in accurate detail, and that he be given his choice of attending what, if any, part he wishes. The chance to make a decision gives him an opportunity for activity at an otherwise helpless time. It avoids the later reproach of his having been excluded and respectfully allows him to gauge for himself what he can and cannot endure. An adult preference that the child participate as a family member may be expressed but only in the context of a guideline, with its being understood clearly that the child's decision will be accepted and honored.

Children vary in their responses, but this approach has one very great advantage to all—it forces the adults to find out exactly what will transpire at the funeral and interment. This can preclude their being surprised and dismayed by some customs that may be upsetting to them; it can also allow them to seek modifications of the usual service to make it more meaningful and helpful. They may prefer a closed casket, a short service, an elimination of exhortations to rejoice because their loved one is now in heaven.

SUMMARY

These then are the few thoughts I would want to express. First, it is important to consider the needs of children at a time of acute grief and the funeral because such consideration might allow the child's needs about mourning to assume the prominence they deserve. Second, as would be true at any other time of life, honesty of facts and feelings at the time of acute grief would seem the only fair approach to a child. Third, the most straightforward thing to do is to explain the realities of the funeral service and let the child decide on his own the degree to which he might wish to participate.

REFERENCE

Furman, Erna: *A Child's Parent Dies.* Hew Haven, Yale University Press, 1974.

CHAPTER 32

THE CHILD AND THE FUNERAL

MORRIS A. WESSEL

WHEN A FAMILY MEMBER or close friend dies, parents often ask their pediatrician how they can be most supportive to children during this time of sadness and stress. I wish to consider here a specific question which is asked frequently. Should a child be offered the opportunity to attend the funeral of a loved one?

I suggest that a child, five years of age or older, be allowed to decide for himself whether he wishes to attend the funeral. Careful consideration of a child's psychological needs suggests that participation in a funeral service can be a meaningful and constructive experience (Furman, 1970).

Many adults assume that a funeral is a painful experience for a child, and that it is kinder to "spare" the child from attending this event. We must remind ourselves, however, that funeral rites have served as a time and place for family, friends and members of a community to gather together to honor the deceased and to support the bereaved individuals as they grieve and begin the process of mourning. To deny a child the opportunity of joining with his family and friends denies him his right as a human being. As a child observes others grieve and mourn, he often finds support for his unique adjustment to the inevitable feelings of desolation (Wolf, 1958).

Those who believe in "sparing" a child from the experience of attending a funeral do so, of course, wtih a child's best interest in mind. I would like to express why I believe that participation in a funeral can be an important and helpful experience for a child who wishes to be present.

[260]

As he comes to the realization that death implies a permanent loss, a child may be overtly troubled and in deep despair. Or he may go about his normal activities acting as though nothing has happened. The behavior in either case is a logical reaction as a young child recognizes and deals with the painful reality of the death of a loved one. If a child "lets go" and sobs with grief, it is likely to be so poignant and distressing that adults may find it overwhelming and unbearable (Furman, 1973). Many adults, when they say "spare" the child, are asking to "spare" themselves from having to deal with a child's reaction to the full meaning of the death of a person he loves.

At what age can a child be expected to understand the finality of death as it relates to any organism? The idea of "absence of living" denoting a cessation of activity is a concept that a nursery school age child can grasp with relative ease as it relates to insects, birds, goldfish and pets (Osborne, 1968). When death involves humans, and particularly human beings a child needs and loves, it is more difficult for him to comprehend and accept what has happened.

Anna Freud and Dorothy Burlingham (1943, 1947) have described the reactions of young children to the death of a father in London during World War II. These children appeared to *understand* the meaning of death. Yet, it was quite another matter for them to *accept* the definitive finality when the death involved their own father. Further anticipated visits of fathers were a frequent topic of conversation among the children. This theme was mentioned *more* often by the children whose fathers had died than by those whose fathers were alive and well. Although talking about "my daddy is deaded" or "killed in the war," many children also spoke endlessly of when their fathers would return. A four-year-old stated, "I want him to come back. . . . My daddy is big. . . . He can do everything. . . ." Another four-year-old said, "We have to wait until after the war. Then God can put people back together again. . . ." And another child of the same age said, "My daddy is deaded. . . . He's in a far away place like Scotland. . . ." These comments reveal with clarity the desperate need children have for the existence of both parents. They keep the deceased parent alive in fantasy because it is so very necessary to possess both a father and a mother as one grows and develops during childhood.

Denial of the loss often expresses itself in a child's desire to return to play, to watch television, and to participate in school and social activities (Wolfenstein, 1965; Wessel, 1973). It is as if to say, "If I return to my usual activities, then life will be as it was before." The strength of the denial may be so strong that adults often consider a child to be oblivious to the death. It is doubtful that this is ever the case, for the absence of the deceased serves as a constant reminder that the person is no longer available.

I believe that if a child of five or older (and, in some instances, even a younger child) wishes to attend a funeral, he is seeking the support of his family, his friends and his community at the funeral rites so that he too may participate in the ritual and be helped as are adults with adjustment to the death of a person he loved.

A short, simple service with a closed casket simplifies the experience for a child. However, whatever ritual and form of funeral service a family finds meaningful, based on their own religious beliefs and cultural patterns, can also be appreciated by a child.

The religious concept of a life hereafter is difficult for a child to comprehend until he is well into the second decade of life. When this philosophy is upheld by the parents, it can be presented simply in this manner: "We like to believe that part of the person, the part we love very much, is somewhere resting comfortably. We like to think of it as Heaven, a place where there is no suffering, no pain, no hunger and no sickness." This provides a religious conceptualization in a form which a child may accept or reject. Later, when a child is older, the religious interpretation may offer him the same comfort it does for many adults. Care must be taken, however, not to present a child a story involving life hereafter when this conceptualization is foreign to the adult's philosophy of life and death. A child is quick to sense any insincerity or dishonesty on the part of adults. To present a concept of life hereafter which one disbelieves, in the hopes that it will help a child, can create only confusion and distrust which are rarely if ever helpful to a child (Becker and Margolin, 1967).

Even when a child is sufficiently mature to understand the finality of death, he still finds it difficult to accept that it has occurred to a person he loves. His conversations may indicate repeatedly a hope that the deceased will return. Lest we assume that this phenomenon is limited to children, it is important to realize, as Parkes has noted in his studies (1973), that wishes, hopes and even hallucinations involving the deceased occur quite frequently for many months among bereaved adults.

Several aspects of a child's experience at a funeral merit careful attention. Care should be taken to explain in advance the details of what will take place. A child needs to know that some members of his family may cry and be preoccupied with their own feelings of sadness. It is imperative that arrangements be made for a close relative or friend to be with the child during the service so that he need not be isolated when he needs comforting. Nothing is sadder than a child standing alone at a funeral with no one by his side during or after the service.

If a child chooses to participate in other ways rather than attend the funeral, this also should be honored. For a child may know better than adults what will help him with his struggles at this very sad time. Some young children who do not wish to attend the service ask to visit the cemetery shortly after the burial. They feel more at ease when they have the opportunity to see the fresh grave. Other children wish to participate by helping with arrangements at home, such as setting the table, hanging up clothes, arranging flowers, etc. These activities allow a child to participate constructively while his family proceeds with the usual funeral rites of their group.

A child may continue to deny the loss even though he attends the funeral. However, the reality of the experience with family and friends provides a base from which he may be able in time, particularly when his physical and emotional needs are well taken care of, to come to terms with his loss and begin the mourning process.

It is difficult for adults to be obliged to observe a child grapple with his feelings after the loss of a loved one. However, a child deserves to have every effort made to help him to deal realistically with his loss. The child who wishes to attend a funeral is asking to be included in the experience as a member of the family. He is telling us that participation in the service will help him in his endeavor to adjust and cope with the loss of someone who has been near and dear to him. The least we as adults can do is to include a child in the activities which for centuries have served to sustain human beings when the final separation from a loved one takes place.

REFERENCES

Becker, D., and Margolin, F.: How surviving parents handle their young children's adaptation to the crisis of loss. *Am J Orthopsychiatry, 37*:753, 1967.

Freud, A., and Burlingham, D.: *War and Children.* New York, Medical War Books, 1943.

———: *Infants Without Families, The Case For and Against Residential Nurseries.* New York, Intl U Pr, 1947.

Furman, R. A.: The child's reaction to death in the family. In Schoenberg, B., Carr, A. C., Peretz, D., and Kutscher, A. H. (Eds.): *Loss and Grief: Psychological Management in Medical Practice.* New York, Columbia U Pr, 1970.

———: A child's capacity for mourning. In Anthony, E. J. (Ed.): *The Child in His Family.* New York, Wiley, 1973.

Osborne, E.: When you lose a loved one. Public Affairs Pamphlet No. 269, New York, 1968.

Parkes, C. M.: *Bereavement.* New York, Intl U Pr, 1973.

Wessel, M. A.: Death of an adult—and its impact on the child. *Clin Pediatr, 12*:28, 1973.

Wolf, A. W. M.: *Helping Your Child To Understand Death.* New York, Child Study Association, 1958.

Wolfenstein, M.: Death of a parent and death of a president. In Wolfenstein, M., and Kliman, G. (Eds.): *Children and the Death of a President.* Garden City, Doubleday, 1965.

CHAPTER 33

THE SCHOOL AND THE FUNERAL

Robert G. Shadick

Most children have uncles but the school seldom sees them, discusses them or has much to do with them. So it is with death. Most children have some personal experience with it, all children must learn about it to some degree. Yet the school usually takes no heed of these matters. A funeral is, perhaps, the only event related to death that is not swept routinely under the rug of silence and neglect by the school as an institution and by its personnel.

A DOUBLE TABOO

Thanatologists and other professionals have long recognized that death is the taboo of our time. David Hendin's (1973) comment expresses this fact: "Certainly death has become the taboo of our time. It is in a very real sense the last remaining one. Sex has been the taboo subject but is no longer. Even elementary school students study it in their classrooms, all is open and above board. But who will talk to us about the death, the inevitable end of life?"

The general taboo appears to be heightened when children are involved. Wiener (1970) notes that "deepseated and ubiquitous feelings of unease are frequently mobilized in staff personnel engaged in caring for a fatally ill child." The intensity of the death taboo as it relates to children has been called "a taboo within a taboo" by Gilbert Kliman (1973).

The author of this chapter has also encountered extreme reactions of avoidance in his own experiences. When he was instrumental in bringing a psychologist with an interest in thanatology to his institution, it was suggested that these thanatological interests and accomplishments be played down in the record of the young man's qualifications to work with prospective teachers.

Another example of this avoidance occurred during a cocktail hour at a professional conference of teacher educators when the author casually mentioned that he had interviewed parents of dying children and recently bereaved parents. Some of his colleagues gasped in disbelief. One expressed the view that the death of a child is too horrible to contemplate. The subject was changed.

TABOO STIRS PARENTAL FEAR

It would appear that all concerned want to pretend that the school is untouched by death. The fear that schools will discriminate against a dying child is widely held and has been for a number of years. In 1960, the author was the principal of a college laboratory school that admitted children on the basis of the date of their applications. The parents of a girl who was eligible for kindergarten called and said that they doubted that their daughter would be accepted because she had leukemia. When they were informed that no rule existed to prevent her being admitted, they were both surprised and grateful. After the child's death, the father approached the author and thanked him profusely for permitting the child to attend the school. He still could not get over the fact that the school had not let the child's grave illness interfere with her admission.

The perceived incongruity of death and the school was even more strongly underlined in the abovementioned interviews with parents of dying or recently deceased children. Parents of sick children took extreme pains to insure that anonymity be maintained. They believed that if word reached the school that their child was terminally ill, he would be treated with discrimination. One mother even sent a friend to speak for her at the interview so that there could not be any possible way to identify her. She feared that if the school learned of her child's terminal illness, he would be dropped from a special class for bright children.

Another parent told of having been advised by her doctor to keep the school ignorant of the gravity or the nature of her child's illness. The doctor's reason for making this recommendation is obscure. He cited no medical or social reason.

The mother did as the doctor suggested, and the school was not informed. As the child became progressively weaker and eventually was unable to attend classes, the school provided homebound instruction. It seemed to the parent that the school personnel would surely either guess the truth and/or inquire about the nature of the illness. If the school personnel did guess the truth, they did not indicate that they had. Nor did they inquire about the nature of the child's problems during the time that home tutoring was being provided.

FUNERALS ARE NOT TABOO

How do school personnel react to funerals? If the school is very large, teachers may commute from outside the community. Their contact with parents and the community is minimal and deaths and funerals may be overlooked in some cases. However, in other cases it is difficult to avoid acknowledging certain facts. If the death involves a pupil in the school, his permanent absence is certainly noted. Siblings, particularly young ones, are apt to call the matter to the attention of their teachers either through overt comment or behavior. If the deceased is a parent, the child's absence is recorded and the reason noted. Most teachers will express their sympathy or make some appropriate comment.

In urban schools where the parents are wellknown to the school, the situation may be different. The parents of one child reported that although the principal and to some extent the teachers resisted the idea that the child was terminally ill, they eventually accepted the fact and were described as "magnificent." The father in particular was very moved by the school's reaction. He felt that the compassion of the teachers and the principal had made the family's grief much easier to bear. He talked at length about this and credited the attitude of educators to the nature of their work. He believed that teachers as professionals saw the best side of people, in contrast to the experiences of policemen or lawyers. For this reason, he felt that educators could be most supportive and helpful.

In the so-called "neighborhood school," the funeral is apt to affect the school in an inescapable manner. This is true whatever the size of the town or city in which the school is located. The critical factor is that in these schools, the teachers and administrators are routinely aware of major events in the community. They may respond to the funeral in several ways. Often, the principal and/or teachers visit the funeral parlor. Classmates may send flowers. In certain instances, members of the school staff may attend the funeral. If the deceased is a classmate or the parent of a classmate, the children in that class may also attend the funeral.

But the taboos associated with death seem to descend upon the school once the funeral is over. There may be a few comments in the teachers room but that is often the limit of the school's notice. In a similar way, children may also discuss the funeral on the playground, but they too drop the subject after a few days. The funeral appears to have served as a way of concluding the matter.

ACUTE GRIEF FOLLOWS THE FUNERAL

In reality, the funeral does not end the effects of the death. Very tangible results remain which the school must live with. Two experiences of the author are suggestive.

In one situation, a boy learned of the sudden death of an uncle from a classmate. Several days after the funeral, a fight erupted suddenly between the two. This seemed puzzling because they had always been good friends. Yet the boy who had lost the uncle had attacked his friend without provocation and could give no reason for his behavior. Apparently, it was an example of punishing the bearer of bad tidings.

In the second instance, the author, as a young teacher, paid a condolence call upon a student who had lost his mother. He drove to the home of the student and was met by an uncle in the yard. He introduced himself and asked to see his student. The boy came over from another house. There was a very brief exchange of greetings and an expression of concern by the author who felt most awkward throughout. However, that particular moment seemed to establish a special bond between him and the student. During the remainder of the school year, the student always chose a seat close to the author. Whenever there were disciplinary problems in the class, this student managed to avoid being a part of the problem. Rather, he seemed to give his teacher a smile of support and sympathy if the teacher looked his way.

Theese two incidents suggest that a funeral can be followed by emotional reactions that impinge upon the school. School personnel are presented with a challenge to their professional skill and there is no escape from this fact.

GRIEF'S LASTING IMPACT

Markusen and Fulton (1971) suggest the gravity of childhood bereavement. In a study correlating the loss of a parent through death, divorce or separation with a child's record of arrests and marital success, they found that there was a significant positive correlation between such loss and trouble with the law as well as broken marriages in later life.

The direct connection with learning, the school's main concern, is made by Kliman (1973): "Continuing with work which is often done well in any psychoanalytically oriented, multi-disciplinary setting we come now to one of the most familiar problems of bereaved children—a combination of intellectual disinterest, learning difficulties, and disturbances in the field of memory. Such children are to be found in every grade school out of proportion to their expected frequency among underachievers."

THE SCHOOL'S RESPONSIBILITY

The teacher's problems and concern are not limited to the bereaved child alone. Where open communication exists between students and teachers, there is bound to be some comment on any death that involves the immediate community. The teacher inevitably finds himself displaying some of his own beliefs, attitudes and feelings. His emotional and intellectual responses to the discussion of death and funerals are bound to influence the child's developing concept of death. An emotionally comfortable and intellectually appropriate reaction is of great importance to the child. This is an inescapable responsibility of all teachers.

Children are subject to much anxiety and stress in relation to the topic of death (Anthony, 1972). This includes all children, not just those who have been bereaved. If the teacher refuses to discuss death, the taboo is reinforced. If, instead, the teacher "honeycoats" reality, as many adults do with young children, there may be many side effects. "Unrealistic explanations about death—that it is merely sleep or that a person has gone away—aside from being untruthful, can also lead to sleep disturbance or anxiety reactions about trips anyone might take" (Furman, 1970). Standard religious answers or naturalistic explanations present other problems in public schools where the separation of church and state is respected and the children are of varied religious persuasions.

The "facts alone" present problems. The emotional response of the teacher adds another, more subtle, burden. Children are very sensitive to the emotional messages of their teachers. The frightened teacher makes death seem frightening. A teacher who is at ease with the thought of death helps the child see death as an inevitable part of life.

If the teacher, and through him the school, is faced with a problem on the occasion of a funeral and the attendant acute grief, then the question of what needs to be done to meet this situation naturally arises. The first step is probably to come to grips with the taboo of death in relation to the school. Here the professions that have begun to explore the thanatological ground must lead the way. How to effect changes in schools remains a puzzling matter for those who have made a lifework of curricular change or have studied the process in depth (Sarason, 1971). Modest results must be expected. If progress is slow and tedious throughout, this is to be expected; efforts should not be abandoned if dramatic results are not immediately forthcoming.

The medical profession may seem to be a logical source of knowledge. But there is little doubt that many doctors are not comfortable enough with death to be of much help to teachers. The doctor's unresolved problems with death are well-documented in thanatological literature (Feifel, 1967) but as thanatology advances, we can assume that progress will be made (Schoenberg, et al., 1970). As it is, we can expect that fewer doctors will advise parents not to reveal a terminal illness to school personnel, as was done in the case cited above. Instead, the doctor might take the initiative and, with parental permission, discuss the nature of the child's illness with the child's teacher or school principal. This would give school personnel time to begin to face some of their own problems related to grief and the funeral.

Those who believe that because school personnel are not medical professionals they should not be involved in medical information concerning the terminally ill must examine the possibility that "non-professionals" have a valuable role to play. Lyall and Vachon (1975) state:

> For many of us to follow her [Kübler-Ross] example too far or too often, may be to put ourselves at a risk of exceeding our capacity to give and to ignore other useful approaches to helping both our patients and their families. In fact, very often there is no one else to meet these needs, and on these occasions having a professional that is willing to undertake either part or all of this task is to answer our highest calling. However, at other times, the natural social supports of the patient are there and are willing to either partially, or totally meet the patient's needs. It would be sad to see professionals 'professionalizing' the care of the dying in a way that made the natural members of the patient's social milieu feel inadequate or unimportant.

Teachers, it would seem, are natural members of the patient's social milieu.

Social workers, psychologists and psychiatrists have established a limited tradition of contact with the school. These contacts should be encouraged and extended. They have an innate limitation however. Those professionals usually deal only with patients who are seen as being disturbed to an abnormal degree. Children or parents who are able to maintain their equanimity would elude this group of professionals. The literature suggests that many bereaved who control their outward behavior may suffer the most, often developing somatic complaints (Lindemann, 1944).

Funeral directors may be another source of assistance for school personnel. The author's niece and nephew were helped most by a funeral director when their father died suddenly and unexpectedly. The funeral director's contribution involved explaining how their father's heart attack occurred, including them in discussions of plans for the funeral, and outlining the steps to be taken to put the family's affairs in order. This experience suggests that funeral directors are in a position to alleviate a young person's bereavement.

Those who are involved with teacher education need to develop more realistic attitudes about death and recognize that like all aspects of life it impinges upon the school. There is little likelihood that thanatology will have a special place in the curriculum of prospective teachers or a spot on the agenda of in-service teacher education. A whole line of other topics and concerns is already being pushed into position for such time allotments. It might not even be desirable to establish a new college course if there were a chance to do so.

A more promising approach would be to incorporate aspects of thanatology whenever and wherever they are relevant. Topics related to death and the attendant problems of grief have an obvious place in the so-called foundation areas of psychology, sociology, philosophy and history of education. Concern about community relations should include some materials and experiences that would make it easier for teachers to interact with bereaved parents. The so-called methods courses should include the information that a grieving child faces learning problems. Means to help a child resume learning even though he is bereaved should be explored and developed.

REFERENCES

Anthony, S.: *The Discovery of Death in Childhood and After.* New York, Basic, 1972.

Feifel, H., et al.: Physicians consider death. In *Proceedings of the 75th Annual Convention of the American Psychological Association,* Washington, A.P.A., 1967.

Furman, R.: The child's reaction to death in the family. In Schoenberg, B., Carr, A. C., Peretz, D., and Kutscher, A. H. (Eds.): *Loss and Grief: Psychological Management in Medical Practice.* New York, Columbia U Pr, 1970.

Hendin, D.: *Death as a Fact of Life.* New York, Norton, 1973.

Kliman, G.: Facilitating Mourning During Childhood, Address delivered at Irene Simon Memorial Symposium, *Bereavement,* co-sponsored by The Foundation of Thanatology and the Department of Psychiatry, College of Physicians and Surgeons, Columbia University, New York, New York, November, 1973.

Lindemann, E.: Symptomatology and management of acute grief. *Am J Psychiatry, 101*:141, 1944.

Lyall, A., and Vachon, M.: Concerns regarding professional role in thanatology. In Schoenberg, B., Gerber, I., Wiener, A., Kutscher, A.H., Peretz, D., and Carr, A.C., (Eds.): *Bereavement: Its Psychosocial Aspects.* New York, Columbia U Pr., 1975.

Markusen, E., and Fulton, R.: Childhood bereavement and behavior disorders: a critical review. *Omega, 2*:111, 1971.

Sarason, S. B.: *The Cultures of the School and the Problem of Change.* Boston, Allyn, 1971.

Schoenberg, B., and Carr, A. C.: Educating the health professional in the psycho-social care of the terminally ill. In Schoenberg, B., Carr, A. C., Peretz, D., and Kutscher, A. H. (Eds.): *Psychosocial Aspects of Terminal Care.* New York, Columbia U Pr, 1972.

Wiener, J. M.: Response of medical personnel to the fatal illness of a child. In Schoenberg, B., Carr, A. C., Peretz, D., and Kutscher, A. H. (Eds.): *Loss and Grief: Psychological Management in Medical Practice.* New York, Columbia U Pr, 1970.

CHAPTER 34

HELPING YOUNG CHILDREN TO COPE WITH ACUTE GRIEF: A BIBLIOTHERAPY APPROACH

JOANNE E. BERNSTEIN

Books have been tools for preventing and solving psychological problems for as long as they have existed. Over the door of the library of Thebes was the inscription, "Healing place of the soul." Literature is a form of vicarious experience which can help people to see themselves, to extend horizons in empathy with those different from themselves, and to contemplate and plan for their actions should *they* be faced with the same situation.

Books can be useful in helping even the youngest children to cope with acute grief. At the preschool level, books can be a vehicle for self-inspection and insight. Through literature, children can see that they are not alone in their reactions to problems. The opportunity to identify with characters and, subsequently, to discuss feelings is presented in gentle, subtle form. Books can be the catalysts for spontaneous release of previously hidden emotions.

For literature to be optimally beneficial, careful thought, selection and planning are essential. The adult (physician, teacher, counselor, parent, and other) who wishes to help the child through the use of books must bear in mind that bibliotherapy is but one component in a program for maintaining mental hygiene. It is an auxiliary technique, used in conjunction with other methods. Just as giving a child a book about the facts of life does not constitute adequate sex education with which to face life, so the offering of a book about dying and bereavement cannot be considered adequate thanatology

[274]

education. Although children and adults can gain some insight from reading alone, openness to discussion is a factor as important as the literature itself.

Timing is important when utilizing literature as a tool for happier living. Books about death and bereavement can be included in a school or home literature collection. Doctors can leave such books around their waiting rooms, along with other materials which have less emotion-provoking content. A major principle in bibliotherapy is that the child plays a central role in selecting the book to be read. The adult does not force the book upon the child, implying "It's good for you!" Rather, the book is to be found among others which might be selected. Many people ask: "Should books about loss be included among possible selections for children who have never experienced loss? Shouldn't little ones be protected from pain for as long as possible?" Children who have not experienced grief through death or divorce can benefit from exposure to books on these themes. Although they are very young and have not had such experiences themselves, in today's world, it is probable that they have had contact with others (in school, around the neighborhood, at home) who *have* had these experiences. These children may have unspoken concerns and questions, and the reading of books on themes of loss gives assurance that "it is acceptable to think about and discuss these matters." Furthermore, the inclusion of such books provides a framework for facing the problems at a future date. The child can look back, however vaguely, upon a vicarious experience and apply the things he remembers to reality.

For children to whom death and bereavement are already matters of reality, the adult keeps the books available. Often, bereaved children will ignore these books within the collection and seek out less threatening fare. At the peak of their grief, it is often the case that people of all ages cannot face mirrors of their emotions. The skilled adult understands and is ready for the moment when the child finds the book or shows definite signs that he or she would be amenable to being given such a book. After a book has been read by or with a child, the adult is available for discussion, but just as the adult did not force the child to use the book, so it is that the adult does not intrude with unwanted discussion.

Before selecting a book for therapeutic use, one should carefully examine it. Factors to be considered include the chronological ages, stages of development, and reading or reading readiness levels of the children. Is the material generally appropriate for the children involved? Will the length, format or level of difficulty impede any possible gains? Is there any misinformation or an attitude contained within the book which the adult might wish to clarify or correct? Is the misinformation of such magnitude that one might wish to discard the book altogether? Most important, is the book worthwhile from a literary viewpoint—is it written with skill, so that fiction or nonfiction does not appear as propaganda? These are among the questions one should ask before including *any* book in a literature collection. When attempting bibliotherapy, one merely asks more thoughtfully.

A search of recent literature for very young children reveals that death has been treated, but those who die are either pets or the elderly. This author has not found a picture book concerned with the death of a parent, sibling or another child. Although death is kept at arm's distance, the existing books often do touch upon developmental themes worthy of discussion.

Nagy (1959) explains that children of less than five years of age see life in death. They are unable to separate death from life, often viewing the dead as living in some limited state either within the grave or in another place. The psychological reason behind such perceptions is the fact that the young child knows he himself is alive. His entire world is seen through egocentric glasses, so he cannot imagine anything being so totally unlike himself. Adults bear remnants of this attitude when they speak of "resting in peace." This childlike conception of death is given fictional form in several books. In *My Grandpa Died Today,* the child who is bereaved performs well in a baseball game and his spirits are uplifted. He looks far away into the clear sky and thinks that his grandfather must feel good, too. In *Nana Upstairs and Nana Downstairs,* the sky is also a medium for communication with the dead. Shortly after the death of "Nana Upstairs," Tommy sees a falling star. "Perhaps that was a kiss from Nana Upstairs," says his mother. Years later, when Tommy is fully grown, his "Nana Downstairs" dies. Another star falls one night and the grown-up Tommy thinks, "Now you are both Nana Upstairs."

In contrast to the above, the death process itself is explained quite well in books for young children. A return to *My Grandpa Died Today* provides an example. Author Fassler writes, "And he stopped rocking. And he didn't move any more. And he didn't talk any more. And he didn't breathe any more. And the grownups said that Grandpa died." The process is further described in Margaret Wise Brown's *The Dead Bird*: "And even as they held it, it began to get cold, and the limp bird body grew stiff so they couldn't bend its legs and the head didn't flop when they moved it."

Sara Stein (1974) also speaks of rigor mortis. She is graphic and explains children's interest in death as seen in their testing of irreversibility in play with insects. Stein uses a unique concept in her book: she provides parallel narratives for her two audiences. Alongside the child's story is detailed information about the psychodynamics of loss.

Kliman (1968) speaks of three areas of mourning work, and these are seen in literature for the young. The first, testing and accepting the reality of the loss, takes place in simple, physical form in *The Dead Bird*. The children feel for the bird's heartbeat. When it is not present, they know the bird is dead. A physical test of the situation is necessary for Tommy, too. After he hears that his "Nana Upstairs" has died, he runs upstairs to her room, where the bed is empty. Tommy realizes the true nature of the loss and asks, "Won't she ever come back?" His mother replies that she will be able to return only in memory, a statement which is closely linked to Kliman's second area of mourning, the working over and decathectization of memories related to the deceased. Memories form the core of two children's books about death. The first, titled *The Tenth Good Thing About Barney,* concerns a family's effort to say farewell to its dead cat. The mother suggests that the child think of ten good things about Barney to recite at the funeral. In the eyes of his child-owner, Barney was regarded as "brave, . . . smart, funny and clean. Also cuddly and handsome and he only once ate a bird." And so on.

Most of Charlotte Zolotow's *My Grandson Lew* is a recitation of memories. Lew had not been told of his grandfather's death for more than four years, simply because he'd never asked. Now, at long last, the mother and son share their thoughts and perhaps Lew's silent, long-hidden pain can begin to be eased. When Lewis tells his mother that he misses the grandfather, she replies, "So do I. . . . But now we will remember him together and neither of us will be so lonely as we would be if we had to remember him alone."

The cultivation of substitute object relationships is the third area of mourning work cited by Kliman. This is most keenly seen in *When Violet Died,* wherein the children psychologically console themselves for the loss of their bird by embracing their cat with rekindled, intense affection. At first, they look towards Blanche as a pet they will have forever, but then they realize that nothing lasts forever. They evolve a plan of action to insure against loneliness for as long as possible. It involves raising a cat, keeping one of her kittens (named Blanche, of course), raising that kitten to motherhood, and starting all over again.

When young children experience a loss, they feel deeply sad for a while, but then, possibly because the sadness is intolerable, they replace their distress with preoccupation with industrious, happy pursuits. Martha Wolfenstein (1965) elucidated this phenomenon and called it the "short sadness span." This reaction is seen in the book that is probably the oldest contemporary book about death for young children, published in 1938. Still in great use, *The Dead Bird* states simply, "And every day, until they forgot, they went and sang to their little dead bird and put fresh flowers on his grave." The accompanying illustration shows children running and playing ball.

Acute grief and funeral ceremonies are depicted in several books. The pet funerals children conduct (as in *The Dead Bird, The Tenth Good Thing About Barney* and *When Violet Died*) can serve as vicarious means for mastering fears and anxieties. The books can be vehicles for answering children's questions about the permanency of death. Witnessing a "burial" reinforces the correct notion that death is not reversible and that it is not a departure for some unknown land. Pet funerals serve in real life and in books as an outlet for sad feelings, just as adult funerals do. The children who found *The Dead Bird* welcomed the opportunity to sing at the funeral, and in their lyrics, they tried to convince themselves of the permanency of the situation: "Oh bird you're dead/You'll never fly again."

Children talk directly to the dead animal at another funeral, the one which takes place in *When Violet Died*: "Vi-o-let, dear Vi-o-let / If you could only see / How sad I am that you are gone / You'd fly right back to me."

Acute grief is aptly described in *The Tenth Good Thing About Barney*. The child states that he cried, and didn't watch television, and didn't eat his chicken or even his chocolate pudding. In *My Grandpa Died Today,* acute grief is described as a funny, empty, scary, rumbly feeling in the stomach. The author states that even the house seems to feel sad.

A reminder of the everlasting cycle of living things is a part of most funeral services, and this is not neglected in fiction either. Violet's owners looked to their cat for continuity, and Barney's owners planted a garden in the area of the yard where the cat is buried. The book explains that Barney will change until he's part of the ground and will help grow the flowers, trees and grass. The child in the family had previously been able to think of only nine good things about Barney, but decides that this is the tenth. An ecology picture book, *The Dead Tree,* stresses this idea also, that even in death, we nurture the living.

Preparation for eventual death is a topic which is almost surprising to find in books for the youngest, but which nevertheless is to be found. On the simplest level, the children in *When Violet Died* realized that the bird was going to die because she had been sick. They were prepared. In *My Grandpa Died Today,* the old man tells his grandson he is very old but is unafraid to die. He explains that this is because he feels that the young boy is not afraid to live.

Annie and the Old One is a story in which a Navajo girl enjoys the daily company of her elderly grandmother. The old woman tells her that when Annie's mother finishes weaving the rug that is presently on the loom, her time in the world will probably be finished. Annie then plots to keep the rug from completion, in order to keep her grandmother alive. At story's end, Annie realizes that she has tried to hold back time, and that all people are part of the earth.

The most subtle story for young children which concerns death is titled *Across the Meadow.* Some children will not understand that death is the ending at all, for Alfred, the cat protagonist, speaks of going on a vacation. He is tired of the hardship his life has become, and the steps he takes before the "vacation" constitute preparation for death: he goes to his animal friends one by one and says goodbye; he takes pleasure in the birds' singing, regretting the times he chased them; he rescues a kitten and guides him to the farm, seemingly to take his place; finally, he goes off by himself to die.

The stories for young children which depict death treat the subject in various ways. Some try to provide information, others try to reassure. Some occasionally promote misconceptions in their efforts to handle a difficult topic. It is the job of the adult who works with these books to be aware of what is in them. With awareness, one can provide the right book, at the right moment, for the right child.

REFERENCES

Brown, M. W.: *The Dead Bird*. Illustrated by R. Charlip. New York, Young Scott, 1938 and 1965.

De Paola, T.: *Nana Upstairs and Nana Downstairs*. New York, Putnam's, 1973.

Fassler, J.: *My Grandpa Died Today*. Illustrated by S. Kranz. New York, Behavioral Publications, 1971.

Kantrowitz, M.: *When Violet Died*. Illustrated by E. A. McCully. New York, Parents' Magazine Press, 1973.

Kliman, G.: *Psychological Emergencies of Childhood*. New York, Grune and Stratton, 1968, p. 86.

Miles, M.: *Annie and the Old One*. Illustrated by P. Parnall. Boston, Little, Brown, 1971.

Nagy, M. H.: The child's view of death. In Feifel, H. (Ed.): *The Meaning of Death*. New York, McGraw-Hill, 1959, p. 81.

Schecter, B.: *Across the Meadow*. Garden City, Doubleday, 1973.

Stein, S. B.: *About Dying: An Open Family Book for Parents and Children Together*. New York, Walker, 1974.

Tresselt, A.: *The Dead Tree*. Illustrated by C. Robinson. New York, Parents' Magazine Press, 1972.

Viorst, J.: *The Tenth Good Thing About Barney*. Illustrated by E. Blegvad. New York, Atheneum, 1972.

Wolfenstein, M.: Death of a parent and death of a president. In Wolfenstein, M., and Kliman, G. (Eds.): *Children and the Death of a President*. Garden City, Doubleday, 1965, pp. 68-9.

Zolotow, C.: *My Grandson Lew*. Illustrated by W. Pène DuBois. New York, Harper and Row, 1974.

CHAPTER 35

STUDENTS WITHOUT PARENTS: AN OPPORTUNITY TO TALK

Marcelle Chenard

Kübler-Ross, in the opening of her book, *On Death and Dying* (1970), writes:

> Death is viewed as taboo, discussion of it is viewed as morbid, and children are excluded (from being near the dead) with the presumption and the pretext that it is too much for them.

A countermovement to this taboo can be seen by the increase of courses on death and dying in the universities, colleges and medical schools; an increase in the number of seminars on the subject in various communities; and an increase in the number of books on the topic. The aim of this paper is to present an alternative to the formal lecture on a college campus. This alternative is an organization for those students who have lost a parent.

The organization discussed here was formed as a result of a request from students who had lost a parent and who had been enrolled in a sociology course in which this topic had been discussed. The student who approached the instructor felt that such an organization could be the place where this topic could be discussed openly "without people thinking you are morbid."

Known as "Students Without Parents," this organization has a loose and informal structure. Initially, it included ten unmarried college students between the ages of 17 to 21 whose mother or father had been dead for two years or more and a college instructor. The instructor serves as its coordinator. Meetings are held twice a month in the late afternoon in a very informal setting on the college campus.

The participants have no assigned tasks. The coordinator has a few tasks. Among these are setting up the meetings, announcing their location formally and informally, and seeking professional assistance when necessary. During the meeting itself, the participants' role is an active one, whereas the coordinator's role is less active. There is only one rule: to listen.

The organization's main objective is to help direct or orient the participants toward the future. To achieve this objective, the students are asked to recall the events following the death of the parent, to examine its impact on their life, and to cultivate a future-orientation.

The participants are asked to recall the most significant changes that they experienced as a consequence of the death of their parent. The majority of them mention "the financial situation," the loss of the parent's income having resulted in a major change in life-style. "You do not have enough money to buy things," said one student. "There is less money every year," added another. A third responded, "It's the women who are left with the financial problems." It would seem that the greatest financial strain occurs in the period immediately following the death of the parent until such time as the estate is settled. In a few cases, when surviving widows returned to work at low-paying positions, the financial strain persisted.

The second major change experienced was the emotional reaction. Some students felt that their mother's behavior changed at the death of her spouse. One student commented, "When my mother got the news that my father was dead, she ran to the bank and withdrew all the money in their account. I felt that she didn't love my father to be able to do that." Others expressed the same reaction, but a few participants said that such an action was necessary. Nevertheless, because of this or other actions, some students now perceive their mother differently. Other, later reactions are resentment and fear. Resentment would seem to be related to an increase of familial responsibilities and a loss of free time. One participant expressed it as follows: "You gotta help. Yet, you feel selfish." This statement was followed with another: "I feel that I'm being robbed of my youth." The fear felt is the fear of losing the surviving parent. "Where would I go?" "Who would take care of my brothers and sisters?" In a few cases, the fear increased when the surviving parent became ill. These have been the main reactions voiced, not necessarily in the order of their importance.

Following the identification of these two major changes, the financial and the emotional, the participants are encouraged to think about their future and how the organization might be of use to them. Selective activities are considered and planned. These can be divided into two categories: structured and unstructured. Among the structured activities agreed upon are planning a budget, preparing the income tax form, and learning about real estate, i.e. the purchase of a house, mortgage rates, and so forth. Professional people from the local community volunteer their time for these activities. Most of the participants have had little to no financial exposure, training or experience and view these activities as a gradual preparation or anticipatory information for their future life.

The unstructured activities are discussions. The topics of these discussions center around the students' present situation. Among some of the topics discussed have been:

"My mother is dating again and I have to help her find dates. How does one go about this?"

"What will I do father-daughter weekend?"

"Now that my father is dead, my grandmother, his mother, keeps telling me what to do. How can I tell her not to bother me?"

"I can't bring my friends to the house and I don't like this. What can I do about it?"

The meetings usually last from one and a half hours to two hours. The structured activities are at the beginning of the meeting so that the time for the discussion is not limited.

Why do the students come to the meetings? "Here I can actually talk about it. I've got to get it out," one replied. Another member feels it's a step in the right direction because "it's helped me." A third participant comes because she finds it easy to talk about her problems at the meetings since "these girls went through it." A fourth student said, "I found myself talking and talking and saying things that I felt. It's helped me. I feel closer to the other girls." A fifth participant summed it up in these words: "I never understood the 'Our Father' until I lost mine."

In sum, the general reaction is positive. The main reason for coming to the meetings is to share the bereavement experienced and its impact. Talking about the death seems to make for acceptance of it. Interestingly enough, though the event has happened two years ago or more, many of these students have only just recently come to accept it as a fact.

In conclusion, an organization such as Students Without Parents is conceived as an attempt to assist those particular students who are looking for a setting to discuss this particular kind of experience. Such discussions of death are not viewed as morbid—at least, by those who have participated in them, giving credence to the possible conclusion that they would have benefited from a therapeutic group experience at the time of their loss.

REFERENCE

Kübler-Ross, E.: *On Death and Dying.* New York, Macmillan, 1970.

CHAPTER 36

THE CONTINUITY OF LIFE

WENDY VEEVERS-CARTER

M^Y PERSONAL EXPERIENCE with death makes me ask four
questions:

1. Is death any easier to bear if you have seen it often?
2. Is some sort of pre-knowledge a help?
3. Can living with the possibility of death mean that when it comes, the mechanics of loss are easier to cope with?
4. Does true sharing, a true partnership in life between two people, mean more or less upheaval at the death of one of them?

Out of my experience, I shall try to answer these questions with the facts as they were for me.

Since 1963, my husband, Mark, and I and our two (and then three) children have lived on isolated islands in the Seychelles Group in the Western Indian Ocean with only brief, and usually separate, visits to "civilization." Our isolation made us as a family very close to one another; the fact that we were so close meant that when we were separated, we felt it the more keenly. Our life is primitive by modern standards. We have been thrown very much onto our own physical resources and mental capabilities: "do-it-yourself" and make-do" are both ways of life to us—exacting, satisfying, frustrating and exciting in about equal proportions, with the overall proviso that in our isolation we have found much peace. Peace *and* space: in choosing this sort of life, we gave ourselves plenty of room to grow, in every sense of the word. It seemed to us that it is precisely this sort of space that is lacking in our ever more congested modern world, and so we paid its price. That we also made others pay involuntarily for the risks we took was itself part of the load we carried: if we had not accepted this, we could never have lived as we did.

All these factors—isolation, closeness to one another, self-reliance, idealism, selfishness, awareness of the risks—form the background against which Mark's death must be seen, and the context in which I ask the questions.

Yes, I think Mark's death was easier to comprehend and accept by the children because of the life we led. They have in many ways seen a lot of death. I sometimes think (because I was not brought up with it) that to see more one would have to live near an abattoir or be in a war. Life is "in the raw" when there are no intermediaries in the food chain. Not for us even the stench of the butcher's shop. We start with the live fish on the hook, the live pig, which we shoot and then dismember upon a table, all guts and blood. We wring the necks of chickens and ducks. We spear crabs. We hunt and are fed and hunt again. And as we deal it out, so do we receive it, at first hand. One by one our dogs have died. A whole herd of goats died of pneumonia. The cows died because of a missing trace element—or so we suppose: we had neither the facilities nor the knowledge to make the right tests.

More seriously, we have had two human deaths as well. On our first island, one of the eight children of a sickly family died soon after they came to us; we learned then what it is truly to accept the belief that God gives and God takes away: for our Seychellois laborers, this is the beginning and end of it and they do not question its rightness. They do, however, take certain "sensible" precautions against the walking of the spirit, in which they also firmly believe, and will not willingly live near the island graveyard or walk past it at night, nor leave their windows open for ghosts to enter. We had a hard time persuading our children, to whom all these beliefs were passed on, that the darkness was safe enough and the night air healthful. They had accepted everything—the realness and finality of the dead body and the realness of the spirit world.

They were older and we were on our second island when Small George, the mason's helper, died of tetanus. He had to be nursed in the house, at first only for a head wound gained in a fight. Two weeks later, he developed tetanus (in the Seychelles, only recently have tetanus innoculations been given as a matter of course) and because he was young and strong, it took him three days to die, in agony, held by us each in turn as this seemed to give him some small comfort. The children saw it all, heard him cry, heard him die, saw him dead. At least an animal can be put out of its misery—this was our agony. But I noticed then and since with animals that the children do not feel this way: their knowledge is less and their hope correspondingly much stronger. "Why do you kill it? It *might* live." They felt the same way about Small George, and were quite cheerful about his suffering in the belief that he might live up to the very moment when he didn't, and then accepted that as—just that. A cessation of being, like all the other beings that had died in their short but full experience.

When the news came of Mark's death, they accepted that, too. Or the two older children did, to be exact. The youngest, then aged 3, could not grasp the fact and for a whole year would not. Not old enough to have seen as much death as the older children nor to have assimilated his experiences, he shared with me (though for different reasons) a feeling of unreality. It was out of the question that his Fafa should be dead like other animals, and so it was not so. Five now, he has at last come to realize that he will not see Mark again, that death is forever; but he still occasionally asks, "Is Fafa really dead?"

Thus my idea: that enough experience of the finality of death at an impressionable age, which experience our children share with the Seychellois people who have worked for us, does help the acceptance of it. And if one truly accepts something, one can at least avoid crying against its having happened, its futility or cruelty, its unjustness. It *has* happened and it must be swallowed; the tears I shed were observed sympathetically by the children but not much understood. They wanted to know about tomorrow.

The fact that Mark had been talking about dying for nearly a year before he died gave me, at the time, no presentiment of disaster; nor did I "feel anything" on the day, at the hour. I am by no means as pragmatic as I used to be in my youth, and no longer dismiss the fact that some people have naturally or can develop a psychic sixth sense; yet, though I believed this might be true of Mark from all the many small incidents of which he had told me, I thought nothing of his gloomy prognostications and dismissed them, often brusquely, since they left a lot to be desired in the way of conversation. I merely thought he was depressed. He had minor but annoying physical ailments at intervals, and we had financial worries, and on our second island so many of our experiments were failures: the fruit trees died, voracious land crabs ate countless budding agricultural experiments, the cattle perished, and so on.

Nor did Mark's real phobia about going to the dentist prevent me from once again nagging him to see one on the trip he was about to take. I knew the phobia to be real enough: he could start shuddering at the mere mention of teeth, and had been physically sick out the window of the car the one time I had been able to get him near a dentist's office. But I dismissed his reactions as a lamentable lack of self-discipline. He had had some very bad experiences, true; but that was no reason to let his teeth rot in his head now that dentistry was so much more sophisticated than it used to be.

Today, however, I wonder—with hindsight, admittedly—whether or not Mark did sense some danger unto death to his person connected with dentistry. Because, of all the unlikely things to have happened in our isolated, island-bound lives, it was in a dentist's chair that he died. And, of course, when the news eventually reached me, all the hundreds of times Mark had returned to his feeling of life being over, a feeling from which he could not distract his mind, flooded back into mine.

It is not much to the point to discuss now whether or not Mark was psychic and did "know"; aside from these two facts, there is no other evidence. Nor could he have had any clear precognition that this particular union of time and place would be fatal to him or, as I suppose, he would not have finally gone to the dentist.[1] Nor was our parting in any way unusual. We were both depressed and edgy; as often before in this life of ours, the thought flashed through my mind that we might never see each other again. But each parting

---

[1]No, I am wrong: if there is precognition, it must be knowing of something unavoidable.

was like that. What I wonder now is how much I may have been prepared by a sort of subliminal awareness—how much this insulated me from complete shock. Because—and I remember every thought quite clearly—I ran the gamut of all the usual emotions except the shock of surprise. And this was a help, a real help. I functioned, was not overwhelmed, even stood aside a little and watched myself suffering and each time examined why.[2] Perhaps I used a sort of induced "fatalism" as a mental crutch, but the shock of surprise seemed to be for others, not for me.

Yet, there was nothing wrong with Mark. The post-mortem revealed a healthy, forty-two-year-old male with no abnormality or malfunction that could have contributed to his death. He died, it seemed, through "anaesthetic accident," of acute cardiac arrest. A fully-qualified anaesthetist was present; the equipment was good; all emergency steps taken. There was no reason he should have died, but he did. And I go on wondering.

In answering the third question, however, I can stop groping for the truth. I *know* I lived with the thought that at some time—any time—something might happen to one of us, and I realize very well that my apparent lack of surprise may do nothing more than bear out the extent of my acceptance of the inherent risks of our life. With our lack of—and lack of interest in—communications, it was true that whoever left the island had to travel over hundreds of sea miles in a small boat, do what was necessary in "civilization," and travel back again the same way, never knowing if during this time anything had happened to those who stayed behind (while the latter were never certain of the well-being of the traveler). What if the boat foundered on its way to Mahe (the main island)? Who would know it was due? Who would look for it? While on the island, all might potter along as usual for two or three months before anyone bothered to think something seriously wrong: trips for spare parts and business transactions could, complete with mechnical failures, often take this long. That there are no radios on the spread-out islands of the Seychelles Group is always unbelievable to visitors, but it is so. Life is like that here: you are on your own. Our accep-

---

[2] If I caught myself crying because of obvious self-pity, I soon dried up.

tance of this is a function both of how much we had been indoc-
trinated by our previous life in many another primitive place and
our general lack of money. Most people would probably have set
up an efficient radio transmitter and receiver before anything else;
we regarded this as an "extra."

So, in a sense, once the parting had taken place, it was almost as
if one's partner had died, in that the ache of missing him/her had
:o be banished, the extra duties taken over, the load carried single-
handedly. Our marriage and our life were such that we were not
often parted and then not willingly—so that when a parting became
inevitable and happened, it was indeed like a "little death."

I would wish every husband and wife as intense a treasuring of
their time together as we treasured ours, and the training for the
final loss that each temporary parting gave us. Nor is my grief
sullied by regrets. We were both lucky to have had each other for
so long; when one has so much good to remember and be grateful
for and when—as our life forced us to do—one also appreciated this
at the time, then, somehow, death is easier to accept.

On the other hand, by how much does taking each parting seriously—and unwillingly—prepare one? Does a treasure horde of
memories of shared happiness really make it easier for the remaining
half of a full partnership to cope with the severance of death? Everywhere one turns, there is that empty space that nothing fills. With
no separateness, it seems as though one has to learn to do everything
over again in order to do it alone. The phrase, "nothing means anything anymore," describes well enough the fact that partners in a
good marriage get incredibly used to sharing perceptions as well as
experience. Half of a sort of extended "self" dies: how does the
remainder function?

What appears to happen—at least in my experience—is that the
whole process of living as a single unit again is so impossible as to
create a sort of reality gap. One is; yet, at the same time, one is not.
Getting at the truth seems to uncover a mass of apparent contradictions. I claim a certain degree of forewarning and forearming;
"therefore, I was not surprised." But, I have to turn straight around
and use the word "incredible." "Unbelievable." I couldn't seem
really to believe that it had actually happened, that this person who
went on being the mother of her children and running the island

and whom everyone seemed to address by my name was really "a widow." It was all a mistake—that was the recurrent theme. How Mark and I laughed (with tenderness) over the ridiculous mixup. How had I ever believed such an unlikely story? Thus my dreams, not limited to the nighttime, and thus my sharing with my young son his feeling of unreality. It wasn't really happening.

Yet it was and, of course, I knew it was. The disbelief was a sort of insulator; long stretches of each day and night were quite bearable because of this drug and I managed the mechanics of the necessary traveling, island management, decision-making, even taking an interest in life and having fun with the children mostly under its influence. While at the same time, I suppose I edged step-by-step toward acceptance. I protected myself and I do not think that this path is dangerous for a sane person because fundamentally the truth is there. It is a kind of self-hypnotism to avoid feeling all of the pain all of the time.

Here is another contradiction: one feels totally "severed" because one is so used to sharing everything, yet because you have shared, to act as the other would is already a habit. The feeling that you know what the other would have done is there without much conscious effort. It gives you courage. You can deal with tomorrow and not falter; it is almost as though there were still two of you. The abyss of desolation and abandonment is still there, but something keeps your feet on the track just to one side of it. Some find this strength in religious faith, of course, but the sheer strength of such a complete relationship with another person has its own kind of "carrying" ability. So much so that while I have given up using "my drug," it still only requires a flick of my mind to bring Mark back.

Giving up using: given up being able to use the device of disbelief is more the truth. I suppose it is some measure of the years that have passed since Mark's death that now "Mark" and "pain" arrive so closely together as to afford no comfort.

"Accepting" and "managing" are just words when this happens, but the security of what we had is still there, rock-like, when the flood subsides. Perhaps this is all that I have learned: that while the present may be grievous enough, death has no power to change the past, and that one's unending sense of loss is really involved with a future of which few of us—mercifully, perhaps—can know much.

INDEX

A

Acceptance of death, and the funeral as a social mechanism, 122-124

Accidents, acute grief and, 134

Acute grief: and accidents, 134; after the funeral, 268-269; a bibliotherapy approach to coping with, 274-280; and children, 257-258; the clergyman aesculapian authority and, 191-193; a description of, 5, 105; and functions of the funeral, 36-40; the funeral, the Italian family and, 142-144; and guilt, 105, 249; and hostility, 105; initial quandries of, 14-15; in literature for children, 278; and murder, 134; observations on the funeral and, 41-53; a physician's viewpoint on, 5-12; psychological function of books for children in, 274-275; role of the pastor in, 190; shock waves of, 194; and suicide, 134; and terminal care, 9-11; use of pharmacologic agents in, 5-6; see also *Grief*

Acute grief crisis, and the funeral director, 50-52

Adaptive funeral, case report of an, 132-133

Aesculapian authority: acute grief, the clergyman, and 191-193; components of 192

Afterlife, and the funeral, 28

Age: of bereaved in relation to attitudes toward funerals and ability to cope with death, 64-68; the deceased, family position and, 68-77

Aged: bereavement, loss, and suicidal potential of the, 223; crying and depression as expressions of grief in the, 226; death and the, 204-205; death anxiety and the, 175; detri-mental effect of grief and the, 221; grief, society, and the, 225-228; income, burials, and the, 149; institutions and the, 227; isolation of the, 218; loss, grief, and the, 218-229; poem by a dying lady who was, 207-208

American Indians, and Spanish speaking people, and the Anglo social culture in the Southwest, 145-147

American society: and death, 73, 109, 122; questionnaire for a study on death and attitudes of, 79-90

Ancient Egypt: embalming in, 23-24; and the funeral, 23-24, 108

Anticipatory mourning, sudden and unexpected death and, 252

Antidepressants, and grief, 6

Anxiety: the aged and death, 175; regarding death and funeral home workers, 174-178; scale on death, 174

Attitudes: a questionnaire for a study on death and American, 79-90; surveyed on the "open casket," "traditional funeral," and "disposal service," 156-168; toward funerals and age of the bereaved, 64-68; toward funerals and religion of the bereaved, 59-62; toward funerals and sex of the bereaved, 62-64

Avoidance, of the topic of death, 265-266

Awareness, of death and crying, 236

B

Behavior: unresolved grief and funeral, 241-247; see also *Social behavior*

Bereaved: attitudes toward funerals and ability to cope with death of the, 59-62; and ceremony, 118; the clergyman and the, 194-195, 197; death, age, and the, 64-68; the funeral and the, 32-40; the funeral director and the, 153-154, 194-197; and the pastor's own discomfort, 188-190

Bereaved child, responsibility of the school and the, 269-272

Bereavement: a definition of, 106; the effects of loss and, 211-225; a family support service post-, 6-9; grief and 234-235; and grief and mourning as realities of loss, 105-113; the process of 219-221; relocation, 224-225; stages of, 219-221; and suicidal potential of the aged, 223

Bibliotherapy approach, to coping with acute grief, 274-280

Books, children in acute grief and the use of, 274-280

3rain death, definition of, 92-93

3urials: family's response to, 16-17; finality of death and, 199; hazards of, 14; the need for wakes, funerals, and, 13-22; reality and, 15; senior citizens, income, and, 149

Businessman, the funeral director as a, 171

C

Case report: of an adopted funeral, 132-133; of a child after mother-loss, 154; of a child's guilt reaction the father's accidental death, 253

Casket, attitudes toward the open, 156-168

Cemetery: and the community mausoleum, 101; and cremation, 101; grief expression and the role of the, 98-101; and memorialization, 98-99

Ceremony: and the bereaved, 118; customs, the community and, 131; death and, 32, 43, 115-116; a definition of, 111; and emotion, 123-124; and ritual as parts of the funeral, 111; see also *Death ceremony*

Change, in traditions, 158

Child: loss of a parent and case of a reaction of a, 253-254; responsibility of the school and the bereaved, 269-272

Children: and acute grief, 257-258; acute grief and funerals in literature for, 278; and adequate education in thanatology, 274-275; areas of mourning weak in literature for, 277; and a bibliotherapy approach to coping with acute grief, 274-280; death denial and, 261-263; death and isolation of, 253-254; death literature for, 274-280; double taboo and dying; 265-266; funerals and, 258-259, 260-264; helplessness and, 252-253; legal disposal of body, 95; and loss of siblings, 256-257; and mourning, 256-259; and talking about death, 254-255; and understanding of death, 261, 267; see also *Child*

Church: discussion of death and the, 75; social strength in the Southwest, 150

Clergy: criticism of the, 179-187; and failure in giving charity and kindness, 182-183; and failure in role, 185-187; see also *Clergymen*

Clergymen: acute grief, aesculapian authority and the, 191-193; the bereaved and the, 194-195, 197; during crisis situations, 198; the family and the, 197-198; lack of empathy and the, 182-183; lack of understanding and the, 183-185; respect and compassion of funeral directors and, 194-199; see also *Clergy*

Community: the cemetery and the, 101; customs, ceremonies, and the, 131

Compassion, and respect of funeral directors and clergymen, 194-199

Coping: with acute grief with a bibliotherapy approach, 274-280; with death and age of the bereaved,

64-68; with death and religion of the bereaved, 59-62; with death and sex of the bereaved, 62-64; with grief, 41

Corpse, viewing the, 16, 111

Cost, of funerals, 51-52, 176-177

Counselor, the funeral director as a, 153-154

Cremation: cemeteries and, 101; and male treatment of spouse's body, 29-30

Crisis: the clergymen during, 198; funeral directors as interveners in situations of, 50-52, 170, 198; of loss and the funeral, 33-34

Criticism, of the clergy, 179-187

Coping: awareness of death and, 236; grief, the aged and, 226; mourning rituals and, 19

Cultures, death ceremony and, 32

Customs: ceremonies, the community and, 131; grief and tribal, 20

D

Data, collection for a study on attitudes toward funerals and ability to cope with death, 56-57

Dead body, legal status of a 93-94

Death: a view of life and, 203-208; age of bereaved and coping with, 64-68; the aged and, 204-205; and American society, 73, 109, 122; avoidance of the topic of, 265-266; burials and finality of, 199; children and understanding of, 261, 276; funeral directors, funerals and, 116-120; funeral home workers and anxiety regarding, 174-178; and the hospital setting, 74; and isolation of children, 253-254; legal aspects of, 92-97; legal definition of, 92; and life history, 107; and memorialization, 16, 98-99; religion of the bereaved and coping with, 59-62; rites and ceremonies, 32, 43-44, 115-116; science, technology and, 110-111; sex of the bereaved and

attitude toward, 62-64; study questionnaire on American attitudes and, 79-90; sudden and unexpected, 252-255; and survivors, 43; the three subdivisions of survivors of, 41-42; understanding, 285-287; in the United States, 26-28; 108, 218; urbanization and, 110; and the young, 205; see also *Hospital death*

Death anxiety: the aged and, 175; of the funeral director, 176; genetic factors and, 175; mourners, society and, 52-53; funeral home workers, 174-178; scale (DAS), 174; and sex, 62-64

Death Anxiety Scale: college students' results on, 175; male vs. female results on, 174-175

Death ceremony: and cultures, 32; major functions of, 32; and mourners, 32

Death denial, see *Denial of death*

Death education, increase of courses in, 281

Death literature, for children, 274-280

Deceased, age and family position and the, 68-77

Definition(s): of bereavement, 106; of brain death, 92-93; of ceremony, 111; of despair, 250; of a funeral, 169-170; of grief, 41, 106, 234; of mourning, 106; of ritual, 111; see also *Description*

Denial of death: children and, 261-263; modern society and, 73-74

Depression, the aged and, 218, 226

Description: of acute grief, 5, 105; of the funeral, 32; of the funeral director, 131; see also *Definition*

Despair: a definition of, 250; and sorrow, 250

Director, see *Funeral director*

Discomfort, the pastor and personal, 188-190

Discussion of death: children and, 254-255; the family and, 75; friends and, 75

Disposal: of a body, 94-95, 111; the hospital and, 96-97; kinship and, 95-96; society and, 97
Disposal service, a funeral director's survey including attitudes toward, 156-168
Drugs, see *Pharmacologic agents*
Dying: funeral directors and the cost of, 51-52; taboo and children who are, 265-266
Dying children, double taboo and, 265-266

E

Effects, of loss and bereavement, 221-225
Elderly, see *Aged*
Embalming, in Ancient Egypt, 23-24
Emotion: and ceremony, 123-124; and rituals, 17
Empathy, funeral directors and, 126-130
Evaluation, items used in a study on grief, 246-247
Expense, see *Cost*
Expression: of feelings and the funeral, 38-39; of grief and the aged, 226; of grief and the role of the cemetery, 98-101

F

Family: as part of the "treatment unit," 10-11; and children, 260-264; and the clergyman, 197-198; discussion of death and the, 75; response to funerals, burials, and wakes, 16-17; social network support of the grieving, 17; structure, 232-233; ties in the Italian, 144; types of, 233; see also *Italian family*
Family position, the deceased, age and, 68-77
Family Support Service: and maladjustment, 7; post-bereavement, 6-9
Fear, taboo and parental, 266-267
Feelings, and expression of, 38-39

Females, Death Anxiety Scale results of males and, 174-175
Finality of death: and burials, 199; and the funeral, 172
Findings: of a study on attitudes toward funerals and ability to cope with death, 59-72; of a study on funeral behavior in relation to unresolved grief, 242-246
Floral offerings, in Italian traditions, 143
Friend: discussion of death and the, 75; grief, the funeral, and the, 231-239
Function: of death ceremony, 32; of the funeral, 24, 36-40, 105, 172
Funeral(s): and acceptance of loss, 33; acute grief after the, 268-269; acute grief and functions of the, 36-40; acute grief, Italian families, and the, 142-144; the adaptive, 131-138; afterlife and the, 28; age of bereaved and attitude toward the, 64-68; in Ancient Egypt, 23-24, 108; as a rite of passage, 18-19; as a social event, 24; as social mechanisms in the acceptance of death, 122-144; and the bereaved, 32-40; case report of adopted, 132-133; and children, 258-259; children and literature on, 278; contemporary society and the traditional, 23-30; cost of 176-177; death, funeral directors and, 116-120; definition of, 169-170; a description of the, 32; design of the, 35-36; expression of feelings and the, 38-39; family's response to the 16-17; finality and the, 172; functions of the, 24, 36-40, 105; grief, the friend, and the, 231-239; hazards of wakes, burials, and, 14; of integration and separation, 28-29; lack of taboo and the, 267-268; loss, mourners and, 33; meaning of the, 35-36; mourners and functions of the the, 16, 36-40; the necessity for wakes, burials, and,

13-22; preserving the psyche and the, 24; reality and, 15, 37, 172; reality, loss, bereavement and, 33-34; reason for the, ix-xv; the recovery process and the, 236-238; religion of the bereaved and attitude toward the, 59-62; ritual and ceremony as part of the, 111; and schools, 265-272; self-actualization and, 206; sex of the bereaved and attitudes toward the, 62-64; sharing and the, 172; social meanings of the, 115-125; some observations on acute grief and the, 41-53; see also *Traditional funeral*

Funeral behavior: and tradition, 149-150; unresolved grief and, 241-247

Funeral ceremony, see *Ceremony*

Funeral director(s): and acute grief crisis, 50-52; as a counselor, 153-154; as an informant, 152-153; as a professional, 109, 171; as technicians and businessmen, 171; the bereaved and the, 153-154, 194-197; compassion of clergymen and, 194-199; and the cost of dying, 51-52; death anxiety of, 176; death, funerals and, 116-120; a description of, 131; and grief, 50-52; as interveners in crisis situations, 170, 198; and mourners, 49-52; purpose for the, 171-173; the hiring and the role of, 151-154; what he does and is, 169-173

Funeral home, death anxiety and those who work in the, 174-178

Funeral procession: grief and the, 111; in Italian tradition, 143-144

Funeral rite: grief and the, 249-251; and hope for the living, 251; and sorrow, 251

Funeral service: description of the humanist, 139-141; physiological need in the, 205-206

Funeral activities: detrimental consequences of lack of, 48; social behavior and, 120-122

G

Genetic factors, and death anxiety, 175

Grief: an aproach to intervention in, 224; bereavement and, 234-235; and bereavement and mourning as realities of loss, 105-113; coping with, 41; a definition of, 41, 106, 234; and its detrimental effect on the aged, 221; failures of the clergy and people in, 182-187; the funeral, 139; funeral behavior in relation to unresolved, 241-247; funeral directors and the crisis of, 50-52; the funeral and the friend, 231-239; and the funeral procession, 111; intensity of, 235; lasting impact of 269; and loss in the later years of life, 218-229; love lost, the funeral rite and, 249-251; social needs and, 206; society, the aged and, 225-228; Southwestern perspectives on the resolution of, 145-150; stages of, 235-239; symptoms of, 5; therapy, 155-168; and traditional customs, 20; tranquillizers, antidepressants and, 6; see also *Acute grief*

Grief evaluation, items used in a study, 246-247

Grief expression, and the role of the cemetery, 98-101

Grief therapy, thoughts on, 155-156

Guilt: and acute grief, 105, 249; reaction of a child to father's sudden death, 253; suicide and, 134; survivors, sudden death and, 252

H

Hazards, of wakes, funerals, and burials, 14

Helplessness, death, children and, 252-253

Home, see *Funeral Home*

Hope, funeral rites, the living and, 251

Hospital, and disposal of the body, 96-97

Hospital death: a personal account of
a, 209-217; see also *Death*
Hospital setting, and death, 74
Hostility: and acute grief, 105; and
rituals, 29
Humanist funeral service, description
of the, 139-141
Husband, and disposal of the deceased, 95

I

Impact, of grief, 269
Indians, see *American Indians*
Institutions, the aged and, 227
Isolation: of the aged, 218; of chil-
dren, 253-254
Italian family: acute grief, the funeral
and the, 142-144; see also *family*

K

Kinship, and disposal of body, 95-96

L

Legal aspects: of death, 92-97; of
disposal and children, 95
Life, the continuity of, 285-291
Literature: on death for children, 274-
280; death and social science, 231
Living, role of the funeral director
and the, 151-154
Loss: acceptance of loss and the, 33;
children and sibling, 256-257; effects of bereavement and, 221-225;
the funeral and the crisis of, 33-34;
funerals, reality and, 33-34; grief,
bereavement, and mourning as the
realities of, 105-113; and grief in
the later years of life, 218-229; reliability questionnaire on predicting maladjustment to, 7-9; rituals
and resolutions of, 123; and suicidal
potential of the aged, 223

M

Maladjustment to loss, and the family
support service, 7

Meanings: of the funeral, 139; the
funeral and social, 115-125
Memorialization: the cemetery and,
98-99; of the dead, 16, 98-99
Method, in a study of funeral behavior in relation to unresolved
grief, 241-242
Mortician, see *Funeral director*
Mortuary, variables in the sociology of
the, 55-79
Mother-loss, child's reaction to, 254
Mourner(s): death ceremony and, 32;
function of the funeral and the,
36-40; funeral directors and, 49-
52; the professional and, 49-52,
194; society, death and 52-53;
wakes, funerals and, 16
Mourning: and children, 256-259;
children and literature in areas of,
277; a definition of, 106; and grief
and bereavement as realities of loss,
105-113; rituals as an occasion to
cry, 19
Murder, acute grief and, 134

N

Need: for wakes, funerals, and burials,
13-22; grief and social, 206; survivors and the security, social, ego,
love, 206; survivors psychological,
sociological, and physical, 47

O

Offerings, of flowers in Italian tradition, 43
Open casket: a funeral director's survey including attitudes toward the,
156-168; see also *Visual confrontation*

P

Parents: discussion opportunities for
students without, 281-284; fear and
taboo, 266-267
Pastor: acute grief and role of the,

190; personal discomfort and the, 188-190; see also *Clergy*

Personal discomfort, and the pastor, 188-190

Pharmacologic agents, acute grief and use of, 5-6

Physical needs, of survivors, 43

Physician: acute grief from the viewpoint of a, 5-12; and psychopharmocologic agents, 5-6

Physiological need, in the funeral service, 205-206

Posta, as an Italian custom at the time of a, 142-143

Process: of bereavement, 219-221; of recovery and the, 236-238

Procession, see *Funeral procession*

Professional: the funeral director as a, 109, 171; mourners and the, 49-52, 194

Psychological functions: of books for children in acute grief, 274-275; of the funeral, 24, 33-35

Psychological needs, of survivors, 43

Psychopharmacologic agents, and the physician, 5-6

Purpose, for the funeral director, 171-173

Q

Questionnaire: reliability in predicting severity of maladjustment to loss, 7-9; for a study on death on American attitudes, 79-90; and tabulations of a survey on attitudes toward the "open casket," "traditional funeral," and "disposal service," 165-168

R

Reality: bereavement, funerals and, 34; function of funerals and, 37, 172; loss, funerals and, 33-34; rituals and, 18; and wakes, funerals, and burials, 15

Reason, for the funeral, ix-xv

Recovery process, and the funeral, 236-238

Relationship, human, 233-234

Religion: death anxiety scale results, college students and, 175; of the bereaved and their attitudes toward funerals and ability to cope with death, 59-62

Relocation, and bereavement, 224-225

Report, see *Case report*

Resolution of grief: rituals, loss and, 123; Southwestern perspectives and, 145-150

Respect, and compassion of funeral directors and clergymen, 194-199

Responsibility, of the school and the bereaved child, 269-272

Rites: ceremonies, death and, 32, 43-44, 115-116; funerals as passage, 18-19

Ritual(s): as outlets for emotions, 17; and ceremony as part of the, 111; a definition of, 111; examination of the hazards in some, 14; and hostility, 29; importance of, 20-22; of mourning as an occasion to cry, 19; and the resolution of loss, 123; underlying reality, 18

Role: the clergy and failure in, 185-187; of the pastor at time of acute grief, 190

S

Sample, description in a study on attitudes towards funerals and ability to cope with death, 57-59

School: the bereaved child and responsibility of the, 269-272; and the funeral, 265-272

Science, death, technology and, 110-111

Senior citizens, income, burials and, 149

Service, see *Funeral service*

Sex: of bereaved and attitudes toward funerals and ability to cope with death, 62-64; death anxiety as related to, 174-175

Sharing, the funeral as an opportunity for, 172

Social behavior, funerary, 120-122

Social meaning, of the funeral, 115-125

Social needs: of survivors, 43, 206; see also *Need*

Social network, support of the grieving family, 17

Social science, literature, 231

Society: the aged, grief and, 225-228; death denial and modern, 73-74; death, mourners and, 52-53; and death taboo, 20-21; and disposal of a body, 97; funerals as events of, 24; the traditional funeral and contemporary, 23-30

Sociology, variables in mortuary, 55-79

Somatic distress, and acute grief, 105

Sorrow: despair and, 250; funeral rites and, 251

Stages: of bereavement, 219-221; of grief, 235-239

Structure, of the family, 232-233

Students, without parents and the opportunity for discussion, 281-284

Study: on funeral behavior in relation to unresolved grief, 241-247; on variables in attitudes toward funerals and the ability to cope with death, 55-91

Sudden death: survivors, guilt and, 252; unexpected and, 252-255

Suicide: acute grief and, 134; and guilt, 134; potential of the aged bereaved, 223

Support: funerals and society's, 111; see also *Family Support Service*

Survey, on attitudes toward the "open casket," "traditional funeral," and "disposal service," 156-168

Survivors: and death, 41-43; individualistic experience of the, 44-46; psychological, sociological and

physical needs of, 43; security, social, ego, and love needs of, 206; sudden death, guilt and, 252; susceptibility of, 47

Symptoms, of grief, 5

T

Taboo: dying children as a double, 265-266; funerals and the lack of, 267-268; and parental fear, 266-267; society and the ritual as, 20-21

Talk: see *Discussion*

Technician, the funeral director as a, 171

Technology, science, death and, 110-111

Terminal care, and acute grief, 9-11

Thanatology, the child and adequate education in, 274-275

Therapy, for grief, 155-168

Thoughts, on grief therapy, 155-156

Tradition: floral offerings and Italian, 143; funeral activity and, 149-150; report on changes in, 158

Traditional funeral: as surveyed by a funeral director, 156-168 and contemporary society, 23-30

Tranquillizers, and grief, 6

Treatment unit, the family as part of the, 10-11

U

Understanding: children and death, 261, 276; the clergyman and lack of, 183-185; death, 285-287

Undertakers, see *Funeral director*

Unexpected death, sudden and, 252-255

United States: death and the, 26-28; 108, 213; resolution of grief in the Southwestern, 145-150

Unresolved grief, and funeral behavior, 241-247

Urbanization, death and, 110

V

Viewpoint: of a physician on acute grief, 5-12; on life and death, 203-208
Visual confrontation, of dead body, 111

W

Wakes: family's response to, 16-17;

hazards of, 14; mourners and, 16; the need for funerals, burials and, 13-22; and reality, 15
Widow: -to-widow program, 224; viewing the corpse and the, 16
Widower, see *Widow*
Wife, disposal and the deceased, 95

Y

Young, death and the, 205